MORAL DEVELOPMENT

MORAL DEVELOPMENT

A PSYCHOLOGICAL STUDY OF MORAL GROWTH
FROM CHILDHOOD TO ADOLESCENCE

A. W. KAY

SCHOCKEN BOOKS

NEW YORK

Published in U.S.A. in 1969
by Schocken Books Inc.
67 Park Avenue, New York, N.Y. 10016

PRINTED IN GREAT BRITAIN

TO MY PARENTS
ALBERT ERNEST
AND
AMY ROSINA

AUTHOR'S PREFACE

In a work of this kind one cannot help being conscious of the debt owed to all who have provided encouragement and information. I would thus like to acknowledge my indebtedness to them.

For those who allowed me to use their unpublished material I owe a special debt of gratitude for much of value often lies hidden in the archives of our universities. I would like too, to thank Prof. H. L. Elvin, Prof. P. Hirst, and Prof. W. R. Niblett of London University; Dr Barry Sugarman and Mr Norman Williams of the Farmington Trust Research Unit, Oxford; Mr E. A. Allen and Dr J. W. Daines of the University of Nottingham; and two head Teachers, Miss M. E. Cooper and Mr V. Conquer, for all giving time to discuss this work with me.

I would particularly like to express my gratitude to those who have helped in specific ways. First to my friend and colleague Jane A. M. Mathison M.Sc., who not only suggested that this book should be written but also supplied the academic judgment which subsequently eliminated some ambiguous arguments and false trails of evidence. I am also indebted to colleagues in the Divinity and Education Departments of my college. Brendan Magill M.A., B.D., and Ron Hanna B.A. B.Ed., B. Mus., both read the manuscript as it was written and made many valuable comments and suggestions; Robin Protheroe M.A., kindly applied his literary expertise to reading the proofs of the text; and John Daines B.D., M.Th., Ph.D., generously agreed to read the proofs in order to check the arguments and psychological data. Finally I wish to record appreciation for the help of my wife Pamela. Without her constant encouragement and practical help —including the compilation of a comprehensive index—this book would never have been completed.

I am glad to say that my colleagues appear to agree with my view in its essentials. But clearly I alone must remain responsible for the opinions expressed in this book.

A. W. KAY

CONTENTS

Literary Note

Any reference to Piaget's psychological system leads to a linguistic dilemma. One may either coin the term *Piagetan* on the analogy of *Lutheran*, or the term *Piagetian* on the analogy of *Kantian*. Although the former is linguistically preferable the latter is becoming accepted by common usage. Therefore throughout this work the term *Piagetian* is used.

INTRODUCTION

Moral education is a subject which is now being discussed with increasing interest in educational circles. Some teachers link this new interest in it with an apparent decline in authoritarianism. Despite the notable success of some totalitarian systems in Europe, it now appears to be generally agreed that a rejection of church, tradition, common morality, parental influence and authority figures in general characterizes our society. The consequence of this is that society is compelled to attempt to introduce deliberate moral education into the state system of education. Whereas earlier one could rely upon the traditional socialization of each generation by the transmission of relatively static value systems and patterns of behaviour, this is no longer possible. A dynamic society with anti-authoritarian and anti-tradition orientated moods will no longer allow this.[1]

Others may argue simply that a society with more leisure and affluence now finds itself increasingly composed of voluntary social structures, and whereas in industrial and commercial organizations behaviour *must* be subordinated to the need to earn a living, this is not so in a club, society or social group. Schools must therefore prepare children to live together as adults when economic restraint does not govern their behaviour.

Perhaps many more will say that the partial eradication of poverty and social deprivation has not resulted in a diminution of juvenile (or adult) delinquency. Therefore, they may insist that we should have moral education to help eradicate this social evil.

The average citizen looks on and cannot help feeling that our schools should be able to produce better citizens. He hears of selfish and irresponsible behaviour in industry while our trading gap widens to the disadvantage of all. He watches motorists display dangerous and selfish aggressive patterns of conduct while slaughter on the roads continues. He becomes involved in the

---

[1] A surprising yet unmarked element in the trial of *Lady Chatterley's Lover* was the closing speech for the prosecution. Here the tradition-centred, authority-orientated mentality shone at its brightest. Rolph records how Mr Griffith-Jones argued that *standards* must be *instilled* in all of us, and that the moral decay he smelt everywhere originated from 'lack of discipline' (pp. 210–11).

spending sprees of our public holidays then ponders over the Oxfam advertisements. He observes the uncritical conformity of his fellows and reflects on the dignity of independent individual decisions. If he works in a profession he sees irrational maliciousness souring relationships between people whose intelligence and good-will should be at a premium. In all this he cannot avoid concluding that the schools should help to produce civilized people who possess moral responsibility, altruism, independence and rationality in a more developed form.

The state in its welfare guise is taking over more and more of what were once family functions. Although Fletcher may argue to the contrary, Musgrove appears to have shown conclusively that the educative family has declined. It is therefore not surprising to find that today many consider moral education to be the duty of professional educators. Dempster summarizes the position succinctly: 'With uncertain standards children must be *prepared for life* with a clear settled mind since the morality of a primitive culture has been left behind.'[1] Indeed it is now not infrequent to hear educators murmur that some of the hours spent teaching children to calculate the volume of a truncated cone might well be spent teaching them to calculate how best to help their neighbours.

Some, too, are emphasizing that we do not teach subjects, we teach people, and pre-eminently we teach *people* to live with *people*. It is thus a salutary thought to realize that at the moment we spend thousands of hours teaching an individual child to live with books, and hardly any time teaching him to live with people. Yet after leaving school he will spend perhaps half an hour each day in the company of books while *all* his time will be spent in the company of people. And further, it is argued, in a shrinking multi-belief world possessing thermo-nuclear power, all nations must learn to live with each other. The age of medieval crusades, whether by Christians or Humanists, is over. We all share the dignity of being human. Let us then live together as human beings.

For many of us the shadow overhanging our culture originates not with any misuse of nuclear power; one must simply hope that man will make good servants of the forces he has unleashed. The real horror for us is the thought that technology without human

[1] J. J. B. Dempster, *Purpose in the Modern School,* p. 30.

values could well be the nightmare of our age. This seems to be what Snow has in mind when speaking of the new technocrats, 'These men, whom we don't yet possess, need to be trained not only in scientific but in *human terms*'.[1]

Of course adults try to be mature in their morality, but if childhood in a competitive and authoritarian school has not allowed the basic moral attitudes to develop, they will find the task extraordinarily difficult. We sometimes feel like men, who having caught the wrong train can only rush madly down the corridor in the opposite direction. Therefore, such adults say, let us have moral education in the schools. Start our children off in the right direction. Help them to become citizens who will grace, and not disgrace, our society.

Teachers too are conscious of this need. Every good teacher of religious education is today deeply concerned to help impart the high moral values which are an integral element of Christian faith and practice. A small group of Humanists is also increasingly emphasizing the need for moral education. These teachers may differ from each other on ideological grounds but all are united (or should be) in their passionate concern to help our children to grow up as mature moral agents. It is this which the committee of Christians and Humanists at London University have said with unequivocal emphasis.[2]

The authorities too are being roused to action. Hitherto satisfied by the simple juxtaposing of religious and moral considerations in official reports[3] they are now supporting activity in many parts of the country intended to improve the quality of our religious and moral education. At the academic and operational level

[1] C. P. Snow, *The Two Cultures: and a Second Look*, p. 47. This however is no new theme. In 1945 the Council for Curriculum Reform observed: 'Twentieth-century society realizes that its citizens must have a maximum of education and that this must include knowledge, skill, creativeness and *moral qualities*, otherwise the twentieth century will transform itself into a totalitarian state.'

[2] *Religious and Moral Education*. Some proposals for county schools by a group of Christians and Humanists.

[3] e.g. The Newsom Report, 'Half Our Future', devotes a chapter to 'Spiritual and Moral Development'. Even the Note of Reservation on Religious Education in the Plowden Report, 'Children and Their Primary Schools', is headed 'Religion and Morals' and notes that 'the force of the moral example which the story of Christ can furnish is certainly not to be discounted' (p. 490).

the Farmington Trust Research Unit, which is studying ways of making moral education a viable element of school life, is now established at Oxford.[1] Its philosopher director, John Wilson is ably assisted by research fellows in sociology and psychology. I have the privilege of co-operating with this unit and in company with many others have high expectations of the help that it will give to us during the ten years of this trust's life. At the practical level Hauser's valuable work is being supported by the Home Office where teachers and social workers are seeking to establish a system of social work in our schools. By this it is hoped that children will at least accept their responsibilities as members of a society which still contains pockets of social neglect.[2]

But if moral education is to be conducted by the schools it must be undertaken as rigorously as any other element in the curriculum. The first essential is that we should know how children *actually* develop morally; not how we think they *ought* to grow. Indeed as Dempster has said, 'We cannot know too much about the children who fill our Modern Schools or about their problems.'[3] Only then can we help them to develop their personal potential as human beings. Secondly we must understand the nature of this moral factor.[4] Only when we understand the nature of child and adolescent morality can we devise the best techniques for advancing its growth.

This book and the companion volume[5] have these aims in common. Here it is shown how children develop morally from infancy to adolescence. The present book analyses this material and suggests the methods to use in order to ensure that moral growth is fostered. Such educational work will meet with co-operation rather than opposition from the great majority of children and adults. There is a vast reservoir of good-will and moral potential to be tapped. We have here what Robbins elsewhere called 'an untapped pool of talent'. The work of pre-collegiate men and women who engage in Voluntary Service Overseas or

[1] Present address: 4, Park Town, Oxford.
[2] See particularly R. and H. Hauser, *The Fraternal Society.*
[3] J. J. B. Dempster, *Purpose in the Modern School*, p. 31.
[4] This is not intended to imply any factorial analysis of morality. It is, to say the least, problematic whether one may speak of a moral quotient in the way that one may speak (guardedly) of an intelligence quotient.
[5] A. W. Kay, *Moral Education; a Sociological Study of the Influence of Home and School*, a forthcoming volume.

work with the Community Service Volunteers indicates this. Moreover, when it is remembered that many large cities each have a leather-clad squad of voluntary motor-cyclists to carry medical supplies swiftly from one hospital to another, it is obvious that there are no class distinctions here.

I have some personal knowledge of this. A friend and colleague of mine, a Methodist Minister,[1] found some homeless and hither-to friendless unmarried mothers in a Lancashire town. His Church rented two houses which they repaired, decorated and furnished. In this work much help in the decorating was given by the clientele of the coffee bar which he runs (for no personal profit) in the town. Today these mothers are valuable members of the community; human dignity has been restored to them; they are working and possess homes for their families for whom they can now provide. On their own initiative these young people are also engaged in other social work. Some, for example, change the library books for housebound invalids; others collect money for Old People's Welfare, and it is salutary to reflect upon the fact that they collect more in a week than many churches do in a year.

So the tale could—and indeed should—continue. Morally mature adolescents *must* emerge from our schools, not merely because shopkeepers object to having their plate glass windows broken, but because society cannot afford to be prodigal and waste this tremendous fund of human potential in our land.

BIBLIOGRAPHY

Dempster, J. J. B., *Purpose in the Modern School*, London, Methuen, 1958.

Fletcher, R., *The Family and Marriage in Britain*, London, Penguin, 1962.

Hauser R. and H., *The Fraternal Society*, London, Bodley Head, 1962.

Kay, A. W., *Moral Education; A Sociological Study of the influence of Home and School*, a forthcoming volume.

Lawrence, D. H., *Lady Chatterley's Lover*, London, Penguin, 1961.

Musgrove, F., 'The Decline of the Educative Family', *Universities Quarterly*, 14, 1960.

[1] The Rev. Dennis G. Fowler, M.A., M.Th.

Newsom, J., 'Half Our Future', the Newsom Report, London, H.M.S.O., 1963.

Plowden, B., 'Children and the Primary Schools' the Plowden Report, London, H.M.S.O., 1967.

'Religious and Moral Education': Some proposals for county schools by a group of Christians and Humanists. London, Blackfriars Press, 1965.

Rolph, C. H., *The Trial of Lady Chatterley*, privately printed, 1961.

Snow, C. P., *The Two Cultures: and a Second Look*, Cambridge, C.U.P., 1962.

CHAPTER 1

THE NATURE OF HUMAN DEVELOPMENT

INTRODUCTION

The evidence supplied by contemporary research into children's morality makes it clear that one can speak confidently of moral development. This is not an entirely original conclusion to reach. In normal social relationships we come to expect different kinds of moral conduct from infants as distinct from adolescents and our behaviour towards both is modified accordingly. It requires no tedious and sophisticated controlled experiment to confirm this. Memories from our own childhood and observations of the children about us every day endorse this conclusion.

Some may cynically suggest that this is what most research of this kind does anyway. It provides massive and unnecessary evidence for accepting what we already know. But even if this is true, such work is still of value. Teachers can teach with greater confidence and certainty if their basic assumptions are confirmed by empirical evidence. In moral education they can do this because the research not only confirms that moral development takes place; it also indicates the sequence and character of the different stages in this process, and furthermore describes the kind of moral conduct that can be expected at each level.

It is true that different research projects have produced varying conclusions, yet in the main they all agree on essentials. Thus parents and educators can accept that children develop morally, just as they develop intellectually, spiritually and physically.

It is from this point onwards that disagreements multiply; and those who are familiar with the work of Isaacs and Piaget[1] will know just what complexities of argument and theory are concealed by such a simple statement. However, the average teacher is well acquainted with theories of development although he may be unfamiliar with the technical details. Common sense and experience have provided him with this information. It is hoped, therefore, that a brief discussion of fundamentals may prompt

[1] Whenever reference is made to a writer by name the full details can be found in the bibliography of references appended to each chapter.

teachers and students to re-read the masters of this subject and assess what these have to say against their own practical knowledge of children.

The one certain fact about our pupils is that they will grow. Teachers may sometimes doubt this, when a year of hard academic work seems to have little effect. Parents, however, have no doubt about this as many a mother sadly surveying outgrown clothes will testify. But children do not only grow out of clothes, they also grow out of knowledge. As they grow, children learn, and possibly the most fundamental educational question being asked today is, 'What is the relationship between learning and growth?' But this presupposes a prior question, 'How exactly are we to understand the nature of human development?'

THE NATURE OF GROWTH

In one sense this is a chapter which the reader could well have written himself. Indeed, it may be a useful experiment at this point, if, instead of reading further, he made a list of the different ways in which things grow or develop, and then attempted to classify the different types of growth contained in that list.

If this were done, it would soon be apparent that there are various kinds of development which can be analysed in at least four different ways.

Firstly, one may note that things grow either qualitatively or quantitatively.

Secondly, they fall into two groups; those which develop by a slow, uniform transition from lower to higher levels, and those which grow by passing through critical points, each of which marks the end of one stage and the beginning of another.

Thirdly, development may either follow a pre-determined course or appear to be haphazard.

Finally, some growth appears to be almost entirely a result of the genetic heritage, while in other aspects it is clear that the environment has played the major role as agent of this development. These four distinctions can now be examined in more detail to throw light on the general problem of human growth.

QUALITY OR QUANTITY[1]

In early times, if an outstanding warrior was killed in battle it was the general practice of those who survived to pay their respects to the slain hero by filing past his corpse. This of course, was all bound up with magical ritual practices and it may be for reasons of this kind that some earth was strewn on the body. The act of casting earth or rock upon the corpse meant that a mound grew. This resulted from the simple addition of more and more material of the same kind making the mound larger and larger. It is believed that in this way the first tumulus or burial mound was made.

In course of time this pile of stones was cemented to prevent animals from desecrating the corpse and robbers from stealing the burial armour. However it may have happened, what is clear is that out of these tumuli grew the pyramid tombs of the Egyptians. Yet despite the increased architectural sophistication of the late pyramids one still finds growth characterized by simple addition. The complexity of the final product must not blind one to this fact. Even the fabulously beautiful Taj Mahal is merely a tomb which grew up in this way.

Now there is another kind of growth which is equally familiar to us. Instead of starting with a single stone we may begin with one egg of frog spawn. As more eggs are laid it looks as though here again is an example of quantitative development. Indeed this is so, but only until the female has finished laying. When all the eggs are laid this kind of growth stops. When it does, another kind begins. Each individual egg then develops into a tadpole, and each tadpole develops into a frog. Here one finds three entirely different stages. Each stage of the frog's growth is so distinct that it demands different foods and environments.

This is the first difference to be noted in human development. Isaacs argued that intellectual growth was characterized merely by the addition of more mental equipment and by a

---

[1] The terms 'maturation' and 'growth' are used synonymously in this book, although some psychologists would prefer to distinguish sharply between them. If there is to be a distinction one may roughly equate the term 'maturation' with qualitative growth, and the term 'growth' with quantitative development. But since it is argued here that moral growth appears in both forms, such a distinction adds little of value.

growing complexity of thought. The only difference between the thinking of an infant and an adolescent was the quantity of knowledge possessed, and the degree to which knowledge and concepts were inter-related.

On the other hand, Piaget says that with the growth of knowledge and conceptual understanding one has a pattern of development which can be divided into clear, qualitatively distinct stages. Just as one can see immediately that there is an obvious qualitative difference between an egg of frog spawn and an adult frog, so by careful observation one can see equally clearly that the thinking of an infant is qualitatively different from that of an adult.

This analogy highlights one of the differences between the theories of Isaacs and Piaget. Isaacs' theory can best be understood in terms of the growth of a single stone into a masterpiece of architecture. Piaget is best understood in terms of the emergence of a frog from an egg. Isaacs argued that different stages of human development are marked by a difference of degree. Piaget believed that they were marked by a difference in kind.

This, of course, is a very elementary attempt to disclose one of the fundamental differences, between the conclusions of both schools of developmental psychology. It is therefore imperfect and thus inadequate. As will be shown later, both theories are of value and in one sense augment each other, but for the moment this analysis highlights one difference between the various theories concerning human growth.

SLOW TRANSITION OR CRITICAL POINTS

Clearly there is a further way in which these two types of growth can be distinguished. In one the development is gradual and consistent. There may appear to be phases of rapid development, but these are only distinct in that the process of quantitative growth is speeded up at certain stages. In the terms of our former analogy, the builders just add more material to the foundation to produce even the most complex architecture. They may work quickly on some days and slowly on others, but this does not affect the way in which the building develops. But in the other process there are critical points which separate qualitatively different stages.

To underline this distinction one may use the analogy of the earth and its satellite moon. Obviously, there is a difference in size, but the most fundamental difference between them is that earth is able to support living matter while the moon apparently cannot. How does this come about?

It is generally supposed that the earth supports life because it can hold an atmosphere. It holds this atmosphere by the gravitational pull which in turn depends on its weight. The moon, on the other hand, cannot support life because it has insufficient mass to hold an atmosphere. Clearly there must be a point midway between these two sizes which is critical. It is that point at which a celestial body is sufficiently large to retain an atmosphere. Anything slightly larger than this can therefore support life; anything just slightly smaller cannot. Thus, although it can be said that they are distinguished by the fact that one is x tons heavier than the other, it is much more true to say that there is a critical point which divides two fundamentally different astronomical bodies.

Here again, one may see this distinction in the work of Isaacs and Piaget. The former says of children's thought: 'It moves continuously on, developing and growing as their practical and social situations change and develop from moment to moment'.[1] Piaget, however, will accept none of this. He argues that there are two critical points in the development of each normal child. Firstly, one where he is suddenly able to see things from another person's point of view; and secondly where he is equally suddenly able to manipulate abstract ideas.

The importance of this for the teacher cannot be over-emphasized. Both are crucial experiences in the lives of his pupils and both occur at critical moments in their school careers. For most children, the first appears as they move into the junior school and the second when they have entered the secondary school.

SEQUENTIAL OR HAPHAZARD

Then there is a third way in which these forms of growth can be distinguished. The course of development can be either predetermined or unexpected. It may be sequential or it may just be haphazard. Here a useful analogy can be found by comparing the growth of a human body with the development of a piece of

[1] S. Isaacs, *Intellectual Growth in Young Children*, p. 49.

human sculpture. The fully mature, human body has had to pass through a series of pre-determined stages before emerging. The sculptor, however, can act upon his material in a haphazard way. He may, for example, decide to begin by roughly hewing the block of stone and then perfecting the facial features, or the torso, or the limbs. It is entirely up to him.

This is an extremely important distinction. According to Susan Isaacs, the course of one's intellectual development can be as much at the mercy of circumstances as is the stone before the sculptor. Surrounded by conversation and books of a high order, children who will benefit from these experiences may make inordinate intellectual advances and proceed to attain a level of conceptual understanding normally only expected in an adolescent. It seems likely therefore, that one may cultivate a particular skill or aptitude in a child just as a sculptor may concentrate on one aspect of his work.

Piaget will not agree that there is any truth in this. Children must grow through all the pre-adult stages, and pass through them in a fixed sequence before attaining intellectual maturity. To do otherwise is to court disaster. Not only will children develop little more than verbal facility, but this forcing of their growth can actually hinder their natural development. They can, of course, have their growth rate accelerated, yet, says Piaget, no stage can be omitted or misplaced in the growth of a child.

ENVIRONMENT OR HEREDITY

This consideration leads naturally to the final way of distinguishing between these theories. The analogy of the sculptor hints at it. It is not entirely true to say that the material is at the mercy of the sculptor. The material itself can partly determine what happens. There is a classic case of this known to many school children. Michelangelo was given a piece of rock which no sculptor wanted because of its shape and grain. Seeing the possibilities in the material he carved a masterpiece—the young David casting a stone from his sling. Here the nature of the material partly determined its development.

So we reach the final question. Does growth depend upon heredity or environment; upon nature or nurture? Is the predominant factor genetic or experiential?

A final illustration can help to sharpen the distinction in this case. One may for example, compare a diamond in a ring with a crystal in a chemical solution. The diamond is shaped by the external application of grinding and cutting tools. This must be done within the limits of its structure but the decisive influence is external to it. The crystal however, takes its shape under the direction of strict physical laws. Its own nature determines its growth. The environment is necessary but it is not the decisive factor.

For Isaacs a child is like a rough diamond. It must be placed in the hands of a skilled craftsman, then ground, polished and set so that the end result is a fully formed human being. For Piaget on the other hand, a child is more like a crystal. It grows according to the laws of its nature. Clearly it must have a favourable environment or growth will be prevented, but the environment merely facilitates that growth, it does not determine its direction. For this reason, Piaget's theories are often referred to as genetic in character.

Before proceeding to argue that these apparently irreconcilable theories can be shown to augment each other, it is necessary to pause at this point, for the discussion now becomes extremely relevant for moral education. Walter, for example, constantly asks the question, 'Are morals inherited?' Hitherto it has been tacitly assumed that they were not. Each individual member of the human race has had to learn how to behave morally. The variety of ethical norms found in works of comparative anthropology can be accepted as evidence for this assumption being well founded.

Such a complacent view has recently been subject to question by a number of facts emerging from medical research. It is now being argued that there is a link between genetic abnormalities found in the sex hormones and the incidence of crimes of violence. Price and Whatmore conclude that men with an extra 'Y' sex chromosome are congenitally liable to come into conflict with the law at an early age. They display severe personality disturbances and indulge in crimes of violence. In addition it has been found that such men are usually tall. This point has been made by Brown, who concluded that there was a link between human height and human crime. This is likely to be received with faint amusement when it is remembered not only that policemen are required to be tall, but that most of the trouble in this world has been caused by little men. Still the facts are self-evident. One's chromosome pattern is clearly an inherited characteristic which may affect human morality.

The evidence is far from conclusive, and the serious researcher would want to know much more about the hidden environmental factors which may also account for this moral abnormality; but it does raise two important issues. One is ethical; the other is educational. Clearly if further evidence comes to light, one must ask these questions.

Should people with such abnormalities be held responsible in law for their actions? That may well be a problem which will have to be faced by society. For our purposes however, the important question is, 'What shall we do with them at school?' There may be a minority for whom sustained ethical excellence is an impossibility. This is a fact which will have to be considered in a course of moral education. It is possible that no matter how sophisticated and effective the techniques used may be, we shall still be left with a minority of amoral or immoral children. In one sense this is to be expected. Despite the extremely efficient English teaching techniques we still have a minority of illiterates in our literate society. Perhaps this will also be true of moral education. We may still have a residue of moral illiterates. There should, however, be a new attitude taken to these unfortunate children. Instead of being treated as culpable, they will be treated as children who need special care and remedial attention of the kind given to genuine illiterates. No longer will we castigate them as hooligan delinquents for whose benefit birching should be reintroduced. Instead we shall treat them as moral invalids whose health should be our first concern since it is desired both by the individual and the society to which he belongs.

THE CONSENSUS OF AGREEMENT

This elementary approach to the problem of growth will not satisfy those who like conclusive answers. Piaget and Isaacs are not the only developmental psychologists whose work can help the practising teacher. They have been chosen not in an attempt to diminish the status of others, but simply because they can highlight the really important problems. This field of inquiry is vast and the exponents of different theories are legion.

Then again, one cannot reach a clear-cut conclusion. This area of inquiry is not only vaster than the average teacher supposes, it is also much more complex. Ideas here have to be held in a stable relationship even though they may appear to be totally irreconcilable.

It may help readers to reach some kind of mental equilibrium, without deciding to reject either Piaget or Isaacs, to hear what an eminent scientist has said. In describing his research, Walter writes, 'We had stumbled on one of those natural paradoxes which are the surest sign of hidden truth'.[1] Here, apparently, one finds a similar paradox. Neither theory is true alone, but both are valuable when held together in a new synthesis. Thus it must be said immediately that the failure to reach a definitive conclusion concerning the nature of human growth is itself a promising sign. Here is a clear guide to that 'hidden truth' of which Walter spoke.

To illustrate this, one may take a simple example. Piaget and Isaacs met on a number of occasions and both recorded their impressions of these meetings. One is particularly interesting for it describes how the redoubtable Frenchman was routed by an indignant English lady. Susan Isaacs tells how she showed Piaget around her experimental school in Cambridge. During this tour he argued that mechanical causality could not be understood till the eighth or ninth year of age. His evidence, he claimed was irrefutable. It was based on child drawings of bicycles which were mechanically improbable; and on subsequent conversations with the children which were equally whimsical.

Her triumph was so complete in this encounter that she must be allowed to describe the incident herself. 'At that moment', she says 'Dan, aged 5.9 happened to be sitting on a tricycle in the garden back-pedalling. I went to him and said, "The tricycle isn't moving is it?" "Of course not, when I'm back-pedalling," he said. "Well", I asked, "How does it go forward when it does." "Oh well," he replied, "your feet press the pedals, that turns the hub round and the crank makes the chain turn that round (pointing to the cog-wheel) and that makes the chain go round and the chain turns the hub round and then the wheels go round—and there you are".'[2]

[1] W. Grey Walter, *The Living Brain*, p. 65.
[2] S. Isaacs, *Intellectual Growth in Young Children*, p. 44.

The suspicious critic may argue that the vocabulary and syntax of this child reveals him to have been a remarkable five-year-old; but the incontrovertible fact remains. In this case, Piaget appeared to be wrong. The hidden truth, however, is that both were right. This has been clearly demonstrated in the last decade. Beard has shown that although the general Piagetian thesis can be confirmed by the most rigorous and sophisticated research, such careful work reveals a rather obvious fact. Children are individuals. It is as simple as that!

Piaget may be right in his view that all children pass through sequential stages and can only accomplish tasks appropriate to each level of development. Yet Isaacs is right too, for Beard found many exceptions. All of these exceptions were either advanced or retarded in their understanding of different concepts. This variety was so pronounced that some young children thought of space in a way which was natural to younger children, while others conceived of time in a way usually associated with older children.

Beard worked with infants and so her findings are relevant to the case of precocious pedal-bike Dan. This deeper truth had been elucidated by a discovery which neither Piaget nor Isaacs noticed. They were so concerned to score points off each other that they forgot the basic maxim of any researcher. Facts are sacred. It is the theory which must be modified to meet the facts and not the facts moulded to fit the theory. Dan's behaviour was merely that of a normal five-year-old in all respects save that in his understanding of mechanical causation he was far in advance of his years.

But polemics of this kind are essential if education is to be a viable, relevant and effective force in our society. While many people tend even today to express regret at the fact that two such eminent people could not agree, the enthusiastic teacher should welcome such conflict. Out of these come deeper truth. Conflict of this kind is the anvil on which we forge our educational techniques.

From this it can be seen there are two ways to reach a consensus. One may either enhance the similarities or devalue the differences. In the first case, one can conclude that most developmental psychologists would agree on four propositions. Firstly, growth in all aspects of his personality can be discerned in every normal child. Secondly, this growth may be gradual and uneven, but it can be analysed into a systematic pattern. Thirdly, age norms are misleading: one must deal with each child as an individual. And finally, all learning is related to this process of development.

In the second case, it is possible to argue that these different views are not contradictory so much as complementary. There is an old Greek legend which illustrates this exactly. Two belligerent warriors approached each other and met at the foot of a statue. One commented on the beauty of the statue's golden shield. The other said immediately that it was silver, so they argued and fought. When both were lying mortally wounded an impartial observer pointed out that both has been right. One side of the shield was overlaid with gold and for economic reasons the other had been overlaid with silver.

CONCLUSION

Such a synthesis can be applied to our view of moral growth. In this development it is possible to see that both Isaacs and Piaget were right. In certain respects the moral development of children proceeds quantitatively. The attitudes of responsibility, altruism, independence and rationality, for example, emerge in childhood and slowly mature. Yet, on the other hand, the different stages of morality may not only be clearly defined and easily recognized, but also located in a fixed sequence.

A young child is clearly controlled by authoritarian considerations, while an adolescent is capable of applying personal moral principles. These two moralities[1] are not only clearly distinct but can be located one at the beginning and the other at the end of a process of moral maturation.

There is an interplay between the quantitative and the qualitative elements which makes it difficult to analyse this development with complete certainty, but in general outline one may trace moral growth through a series of sequential, qualitatively differ-

[1] For convenience this book refers to 'moralities' to avoid cumbrous phrases. It is, of course, not strictly accurate, but is used in preference to the lengthy and technical terms which purist psychologists may prefer. However it has impeccable credentials: Piaget himself refers to the two moralities of childhood.

ent stages *and also* along a line of growth marked by quantitatively increasing stability and complexity.

BIBLIOGRAPHY

Beard, R. M., *An Investigation of Concept Formation among Infant School Children*, Unpub. Ph.D. Thesis, London, 1957.

Brown, W. M. C., Director of Medical Research, Research Council, Western General Hospital, Edinburgh, reporting to annual British Association Meeting, Leeds, 4 Sept., 1967. (See *Guardian Journal*, 5 Sept., 1967.)

Isaacs, S., *Intellectual Growth in Young Children*, London, Routledge and Kegan Paul, 1930; New York, Schocken Books, 1966.

Piaget, J., *The Moral Judgment of the Child*, London, Routledge and Kegan Paul, 1932; New York, Free Press.

—: *Logic and Psychology*, Manchester, Manchester University Press, 1953.

Price, W. H., and Whatmore, P. B., *British Medical Journal*, London, February, 1967. *Nature*, London, March, 1967.

Vernon, P. E., *Intelligence and Attainment Tests*, London, U.L.P., 1960.

Walter, W. G., *The Living Brain*, London, Duckworth, 1957; New York, Norton, 1953.

CHAPTER 2

RESEARCH RELATING TO MORAL DEVELOPMENT

INTRODUCTION

Before reviewing the relevant literature two important points must be made. Firstly, although there is a surge of renewed interest in moral education, the amount of empirically confirmed data available to the worker in this field is very limited indeed. Secondly, as a natural consequence of this, the revival of interest has meant that the limited material available has been thoroughly examined and re-worked by educational researchers in England during the post-war years.

Such a situation has naturally resulted in a dangerous state of academic in-breeding. Almost every bibliography appended to any article, book or thesis on this subject tends to replicate the others in its contents.[1]

In one sense this is disappointing and frustrating. One looks perpetually for some new insight or conclusion and finds little more than a re-working of familiar material. Yet this is also a situation which engenders hope. One soon becomes familiar with the standard works which form the basis of study in this subject. Then the ease with which such a clear view of the problem is gained, and the paucity of material to be mastered is a clear advantage. It enables one to hope that here is an area of educational inquiry which although presenting innumerable problems and difficulties to the research worker may provide clear guidance to classroom teachers. For one thing is certain, many teachers today are desperately concerned to do something viable and effective about the moral education of their pupils. It is to help them that this book has collated most of the material available at the moment.

The potentialities of this work are enormous. This is an important area of educational research which is hardly worked at all. It

[1] This book was written before the publication of *Introduction to Moral Education* (Penguin) the report of the Farmington Trust Research Unit at Oxford.

is almost virgin soil and one cannot yet tell what educationally nutritious crop it may yield. If this book provides teachers with the tools to reap such a harvest its purpose will have been well fulfilled. But before this the basic digging must be done. We must see firstly the results of other men's labours.

THE WORK OF EARLIER RESEARCHERS

Macaulay and Watkins, 1925
When Macaulay and Watkins published the results of their study on the environmental influences which affect the development of moral values, they could scarcely have known that this work would remain the solitary contribution of English scholars for many years to come. Yet such is the case. Until recently, apart from Piaget's contribution, one has to refer to work done mostly in America. The English remained singularly silent on this subject. It is possible, that a nation with a tradition of religious education may have been deceived into inactivity by the doubtful conclusion that moral education was thereby assured.

This conflation of religion and morality appears to have been a constantly unexamined axiom in English education. At the beginning of the nineteenth century, for example, one finds Lancaster recording the minute of a local committee thus: 'Resolved that, as the Education of the poor, by enabling them to read the scriptures has a direct tendency to improve their moral condition and to make them more useful and respectable members of the community in which they live, any plan, which promotes this object at the smallest expense, ought to be encouraged.'[1] And at the close of the same century one finds a popular expression of this idea at the other end of the social scale. In *Tom Brown's Schooldays* the author records Squire Brown's meditations before sending Tom to Rugby: 'Shall I tell him to mind his work and say he's sent to school to make himself a good scholar? . . . If he'll only turn out a brave, helpful, truth-telling Englishman, and a gentleman and a Christian, that's all I want, thought the squire.'[2] However, this is a problematic point which cannot be examined here.

Macaulay and Watkins studied over three thousand school-

[1] J. Lancaster 'The British System of Education', 1810. Minute of meeting on March 17th at Bury St Edmunds.
[2] T. Hughes, *Tom Brown's Schooldays'*, pp. 60–1.

children of every age group. Their data was obtained in the first instance by asking these children to make a list of, 'the most wicked things anyone could do', and in the second instance, by asking the children to choose a person whom they would most wish to be like, and to then give reasons for their choice.

This singularly unsophisticated device reminds one very much of the technique used thirty years later by Rowland. Wishing to discover the standards of interpersonal behaviour amongst secondary school pupils, he asked all the children in three secondary schools to 'Write down what you consider to be the most important rules of conduct of boys in the presence of girls, and of girls in the presence of boys'. However, in each case sufficient evidence was provided for some sort of analysis to be made.

In the case in point, Macaulay and Watkins were able to use their data to reach some general conclusions about morality. Amongst these there are two of importance. The first is that children build up a value system by the acceptance of social conventions. The second, that there appears to be a pattern of development in this growth. These two ideas are naturally related and Macaulay and Watkins finally argue that although social conventions are accepted in early childhood it is still possible to trace a general pattern of moral development.

Hartshorne, May and Maller, 1928–1930
These researches, generally referred to as the Character Education Inquiry, provide little of value to those attempting to elucidate the nature of moral development in terms of a single coherent theory. The importance of this work lies in the fact that their five year project, examining the conduct of children of secondary school age, revealed the inordinate complexity of moral behaviour. The authors concluded that so complex were the factors producing moral actions that it was impossible to make any generalizations at all about moral behaviour, and this applies equally to any pattern of moral development.

In an extremely important discussion on the specificity of moral conduct, attitudes and motives they reach a clear conclusion. This establishes for them the fact that morality is specific to each situation. 'Following this effort to scale the attitudes involved in a particular situation', they say, 'we endeavoured without success to form a scale which would include the tests representing a

variety of situations both in the classroom and out. That is, the
attitudes associated with an act or distinct type of deception are
apparently bound up with it in such a way as not to be operative
in other acts or types of deception. They are, like the act itself, *a
specific mode of response which is as much a function of the
situation as of the individual* or better, which is part of the total
functioning complex that includes both the individuals and the
occasion.'[1] This conclusion was reached simply because it was
impossible to find any significant correlations between the results
of their different tests with the children concerned.

Unfortunately, there was a basic flaw in their argument. The
fundamental confusion seems to have been between two concepts: that of morality in itself and that of moral traits. The tests
used were clearly designed to examine particular traits. But their
project, as its title discloses, was concerned with morality itself.

This is not a subtle linguistic complexity; it is merely a matter
of verbal definitions. In this American context the term 'character' means 'moral'. Their academic heirs, Havighurst and Taba
are quite explicit on this point. 'Character is a word with many
meanings. It is used here in the current sense of "moral character". Thus, for the purposes of these studies, character is that part
of personality which is most subject to social approval. For example, honesty but not humour is part of character. An honest
person is highly approved of by society, while a dishonest person
is disapproved of, and may even be put in jail. But a person with
a strong sense of humour, though he may be said to have a more
pleasing personality, is not therefore said to have a better character.'[2]

In order then to examine morality Hartshorne and May
tested specific moral traits. It is therefore no surprise to learn that
they foundered on this rock of moral specificity, and once
grounded had to weather the subsequent storms of violent criticism.

An Early Antithesis

At this stage in the review a rather obvious point needs to be
made. In this reference to the two earliest researches in the field

---

[1] H. Hartshorne and M. A. May, *Studies in Deceit*, p. 238. (Author's
italics.)

[2] R. J. Havighurst and H. Taba, *Adolescent Character and Personality*,
p. 3.

of moral behaviour one finds a fundamental difference of opinion. For Macaulay and Watkins there appeared to be 'broad lines of moral development'. For Hartshorne and May there was clearly no such thing.

Thus at this stage in the review a clear question is posed. One must decide whether to come down generally on the side of Macaulay and Watkins or on the side of Hartshorne and May. This is a reasonably simple decision to make for important factors other than those relating to the research conclusions help in this choice.

If Hartshorne and May are correct in their general conclusion that there is little evidence for the existence of constant moral factors in human personality and motivation, there can be no systematization in this area of inquiry. But the reverse is not true. To accept the Macaulay and Watkins conclusions does not necessarily mean that one has also to reject the view that moral acts may be specific to situations. Thus our understanding of morality is advanced. We may now argue that a pattern of moral development can be clearly traced in the growth of each individual, but also that the particular actions are effected by factors specific to particular situations. Now with the inclusion of this factor of moral specificity, it is possible to argue that individual differences may be apportioned within this dimension.

The actual methodology employed in this research suggests that this is the kind of conclusion to which an impartial reader would come. The methodology of Hartshorne and May emphasized the specific elements in moral behaviour. They then mistook this part for the whole, the secondary for the primary, and so did not realize the full significance of their research findings.

Edwards has shown that it is this imperfection to which later writers perpetually allude, and thus how it is this concomitant conclusion which has been most severely criticized by a series of eminent researchers. Allport argued that some account ought to have been taken of a developmental pattern. Indeed, he continues, it could be argued that the failure to discover a moral constant in the context of this methodology points just as much to the conclusion that morality develops, as it does to the conclusion that moral behaviour is specific to situations.

Valentine criticized this conclusion in a similar way. Whereas Allport could systematize the data by hypothesizing a developmental structure, Valentine suggested that this could be equally organized within a socio-economic framework. A closer examination of the data reveals that many differences in moral behaviour suggested not moral specificity, but the existence of socio-economic and sub-cultural levels.

Thus, the least that can be said at this point is that the apparent specificity of the moral conduct of these children can be interpreted in a number of different ways, and most of these in fact point to the possibility of a hypothetical structure with psycho-social constants at each stage.

A further criticism originated with Eysenck who argued against the Hartshorne and May conclusions in a novel way. He employed the analogue of intelligence testing. In such tests, he said, children may or may not be successful within that frame of reference. One does not thereby conclude that there is an essential specificity in intellectual activity, nor that the level of intelligence is not a relative constant. Therefore, he continues, Hartshorne and May should not have reached a parallel conclusion on the basis of their moral tests.

The list of eminent critics can be concluded with Vernon. He believed simply that he could discern a moral constant or common factor when he re-analysed the data supplied by these tests.

A Possible Synthesis

In these two early studies one finds two extreme positions. It seems natural to conclude therefore that the truth may lie somewhere between them. This suggests that moral conduct is neither as general as Macaulay and Watkins supposed nor as specific as Hartshorne and May believed. In a more recent work Swainson has commented pertinently on this point: 'children absorb, practise and think out moral ideas more fully in a unique and concrete situation—a totality of which they themselves are an integral part—than from generalized theory or precept.'[1] And Eysenck later and much more specifically added: 'Although Hartshorne and May have failed to show that human conduct is completely specific, they have shown conclusively that it is far

[1] B. M. Swainson, *The Development of Moral Ideas in Children and Adolescents*. Unpub. D.Phil. Oxford. 1949. p. 6.

less general than we tend to imagine, and far more strongly determined by the specific situation in which it occurs.'[1]

This is precisely what one would expect. In examining moral conduct one is making conclusions about moral attitudes, and an essential characteristic of an attitude is that it is motivated into action by a specific relationship with a particular referent. Thus, in this sociological sense, although the attitudes are themselves enduring, and so produce consistent behaviour patterns, they are still brought into operation by the specific situation containing the moral referent which activates the agent in a moral way. But equally, one would not expect this conclusion to affect the general thesis that moral growth proceeds by sequential stages. It merely adds another dimension. Actual moral behaviour depends not only on the moral maturity of the agent but also on the situational circumstances of the particular moral dilemma.

Thus the conclusion that moral conduct is so specific to situations that it precludes one from attempting to trace a scheme of moral development, seems on the whole to be inadequate. One may thus return to the evidence of Macaulay and Watkins; accept the hypothesis that they presumably validated; and so pass on from this inchoate form of the theory to consider later research evidence.

PIAGET, 1932

Introduction

Piaget's work marks a further stage in the emergence of some such scheme of moral development. He was evidently impressed by the work of four contemporaries—Durkheim, Fauconnet, Bovet and Baldwin. In fact he based his research and the subsequent report upon their work. Each of them had dealt with a problem which he considered to be relevant to his own studies on the development of moral judgment. These were:

(1) The influence of adult constraint on the child.
(2) The effect of social co-operation on moral judgment.
(3) The reflection of intellectual development on the processes of moral thought.
(4) The interaction of these three factors.

[1] H. J. Eysenck, *The Structure of Human Personality*, p. 8.

In order to throw more light on to these problems he individually interviewed about a hundred Swiss children of primary school age. The social class factor was partially eliminated by choosing children from lower status homes.

The Research Report

Piaget's published report is therefore neatly divided into four sections. The first reports the attitudes[1] of these children to the rules of the game when playing marbles. The second and third chapters report the results of telling children stories which require them to make moral judgments on the basis of the information given. And the last section reviews his findings in the light of social psychology, with particular reference to Durkheim, who had argued that society and its sanctions are the only source of morality.

The complete book is bound together by a single developmental theory, which in its simplest form argues that there are two sequential types of morality, heteronomous and autonomous.

This single theory dominates. In studying children's attitudes to the rules of the game he was led to conclude that there was firstly a morality of constraint and secondly a morality of co-operation. He then examined these two notions more carefully in the subsequent sections of his book. By doing this he discovered that the context of any moral judgment did not invalidate the theory. Finally he moved from psychology to social philosophy in his concluding, subtly speculative last chapter.

It is of course, possible to criticize Piaget's findings in a number of ways and Flavell offers a definitive list of these for the interested reader. Yet, despite these criticisms it is invariably admitted that this method and research programme produced some valuable conclusions.

The Research Conclusions

In the early stages of moral development he found that children began by 'regarding these rules not only as obligatory, but also as inviolable'.[2] At this point the coercive rules, it seems, reflect parental authority. These rules, like parents, constituted part of

---

[1] It should be noted that Piaget nowhere defines what he means by an 'attitude' and so does not use the term in its technical sense.

[2] J. Piaget, *The Moral Judgement of The Child*, p. 104.

the 'given' order of existence, and like parents they too had to be obeyed without question. Later, as a result of social interaction and co-operation it is seen that rules are not absolute. They are created by society. This, it must be emphasized, was not merely a repetition of Durkheim's sociological theories of morality. Piaget concludes that children no longer considered these rules to be unchanging because they did in fact actually alter them on the basis of social consensus. In general then the process is clear. 'Autonomy follows upon heteronomy; the rule of a game appears to the child no longer as an external law sacred in so far as it has been laid down by adults; but as the outcome of a free decision and worthy of respect in the measure that it has enlisted mutual consent.'[1]

In the second section of the report Piaget passes to the nature of children's moral judgments. He discovered two clearly distinct forms. There was firstly the judgment based solely upon the material consequences of wrong-doing. Secondly the judgment which took cognizance of intention or motive. Thus Piaget believes he found a growing pattern of operational thinking. It must however, be remembered that subsequent researchers have queried this.

Edwards for example, found that his older adolescent boys paid no greater attention to motive or intention than the younger. Piaget however, is quite explicit on this point. 'These two attitudes may coexist at the same age and even in the same child, but broadly speaking they do not synchronize. Objective responsibility diminished on the average as the child grows older, and subjective responsibility gains correlatively in importance. We have therefore two processes partially overlapping, but of which the second gradually succeeds in dominating the first.'[2]

Thus the first stage is superseded when children deem the motive or intention to be of prime importance. This implies two things; the rejection of adults as the normative restraining influences, and the admission that parental wishes are not necessarily immutable laws. In a suggested technique which would enable parents to facilitate this moral development Piaget makes the point perfectly clear. 'Such is the prestige of parents in the eyes of the very young child, that even if they lay down nothing in the form of general duties their wishes act as law and thus give

[1] *Ibid.* p. 57.   [2] *Ibid.* p. 129.

rise automatically to moral realism. In order to remove all traces
of moral realism one must place oneself on the child's own level
and give him a feeling of equality by laying stress on one's own
obligation and one's own deficiencies.'[1]

Brennan is quite convinced that his research has confirmed this
conclusion, but he takes it a step further and argues that adults
must deliberately and consciously withdraw their influence and
so allow moral realism in children to diminish more rapidly.
However, the point Piaget makes here is that each child has as
much right to an expression of opinion as any other person. In
practice this development is furthered by the slow realization
that adults are sometimes unjust. Young children, as Bovet
discovered, may begin by deifying their parents but the
passing of this unhealthy stage is inevitable. The morality of
obedience is left behind and the morality of social sanction then
emerges.

It is precisely this to which a consideration of motive rather
than consequence points, as Piaget makes quite clear: 'The child
finds in his brothers and sisters or in his playmates a form of
society which develops his desire for co-operation. Then a new
type of morality will be created in him, a morality of reciprocity
and not of obedience. This is the true morality of intention.'[2]

The ease with which one may identify moral reciprocity and
intellectual reversibility can lead to the view that here one has
the ethical parallel of operational thinking. But Piaget does not
pursue that point. He concludes this section by referring again to
the two types of morality which were seen to operate when children had to subscribe to the rules of the game.

He is careful to note that one must not assume that these form
successive stages of moral development. But he is equally clear
that the evidence *suggests* that one has in fact a sequential relationship separated by an intermediate phase. Thus he argues that
these two moralities are due to formative processes which broadly
speaking follow on one another without, however, constituting
definite stages. It is possible, moreover, to note the existence of an
intermediate phase. 'The first of these processes is the moral
constraint of the adult, a constraint which leads to heteronomy
and consequently to moral realism. The second is co-operation
which leads to autonomy. Between the two can be discerned a

[1] *Ibid.* pp. 133-4.   [2] *Ibid.*

phase during which rules and commands are interiorized and generalized.'[1]

The development of moral judgment from the heteronomous to the autonomous stage must inevitably include a process which can legitimately be described as the interiorizing of rules. Thus one is brought again to this enticing problem, for this section actually closes with his observation—'Autonomy therefore, appears only with reciprocity, when mutual respect is strong enough to make the individual feel from within the desire to treat others as he himself would wish to be treated.'[2] Here the analogy with intellectual development is very close. In passing from pre-operational to operational thinking children must begin to think (as the term implies) in operations. Now an operation is an internalized mental activity capable of reversibility; and psychologically speaking this describes the process, in children, of passing from pre-moral to genuine moral judgment. In this growth one must expect to find the internalizing of rules and the admission of reversibility in their application. This in fact is what his research indicates.

However, after this fascinating and complex disquisition Piaget concludes the second section by saying simply: 'The results obtained in the course of our study of moral realism confirm those of our analysis of the game of marbles. There seem to exist in the child two separate moralities. . . . The first of these processes is the moral constraint of the adult which leads to heteronomy and consequently to moral realism. The second is co-operation which leads to autonomy.'[1]

Thus Piaget passes to the third section of his report. This focuses attention on a more developed form of moral judgment. Since this basic development is a process from moral restraint to moral co-operation he passes from a consideration of the former, which was characterized by moral realism, to a discussion of the latter which is characterized by justice. This latter assumption, that moral co-operation inevitably involves one in a consideration of justice is justified by his view that: 'the sense of justice . . . requires nothing more for its development than the mutual respect and solidarity which holds among children themselves.'[3] And

---

[1] *Ibid.* p. 193. N.B. Moral realism is a technical phrase in Piaget's work. It refers to a child's tendency to submit meekly to the demands of law. cf. pp. 106–7.   [2] *Ibid.* p. 194.   [3] *Ibid.* p. 196.

his conviction that moral co-operation, and its corollary of justice in conduct, characterizes an advanced moral stage in the development of children is made explicit in the sociological observation that: 'As the solidarity between children grows we shall find this notion of justice gradually emerging in almost complete autonomy.'[1]

This moral attitude is totally autonomous. It in no way depends upon adults. Indeed Piaget's central argument is now that this growth is often at the expense of adults. Notions of justice best emerge in children's minds when adults are consciously precluded from bringing any influence to bear. It is this social circumstance, which Brennan emphasized in his work, later noting that for moral development 'It is essential that children should have the experience of living without direct adult supervision.'[2]

Then follows a study of children's views of justice and punishment, and once again the two general kinds of morality are apparent. There emerge two concepts of punishment. Firstly those punishments which result from the transgression of an externally imposed regulation, and secondly those which do not. Of the first kind Piaget writes: 'There are what we shall call expiatory punishments which seem to us to go hand in hand with constraint and the rules of authority.'[3]

The second kind of punishment is more subtle. Here it does not refer to a transgression of any external law, but the violation of a rule or command which had been 'interiorized and generalized'. Thus a child who refused to co-operate and so broke one of the basic rules of social life, needed no punishment to be imposed from without.

This must not be identified with remorse or conscience. The concept is much more complex than this. Once the principle of moral reciprocity is brought into operation, the transgressor is denied normal social relations and is isolated from the group by his own action. Thus his punishment is self-imposed. It is brought about by the operation of reciprocity, which the agent, in this instance, has flouted. Speaking of this kind of punishment Piaget writes: 'There are what we shall call punishments of reciprocity

[1] *Ibid.*
[2] W. K. Brennan, 'The Foundations for Moral Development', *Special Education,* Spring 1965, Vol. LIV. No. 1. p. 7.
[3] J. Piaget, *The Moral Judgement of the Child,* p. 203.

in so far as they go hand in hand with co-operation and rules of equality.'[1]

Once again he finds confirmation of his view that there are two moralities operating in pre-adolescent children and so concludes this section by commenting on both ethical systems. 'The ethics of authority, which is that of duty and obedience, leads in the domain of justice to the confusion of what is just with the content of established law and to the acceptances of expiatory punishment. The ethic of mutual respect, which is that of good as opposed to duty and of autonomy, leads in the domain of justice to the development of equality, which is the idea at the bottom of distributive justice and of reciprocity.'[2]

Finally, one reaches the fourth chapter where this notion of the two moralities is discussed at a speculative level. Here an obvious problem must be solved. If children pass from heteronomy to autonomy in their moral development, how is it possible for them to live in a society which must be regulated by law and stabilized by a legal structure?

The arguments here are tortuous and involved and the difference in the quality of varying sections of the book becomes most pronounced.

Harding suggests that this partly results from the fact that in the first section of the report Piaget functions as a psychologist, whereas in the last he approaches the problems as a sociologist. Thus he notes: 'The sociologist will feel that in this latter part Piaget is at last coming to the heart of the problem; the psychologist will be bored and dissatisfied, feeling that after a good beginning Piaget has let himself sink back into an armchair furnished with the air cushioning of polysyllables. Most psychologists would want their eventual generalizations to refer not to broadly described social trends but to innate psychological processes in the individual members of the group.'[3]

However, Piaget succeeds in solving this sociological problem by basing most of this chapter on the thinking of Durkheim and pursuing the argument to the end. His solution is simple. Following Durkheim he assumes that: 'Society is the only source of morality'.[4] One needs only to place besides this, Piaget's earlier

---

[1] *Ibid.*   [2] *Ibid.*

[3] D. W. Harding, *Social Psychology and Individual Values*, p. 44.

[4] J. Piaget, *The Moral Judgement of the Child*, p. 326.

assertion, 'All morality consists in a system of rules'.[1] Now the problem is solved. Such rules require a sociological context for their development! 'Morality presupposes the existence of rules which transcend the individual and these rules could only develop through contact with other people. Thus the fundamental conceptions of childish morality consist of those imposed by the adult and of those born of collaboration between children themselves. In both cases that is to say, whether the child's moral judgments are heteronomous or autonomous, accepted under pressure or worked out in freedom, this morality is social, and on this point Durkheim was unquestionably right.'[2]

Before closing this review of his conclusions there is only one further observation which needs to be made. There is here an implicit reference to a further stage of moral development. These autonomous, freely constructed rules constitute ideals which are always approved by society. There would thus appear to be a normative autonomy in moral development, which is reflected both in society and the individual. The grave weakness of this position is unfortunately too evident in the history of mankind. It cannot explain the lives of outstandingly moral men, like Christ and Socrates, who were rejected by society. This is a further problem for which Piaget finds no satisfactory solution. The nearest he comes to an answer consists simply of a quotation from Durkheim: 'Socrates expressed more faithfully than his judges the morality that suited the society of his time.'[3]

Having now established that children are social beings whose learning takes place in the context of a social group, he concludes with the educational precept which Brennan recently emphasized. 'If then we had to choose from among the totality of existing educational systems those which would best correspond with our psychological results we would turn our methods in the direction of what has been called 'group work' and 'self government'.[4]

An Assessment of Piaget's Conclusions
The importance of this work cannot be over-estimated. Thus the powerful support which it gives to a developmental theory of moral growth must now be assessed before proceeding to the next publication on this subject.

[1] *Ibid.* p. 1.   [2] *Ibid.* p. 344.   [3] *Ibid.* p. 346.   [4] *Ibid.* p. 412.

Probably the most redoubtable critic of Piaget was Isaacs. She attacked him in a number of ways. She criticized his terminology and complained that he: 'Underestimates the richness and complexity of the emotional life and personal awareness of the child.'[1] But the most damaging criticism for the purposes of this study is her rejection of Piaget's developmental stages. She had earlier argued from her observations in the Cambridge experimental school that any advance in conceptual understanding was characterized not by sequential stages but by a growth of complexity. 'Intellectual growth certainly shows a psychological coherence; but this coherence has the elasticity and vital movement of a living process, not the rigid formality of a logical system.'[2]

She further continues: 'It is not that one kind of structure gives place to another it is rather that there is a progressive penetration of feeling and phantasy by experience, a progressive ordering by relational thought of the child's responses to the world.'[3]

Here one finds an echo of the sharp clash between educators who adopt a genetic view and those who advocate an experiential view of learning. For this study, however, the important point is that Isaacs sharply opposed Piaget's developmental scheme. Thus within a decade the problem of hypothesization was again planted firmly in the path of the researcher. If Isaacs was right then one must abandon all hope of tracing a scheme of moral development. The dilemma faced when studying the work of Macaulay and Watkins and Hartshorne and May thus has once more to be resolved. It is true that Isaacs' strictures are directed against Piaget's view of intellectual rather than moral growth. But this makes little difference.

There was an almost immediate confirmation of Piaget's position by Smith. Yet later it looked as though Piaget's general conclusion about moral development needed to be revised.

Smith said that he could trace three clear stages in moral development from childhood to adolescence. The first he believed was characterized by obedience to parents; the second by subscription to law; and the third was governed by personal relationships. However, the need for some revision seemed to be

---

[1] S. Isaacs, *Mind*, Review, pp. 85ff. Reference from p. 98.
[2] S. Isaacs, *Intellectual Growth in Young Children*, p. 97.
[3] *Ibid.* p. 107.

established by the fact that Isaacs' comment was only the first of a series of pungent and penetrating criticisms.

Harrower disagreed with Piaget's view that a sense of justice developed independently of adult influence. She claimed also that she could find no clear developmental stages even though she had specifically set out to do this. Lerner made a close study of 'moral realism' and became convinced that Piaget had been far too superficial in his view of morality as adult constraint. He thus considerably modified the concepts of this stage in Piaget's developmental scheme.

MacRae too was a critic of Piaget. He believed that both Piaget and Lerner were wrong. They had mistakenly assumed that there was only one dominant factor in moral development. He criticized Piaget's methodology complaining that his interview questions implied that, apart from age, there was only one relevant factor to consider. For MacRae, therefore, the stages of development were an illusory corollary of the methodology. They indicated no more than the fact that other elements needed to be considered. The impact of parental pressure, the emotional response of children in an identification situation and the predisposing elements within different social class and societies, all needed to be considered: all of which is similar to Valentine's criticism of Hartshorne and May.

However, one can find support for the Piagetian position in the work of Brennan. He has not only sustained the view that one may clearly discern four stages in the growth of moral judgment, but believes further that the withdrawal of adult influences enhance the prospect of this growth towards equity. His work happened to be with educationally sub-normal (E.S.N.) and maladjusted children and is thus open to some criticism. Yet Brennan remains convinced that a programme of social education, built upon the Piagetian plan, will succeed. Thus he concluded later: 'It is essential that children should have the experience of living without direct adult supervision or direction . . . It is in such free time that children form spontaneous play and peer groups in which they may experience the basic emotions necessary if constraint is to be replaced by co-operation. The aim is to re-create as far as possible the "Rich democracy of the Street", so important in the development of the working class child living at home. But within the group the individual child moves but slowly through the socializing process from unconcern for others, through conflict to co-operation, so that it is essential that children have time to attempt their own solutions to their own problems, to settle their own quarrels without immediate adult intervention.'[1]

Goldman too has supported Piaget in an oblique way. His work has been the most recent comprehensive confirmation of the Piagetian scheme outside the realm of intellectual development. But one must immediately admit that Goldman's bibliography omits any reference to the work of Fleming which vigorously rejects this theory. Therefore, in order to balance this presentation of Piaget's work one must end on a polemical note.

The Piaget/Isaacs conflict appears now to be a Goldman/Fleming confrontation. In this phase of the debate one may perhaps allow Dr Fleming to have the final word. In a recent publication she has said of Goldman: 'He does not take seriously the evidence from long term studies that growth is gradual and continuous and that variability and disharmony are characteristic of all human development.'[2] Had she been alive today Susan Isaacs would undoubtedly have subscribed to this view and been as pungent and pointed in her remarks!

But despite these criticisms Piaget's view that one can trace a scheme of moral development seems to be assured by at least two considerations. Firstly Piaget's subsequent work in other fields has confirmed this general developmental view. Secondly many later studies of moral development have each presented a similar developmental scheme. One of particular value is the work of Loughran (*see* pp. 178ff. below). He deliberately replicated Piaget's research with adolescent children and found that Piaget's general conclusions were not only still valid over forty years later with children of a different nationality, but also that his developmental scheme was applicable to adolescents as well as children.

HAVIGHURST AND TABA 1949

Introduction
Havighurst and Taba worked, with a team of researchers, in the small American middle-west town of Morris, Illinois. This has

[1] W. K. Brennan, *op. cit.*, p. 7.
[2] C. M. Fleming, 'Research Evidence and Christian Education' in *Learning for Living*, September 1966, p. 12.

been variously designated Elmtown and Prairie City in different reports. Under the auspices of the Chicago Committee on Human Development they studied the character and personality of 'all boys and girls in the Prairie City area who became ten years old in the calendar year 1942 and all those who became sixteen'.[1]

By the term 'character' (as has already been observed) they meant something quite specific and moral in its connotations. 'Character is a word with many meanings. It is used here in the current sense of "moral character". Thus for the purposes of these studies "character" is that part of personality which is most subject to social approval.'[2]

Research Procedure

Havighurst and Taba argued that character develops as a result of three forces: reward and punishment, unconscious imitation and reflective thinking. One may be forgiven perhaps for finding here a clear reflection of the view that morality passes from the prudential stage of reward and punishment, through the social stage of unconscious imitation, into the personal stage of reflective thinking.

They, however, postulated only two levels of character, the first is controlled by social expectation and the second by moral ideals. They then defined character in terms of traits, deeming it to be an amalgam of moral traits; and fortunately they achieved this without falling into the error of Hartshorne and May. Thus they occupy a position midway between the conclusions of Macaulay and Watkins and those of Hartshorne and May. Having postulated a developmental pattern of morality but at the same time recognizing its complexity, they systematized this complexity by their treatment of moral traits and decided that there were five. These were the most outstanding: honesty, responsibility, moral courage, loyalty and friendliness. They then turned to the problem of research and concluded: 'It was necessary to find something about an individual which would serve as an index of his honesty, responsibility, moral courage, loyalty and friendliness.'[3]

Havighurst and Taba then reviewed the techniques which had

[1] R. J. Havighurst and H. Taba, *Adolescent Character and Personality*, p. 20.　　　　[2] *Ibid.* p. 3.　　　　[3] *Ibid.* p. 9.

been used earlier by the Character Education Inquiry and carefully considered the ingenious test situations of Hartshorne and
May. At first these commended themselves as empirically controlled substitutes for everyday experience in which honesty and
other traits could be tested, but they finally decided not to employ
artificial techniques. Everyday experiences, they argued, cannot
be faithfully re-created under such artificial conditions. 'In the
light of these considerations it seemed desirable to use reputations
as an index of character. A person's reputation is based primarily
upon long observation of his behaviour by his associates. Although
not trained to record and interpret their observations objectively
a person's associates have the advantage over professional
observers that they have observed the person in real life over a
long period of time.'[1]

Character reputations were thus given tremendous weight. The
fact that misgivings about this method thread their way through
the report, show their methodological dilemma. However, they
are quite explicit about their resolution of this dilemma. 'For the
purposes of these studies reputational ratings were used as the
principle means of measuring character.'[2]

As the investigation progressed the team tried to systematize
the data in order to delineate some character types. These they
called the self-directive, the adaptive, the submissive, the defiant
and the unadjusted persons. The first three had high character
reputations and the last two had low ratings. Almost all the children fell into one of these categories, but the largest number
seemed to belong to the self-directive group. The authors then
gave comprehensive case studies of each character type to complete the picture, finally ending with some practical suggestions which should be considered in framing a course on moral
education.

In conclusion it should be said that a scheme of this kind,
which suggests a parallel between personality types and moral
development, can leave a false impression. Most children were
classified as belonging to the highest group, yet almost a third of
the children could not be classified in terms of a dominant personality type. Apart from the fringe 4 per cent of defiant personalities, the population sample was not too dramatically disparate
in its character grouping. In terms of percentages, the 65 per cent

[1] *Ibid.* pp. 9–10.   [2] *Ibid.* p. 10.

of the sample left were divided as follows: self-directive 21 per cent, submissive 17 per cent, unadjusted 16 per cent, and adaptive 11 per cent.

General Conclusions

Before passing to the general conclusions of Havighurst and Taba it is worth emphasizing again that these stand roughly midway between the extremes already referred to earlier.[1] This is further confirmed by the fact that they posed a counterbalance against this clear systematization. This corrective is their emphasis on the importance and value of particular and isolated actions in the context of moral development. Indeed they are so convinced that it is through an accumulation of reactions to specific and immediate situations, that moral beliefs and values develop, that they conclude that moral education must take place with reference to concrete acts. But this is only an accommodation to the existing situation for they quickly add, 'This reflects the fact that teaching of what is right and wrong is done with reference to isolated, concrete acts of behaviour; relatively little effort is made to help young people generalize from these situations or to help them to develop a coherent moral philosophy.'[2]

This clearly implies that moral education is that process which helps children to develop their own moral philosophy. And this suggests that they should live self-directive lives based on a coherent value system, which springs from rationally held ethical principles.

This is also interesting in that it not only refers backwards to Hartshorne and May, but forward to Swainson, Eysenck and the conclusions reached in a later report of the Committee on Human Development. Hartshorne and May had argued that moral education should consist of teaching children to have socially acceptable habits in specific situations. Swainson is convinced that moral requirements are only really discerned in a concrete situation. Eysenck believes that the imperative springs from a conscience which is primarily a generalized conditioned response arising from a whole series of responses to specific and particular situations. And Peck and Havighurst believe that the rationally held and applied principles, which emerge from experiental data, are the hallmark of the morally mature person.

[1] See pp. 36ff and pp. 46ff above.   [2] *Ibid.* p. 95.

In addition to this conclusion they reached others. They believed that in the matter of moral values, adolescents are strongly conditioned by family and peers, the community mores and church attendance. At the age of sixteen children are mostly unable to apply their moral values in an increasingly complex society. Emotional adjustment, as MacRae later noted, is an extremely important contributory factor in moral development. And Prairie City (like any other 'folk' society) imposed a rigid code of behaviour in which it was difficult to reach moral maturity.

Perhaps the only corrective necessary here is that of Neubauer. She studied these children in relation to church attendance, and although Havighurst and Taba acknowledge what seems to them to be the self-evident influence of Christian belief upon moral development, she concludes, as did Swainson, that: 'Church membership itself is not an independently powerful influence in the development of character, but that church membership is often associated with other factors that tend to produce good or bad character reputations.'[1]

A Tentative Assessment

This comprehensive and extremely valuable report avoids the error of Hartshorne and May by establishing that traits must be classified within a developmental system. But it tends to fall into the error which Piaget only avoided with the greatest of difficulty and subtlety of thought. In defining character as a composite of moral traits and then concentrating upon the traits of honesty, loyalty, friendliness, responsibility and moral courage, it can be too easily and falsely assumed that the highest moral character still requires social approval.

Individuals must grow from the stage of social morality to that of personal morality. Yet they must live in a social context while doing so. Piaget solved this rather unconvincingly by quoting Durkheim's comment about Socrates. Havighurst and Taba unfortunately leave this problem unresolved. For them the most desirable moral traits have social connotations even though the self-directive persons, for whom social sanctions have little force, are the ones of whom they speak with most approval.

It may be that a methodology which places such emphasis on

[1] D. Neubauer, 'The Relation of the Church to Character Formation' in *Adolescent Character and Development*, Havighurst and Taba, p. 68.

character reputations and so derives its data from social sources, leads inevitably to this dilemma. If one assists at childbirth with a pair of sharp forceps the impressions left may look very much like birthmarks. Consequently a whole system of paediatrics may grow up around babies and these marks. Thus the problem of methodology is both central and crucial.

GESELL, AND HIS ASSOCIATES, 1946–56

Here one finds a comprehensive account of the development of children from the age of five to sixteen years. Their work covers every aspect of this growth and so includes some very important sections on moral development during the school years.

In general these writers believe that the moral growth of this period is presaged during the first five years of life. From this they conclude that the next two cycles of development, i.e. from six to ten years and then from eleven to sixteen years, simply build upon this early foundation. This building process is facilitated by increasing intellectual power and widening social relationships. Although the ground plan for morality is laid down in the pre-school years the edifice erected upon this can be modified considerably as the child grows. This point comes out clearly when after having given, in outline, some idea of how the ethical sense emerges in the early years, they add, 'To a remarkable degree equivalents of these ethical stages reappear in the cycle of years from five to ten and emerge once more in the cycle from ten to sixteen. In general, each of these cycles registers an improvement and broadening of ethical attitudes.'[1]

At first glance it looks very much as though their thesis replicates that of Isaacs. Both she and Gesell suggest that development proceeds by a process of increased comprehension and an enrichment of interpersonal relationships. This clearly suggests a merely quantitative growth in complexity. But this is a false impression, and two sound reasons can be adduced for supporting this contention. The first is implicit in all Gesell's studies. The second is explicit in the work now under review.

In all his writings we find Gesell coming down heavily upon the side of those who view all growth as sequential. He is certain

[1] A. Gesell, F. L. Ilg, and L. B. Ames, *Youth: the Years from Ten to Sixteen*, pp. 464–5.

that each step is only possible because of the preceding stage. But this, one may argue, merely emphasizes his cyclical view of development. Thus, secondly, one must add the explicit statement which suggests that here too is confirmation not only of a sequential development scheme, but of one which supports the Piagetian view in its general outlines, for he continues: 'There is an unmistakable trend from the specific to the general and from the concrete to the abstract. Another trend shows increasing tolerance, a quality of judiciousness, and a regard for the relativities of conduct. Most impressive is the consistent concern for fairness, which shows up at all the ages from ten to sixteen. For youth this seems to be a cardinal moral virtue, which progresses from fairness claimed for the individual to fairness claimed also for others.'[1]

All the Piagetian elements are here and the value of this evidence lies in the fact that the records of Gesell are based on longitudinal studies of children from birth to adolescence. Both facts explain the biological orientation of the records and the tendency to be descriptive rather than analytical in their accounts of behaviour. But this deficiency is insignificant when placed beside the advantages of such a methodology.

The general hypothesis too is interesting. Growth is the result of a tension between stability and plasticity in human experience. In this it is possible to discern another Piagetian conviction, for this notion is very similar to that of Piaget. He believes that intellectual development proceeds through a series of equilibria. These are transitional stages, when for a while the tension existing between the tendencies to assimilate and to accommodate has been resolved. However, for Gesell, behaviour emerges in the need to adapt and in this adaptation the active organism grows. This growth or maturation is indexed by maturity traits. Each one is assigned a development quotient and these quotients are then the guide or criteria whereby growth is assessed.

The three volumes of Gesell's reports,[2] referred to below, leave one with two positive convictions. Firstly that his contribution towards an understanding of maturation is more useful in the early years when analytical diagnoses are not so essential to our understanding of child development. Secondly, that this wealth of evidence points clearly to moral development as sequential,

[1] *Ibid.* p. 465.   [2] See p. 104.

and thus provides further support for the main argument of this chapter. Unfortunately, the insights afforded do not extend to a definition of maturational levels. One is told more about *what* children think, than *how* they think. Thus in turning to Gesell for help one is provided with descriptions and not analyses. Although it is clear throughout that some attempt is made to define moral age-norms.

SWAINSON, 1949[1]

Swainson's study is both exhaustive and comprehensive. It attempts to trace the development of moral ideas from childhood to adolescence and appears to have used every conceivable kind of relevant available research technique for this purpose.

Her review of the pertinent published literature laid bare the plan of hypothesization. It was that 'moral development consists of progressive integration of the psyche in increasing mutual relations with an ever widening environment'.[1] Apart from her re-affirmation of the opinion of Hartshorne and May, that moral activity can only be judged specifically and in concrete instances, this echo of Isaacs constitutes the primary conclusion to which her study points.

In the development of this theme, however, three important elements emerge. There is firstly the view that Gestalt psychology offers many insights which can clarify this process. This theory asserts that man's conduct is motivated by his need not only to re-establish equilibrium at higher levels, but also to perceive more complex and comprehensive patterns to explain his experience. Secondly, she affirms the centrality of the concept of a 'love-morality' which she deems to be the integrating element in both society and the individual. Thirdly, the work is clearly explicitly involved with an attempt to understand how a sense of moral responsibility emerges. For her it is this sense of responsibility which constitutes the essence of morality.

That these three elements cohere into an integrated whole is made quite clear by her comment in reference to moral responsibility. Speaking of this as a moral imperative she remarks: 'To

[1] B. M. Swainson, *The Development of Moral Ideas in Children and Adolescents*, Unpub. D.Phil. Oxford, 1949. Preface.

obey this imperative normally results in happiness owing to the achievement of harmony with the whole.'[1]

Thus her final conclusion that the moral development of children 'is due not solely to thwarted impulses nor solely to social pressure',[2] so successfully repudiates the Freudian view, that one finds a contemporary critic of Freud almost echoing this conviction. Stafford-Clark dealing with the same problem observes: 'It is arguable that the ultimate source of morality, as experienced subjectively in conscience, must be something beyond the individual traditions and environment if it is to be meaningful; it cannot be merely the distilled or distorted relics of infantile experience and environment.'[3]

Thus, by this path Swainson reaches her conclusion. It is simply that, 'Child morality ... springs primarily from the positive impulse to love-relationships within the individual and develops in proportion as he becomes a more complete person in response to an ever widening environment. Development takes place by means of creative tension between the morality of being true to oneself and the morality of relating to the other. Yet these apparent opposites become reconciled in the realization that the self is not fulfilled without the other, so that in moral maturity the conflicts of youth are resolved into a glad acceptance.'[4]

The Methodology of the Project

In order to reach this comprehensive conclusion Swainson gathered and analysed a tremendous amount of empirical data from children of all ages and social classes. In this she took great care to see that her sample did not reflect any topographical subculture.

The techniques employed were varied. She used questionnaires and free essays, substituting the latter with free pictorial expression for the primary school children, and augmenting all this material with depth interviews. Her questionnaires are very interesting. In these she recounted incidents upon which the children had to pass a moral judgment. In the presentation of this

[1] *Ibid.*, Introduction.
[2] *Ibid.* p. 126.
[3] J. Stafford-Clark, *What Freud Really Said*, p. 204.
[4] B. M. Swainson, *The Development of Moral Ideas in Children and Adolescents*, p. 126.

material she stands in a line of developing methodology from Piaget, who simply recounted such stories, to McKnight whose alternative answers, supplied with the story, had been structured into an attitude scale, from raw data supplied by other means. Her stories are similar to those used by Piaget, but the possible answers are supplied in the form of alternatives, as in the case of McKnight. Thus here one has a technique which is not only employing a projective device, but incorporating an attitude scale.

The Development Scheme

For the purposes of this introductory review it is not necessary to study the developmental scheme which emerges from this important piece of research. This will be examined in greater detail when outlining the hypothesis of moral development by stages. It is important however, to note here that such a scheme emerges from the study.

For Swainson there appear to be three stages. They are organized around the central thesis that morality emerges from the inevitable tensions which exist between the social-self and society. But they clearly fit into a scheme of development of the kind outlined by Piaget. These stages, like those of Smith cover infancy, childhood and adolescence. In infancy the 'I-thou' tension not only involves one in the need to be acceptable to others but also in the attempt to reduce the world to manageable proportions. Thus, she argues, prudential and authoritarian modes of thinking govern moral conduct at this stage.

During childhood further tensions emerge which cause the moral sanctions to undergo drastic change. The authoritarian structure is perpetuated since children at this stage require a stable external framework. This imposes control, but it also supplies a sense of security within which development takes place. At the same time this self-regarding claim meets the demands of society in a new form. At this stage it is the collective morality of the peer group which begins to grow in importance. Thus one finds the social sanction emerging with new force.

Finally in adolescence, this 'self-society' tension is internalized so that where previously there had been imposition from without there is now control from within. Thus although the fundamental problem remains, morality at this point ceases to be an approximation to an external requirement and becomes essentially a process of personal adjustment. Now personal sanctions emerge, for as external control becomes self-control the process leading towards moral autonomy is virtually complete.

MCKNIGHT, 1950

Although this work is contained within a slender volume, it is a clear report of great value. McKnight tested 159 Scottish children between the ages of eight and fourteen years, primarily to study different types of moral sanction. His full aim, however, was fourfold. He wished to elucidate the moral controls operating within this age range; the relationship between general intelligence and moral-test performance; the relationships between the economic and social environment; and finally the influence of the respondent's sex on test performance. His work makes it quite clear however, that he is primarily interested in the nature of the moral controls in children of this age range. Indeed he calls his thesis 'The Moral Sanctions of the Child'.

His method of testing has been described above. It consisted of a simple test which was projective in form and allied to one of the tests used by Swainson. McKnight himself admits that the application of such a simple test in one Scottish school in a rural area may not produce results which could be validly generalized. Yet his findings are extremely important for this present study.

Limited though the sample and techniques of testing may have been, he was able to show that the four primary moral controls, described by McDougall and later designated by Kennedy-Fraser as the prudential, the authoritative, the social and the personal, were in fact effective amongst the children studied. But in addition he discerned some general trends in development. 'With increasing age the authoritative level exercised rather less control and the personal level distinctly more.'[1]

His tabulated data shows too that the social control slowly overtakes the authoritarian control during the ninth to twelfth years. Thus amongst his general conclusions he can say: 'There is considerable correspondence between chronological age and level of moral control.'[2] But it is quite clear that there is no

[1] R. K. McKnight, *The Moral Sanctions of the Child,* Unpub. B.Ed. Glasgow, p. 27.
[2] *Ibid.* p. 32.

inevitable maturation of moral development since the correspondence between *mental* age and the kind of moral control exercised is even greater. Thus the highly intelligent children reach the personal stage of morality before their less gifted fellows.

Once again however, one finds McKnight's conclusions midway between those of Macaulay and Watkins and Hartshorne and May. He believed not only that a scheme of development could be traced but also that there is a certain degree of moral specificity. 'The principles involved in a situation are important factors in the response which occurs.'[1]

However, this work presents one with a clear developmental scheme within which the specificity operates in terms of varying moral controls. These are specific to each situation and vary with the concrete circumstances which determine their operation.

MORRIS 1955

From our clear confirmation of the general thesis we must turn to a subsequent research report, which partially contradicts this view. Here we find clear empirical evidence for rejecting the view that it is possible to trace a simple and clearly defined pattern in moral development. But this is a rejection which must be modified in terms which would also qualify it as an acceptance of the developmental view. As will be seen, it is Morris's emphasis on the specificity of moral conduct, which leads to this conclusion.

He took up the problem of moral development at the point where it had been left by Piaget. Recognizing the validity of Piaget's distinction between moral heteronomy and autonomy and noting that Piaget had limited his investigation to preadolescent children, he decided to continue this study into the adolescent age range.

This he did by studying a random sample of three hundred secondary school children in London and Manchester. He centred his interviews with them around the 'problem situation tests', to which reference has already been made above. Thus his original impetus originated with the work of Piaget. This apparent predisposition towards accepting the viability of a developmental theory of moral growth is revealed by his later observation: 'What remains still unclear is the relationship be-

[1] *Ibid.* p. 33.

tween age and moral development in Britain during the period of adolescence.'[1]

Yet Morris was critical of Piaget's conclusions. One of the main difficulties in the way of accepting Piaget's scheme of moral development, he argued, was the disparity between empirical observation and theoretical deduction. Thus Morris criticizes Piaget's 'use of analytical categories of a much higher order of abstraction than the observations on which they are based'.[2]

It is not therefore surprising to find that on the whole Morris is convinced that his research findings do not fit into any clearly defined theory of moral development. He concludes his study by observing: 'Those who hold the view that character development consists in the acquisition of a body of explicit principles to which conduct is referred, will find little of comfort in the data we have presented.'[3]

Despite this pessimistic assessment of his own data, it should be noted that one of his primary conclusions was that there appeared to be a general decline in the dependence of morality upon authority and a corresponding increase in a morality which was independent of heteronomous regulations. On this important point he is unequivocably concise. 'Our results show clearly that the trend postulated by Piaget towards increasing equity can be discerned in our material.'[4]

Morris himself indicates two important considerations to be borne in mind when assessing his apparently non-Piagetian conclusions. Firstly unlike Piaget, he was inordinately interested in what he calls: 'The discrepancies between value-judgments and expectations of what is actually likely to be done.'[5]

Secondly, again unlike Piaget, he was extremely anxious to review the situational nature of value judgments. Thus he remarks: 'Each respondent brings to the standardized problems which we provide a fund of experiences of situations which he considers to be relevant to those given. Variations in the responses appear quite comprehensible when one knows the points of reference that the respondent is using and his expectations of antecedent and subsequent conditions in the problems with which he is dealing.'[6]

---

[1] J. F. Morris, 'The Development of Adolescent Value-Judgements', p. 8.
[2] J. F. Morris, 'A Study of Value-Judgements in Adolescents', p. 26.
[3] *Ibid*. p. 378.   [4] *Ibid*. p. 376.   [5] *Ibid*. p. 378.   [6] *Ibid*.

Because he emphasized situational differences he worked more closely to the methods of Hartshorne and May than those of Piaget. It is therefore not surprising to find him concluding that: 'Our findings, like theirs (i.e. Hartshorne and May) show situational differences.'[1] Again a medial position is reached in which both the specificity of moral conduct and a scheme of development are then partially admitted. The only difference in all these conclusions seems to be one of emphasis—an emphasis which places each conclusion at a different point in a continuum between these extremes.

Whether this indicates that the results of research are implicitly related to the methodology employed, is a fundamental question, which cannot be pursued here. What is clear however, is that although his results do not readily fit into any clear theory of moral development, a general trend can be discerned in the pupils' progress from heteronomous to autonomous moral conduct.

PECK AND HAVIGHURST 1960

Introduction
This is the latest report of American research into moral development. The first had originated with the Character Education Inquiry, under the direction of Hartshorne and May. These earlier findings, it will be remembered, were published between 1928 and 1930 and were followed by considerable discussion but little research. Morris claims that this prolonged inactivity, 'May have been due to the paralysing effect of the Hartshorne-May work upon the settled preconceptions of educators'.[2]

Peck and Havighurst were much more explicit in their view. 'An unfortunate effect of the Character Education Inquiry was that it stunned and discouraged the proponents of experimentation and objective study in the field of character education. Thus it was a decade before people began to theorize and experiment again.'[3] A view incidentally, which was repeated literally by the same committee ten years later. 'One unintended result of the Character Education Inquiry was that it apparently discouraged proponents of experimentation and objective study in

---

[1] *Ibid.* p. 381.   [2] *Ibid.* p. 44.
[3] R. F. Peck and R. J. Havighurst, *Educational Research in the Field of Character Development.*

the field of character education. Most educators and psychologists reacted to the Inquiry by turning away from this complex area of human behaviour. Thus it was a decade before people began to theorize and experiment again, with the conviction that they could accomplish something useful in this field.'[1]

It was left to Havighurst and Taba to reopen the research inquiries in this area of personality development. This second report consisted of work produced by the members of the Committee of Human Development, and was published under the names of Havighurst and Taba. As has already been noted this work was conducted in the small mid-western town of Morris in Illinois. Even a cursory reading of that report (which was in fact a selection of interim reports on work which was still in progress) reveals the importance of this publication. Thus Morris says with confidence: 'There seems no doubt that this study ranks with the Columbia Education Inquiry as a landmark in the study of adolescent values in the United States.'[2]

Research Report

We thus come to the latest report in this series. This has been published under the names of Peck and Havighurst. In it the earlier promise of a longitudinal study on moral development has been kept.

Peck and Havighurst begin by reviewing previous research projects but finally decide to place their emphasis not upon the specificity of moral conduct, but upon its general persistence and predictability. Of this they say: 'If behaviour were viewed from a different angle from the one the Character Education Inquiry adopted, that of persistent attitudes and ways of relating to people, it seemed to us likely that "popular opinion" about the generality of moral character, which Hartshorne and his colleagues felt was discredited by their studies, might turn out to be not so far wrong at all.'[3]

But it must be noted that although they adopted a different vantage point from which to survey this field, they still secured

[1] R. F. Peck and R. J. Havighurst, *The Psychology of Character Development*, p. vi.

[2] J. F. Morris, *op. cit.*, p. 61.

[3] R. F. Peck and R. J. Havighurst, *The Psychology of Character Development*, p. vi. Cf. Chapter 9 below.

the all-important continuity of sample. This was done by a deliberate policy of studying the adolescents who had already been surveyed by the earlier (1949) team of researchers. Thus they could also draw upon earlier findings to supplement their own research.

They begin with the perennial question, 'What is moral character?', and proceed to consider not only its constitution but also the various environmental influences which affect its development. Basing their hypotheses upon Freud's view that the stages of development can be categorized as oral, anal, phallic and genital, they augmented this with Fromm's adaptation of these stages into the specifically moral classifications of receptive, exploitative, hoarding and marketing personalities. Thus, Peck and Havighurst produced a motivational theory of morality in terms of psycho-social development. They hypothesized five character types. These were designated as amoral, expedient, conforming, irrational-conscientious and rational-altruistic. It must however be emphasized that: 'These types are merely a descriptive device. It was found as anticipated, that no one was entirely of (one) type.'[1]

From this hypothetical categorizing, emerge two very important secondary hypotheses. Firstly, these different personality types constitute five primary types of moral motivation. Thus they begin their report: 'This set of character types was intended to: (1) be defined and labelled in terms of the control system the individual uses to adapt his search for satisfaction to the requirements of the social world: (2) include all the possible modes of adaptation. (3) be defined in terms of motivation (so long as it achieves behavioral expression)'.[2]

Secondly, that each of these types is not only a component of character and thus a motivational factor, but also represents a definite stage in a developmental scheme: 'A set of five character types was defined, each conceived as the representative of a successive stage in the psycho-social development of the individual.'[3] But there is the further advantage that, 'This serves the additional purpose in thinking about the motivation patterns as an ascending developmental sequence, from childlike reasons to mature reasons for behaving morally'.[4]

[1] *Ibid.* p. 166. [2] *Ibid.* p. 4.
[3] *Ibid.* p. 3. [4] *Ibid.* p. 4.

They then proceed to show that this hypothesization is supported by the empirical evidence and further claim that their definition of character types can be expressed in terms of moral motivation. This motivation therefore, alters with the maturing of individual personality. Finally, although the *form* of motivation changes the basic personality structure of the individual's morality remains stable. Conduct is therefore relatively predictable.

Before continuing with this important point, namely that the basic moral structure persists in each individual, it is worth noting that the sociological orientation of this study provides some extremely valuable psycho-social data. They study and report upon the various influences acting upon the respondents in this research. By drawing particular attention to the family, the peer group and the social environment they show how each makes its contribution to the moral development of the individual children studied.

However, their point concerning the permanence of individual moral structures, is more relevant to this book. This permanence they insist, is only relative even though it can be described as persisting. On this point they conclude: 'This persistence is observable in two ways. The adequacy of an individual's moral motives and behaviour relative to his own age group seems to stay at about the same relative level as he develops . . . the ones who have relatively best control at ten are likely to have the best self-control in their age group at sixteen.'[1]

Thus, although the expected pattern of moral maturation emerged from these studies, moral character, as they saw it, displayed this remarkable consistency. Thus there is no insoluble dilemma met in the consideration that consistency can be maintained as maturational processes produce change in the personality. 'As the children were studied from age ten to seventeen, each individual tended to show a stable predictable pattern of moral character. Many of their overt actions changed, of course, as they grew older, learned new social and intellectual skills, and developed through puberty. However, each child appeared to maintain very persistently his deeply held feeling and attitudes towards life, and the modes of reacting which we call his character structures.'[2]

[1] *Ibid.* p. 165.   [2] *Ibid.* p. 155.

This point needs to be underlined because of its educational implications. This conclusion ascribes such immutability to moral attitudes that any attempt to modify anti-social attitudes may be a harder educational task than is at present realized. It is argued later in this book that such a conclusion is double-edged. If it is true that moral attitudes have this enduring quality, then successful processes of moral education will create socially desirable attitudes which are equally enduring.

The Developmental Pattern

Finally, the conclusions of this study can be briefly outlined. The evidence supports the view that there is an enduring basic pattern of moral character. Morality can be designated as a particular aspect of the whole personality, and each moral type of person displays a distinctive personality pattern. The parental and familial experiences of children are the most potent forces moulding their moral character. The peer group, is thus not an originator, but a reinforcer of the moral values developed in the family. Even siblings seem to exert little influence.

The family exists in a specific cultural milieu. Indeed the interaction between the values of the family and the community constitute the mores of the society and this emerges as an ethical value system, to which all its members would naturally subscribe. Thus the influence of the community cannot be discounted even though it operates in such a pervasive and indirect manner.

The most important conclusion for this book, however, is that the hypothesizing of personality types in terms of moral stages of development, was substantiated by the empirical findings of this research project. It must be accepted, as was noted above, that this typology is purely descriptive. No one person has such a consistent and unalloyed moral character that he or she can be classified as belonging exclusively to one of these categories. Yet when the respondents are classified, according to their dominant moral characteristics, they form clearly defined groups of the kind hypothesized. Thus Peck and Havighurst can conclude: 'judging from the present research it appears possible and useful to define "basic character" in a series of five types arranged on an ascending scale of psychological and moral maturity.'[1]

Before concluding the review of this work, it might be useful to

[1] *Ibid.* pp. 165–6.

emphasize again the central paradox. These research reports show that moral development contains both dynamic and static elements. The dynamic quality is most obvious in the fact that children develop morally and pass through different sequential stages in this process. The static element is apparent when one considers that despite this growth the characteristics of an individual's moral conduct remain essentially the same. The relationship between the two elements seems to be one of mutual dependence. Both are inherent in any moral conduct. In the terms of our thesis it can be simply said that this developmental scheme contains enduring and persistent characteristics which emerge as moral attitudes.

In an earlier work Havighurst expressed the belief that there are 'development tasks' appropriate to each stage of development. This basic truth can thus be expressed differently, in the terms of a related thesis. Here it can be argued that the way in which each child approaches his own development tasks displays a high degree of consistency, even though the tasks and the techniques employed to master them perpetually change. Thus what one finds in both the theses, is simply a longitudinal dimension of personality rating.

However, this last American report comes down firmly on the side of researchers who have tried to discern a scheme of moral development in children. Indeed the writers even go further and make the tentative suggestion that these developmental stages may be located from infancy to childhood as follows: 'Amoral type=infancy; Expedient type=early childhood; Conforming type=later childhood; Irrational-conscientious=later childhood; Rational-altruistic = adolescence to adulthood.'[1]

It now only remains to review the foregoing accounts to decide finally whether it is legitimate to hypothesize a scheme of moral development without doing violence to the evidence at hand.

CONCLUSION

The above review of relevant literature on moral development has necessarily been simplified in order to see more clearly whether it precipitates a basic hypothesis or not. The evidence suggests that it does, and also indicates the general form which

[1] *Ibid.* p. 3.

such an hypothesis will take. The reason for reaching such a clear conclusion lies in the fact that as one progresses through the research conclusions, it becomes more and more apparent that the weight of evidence lies on the side of those who claim to be able to discern a clear pattern of sequential developmental moral growth.

Macaulay and Watkins concluded that there was a general pattern in moral development. Hartshorne and May were convinced that there was not. Thus the two earliest works present the reader with two apparently incompatible and diametrically opposed conclusions. The subsequent criticism of the Hartshorne and May conclusions suggests that moral behaviour is not as specific as they suggest. Yet this does not mean that a scheme as simple and unspecific as Macaulay and Watkins supposed has to be accepted. The truth, as many have indicated, lies somewhere between these two extreme views.

While the balance was thus tipped slightly in favour of a developmental pattern, Piaget added his conclusions and brought the scale down heavily on this side. The subsequent criticism of Isaacs, Lerner and MacRae modified, but did not reject, the basic conclusions of Piaget, and he subsequently confirmed it in his parallel studies of intellectual development.

Havighurst and Taba suggested next that a developmental pattern could be discerned. This is based on the fact that different personality types emerge in the maturational process and these types display common patterns of moral behaviour.

The work of Gesell then revealed a vague generalized Piagetian type scheme of moral development. Swainson, in her 'tension' thesis, supports this. McKnight shows clearly that the different moral controls coincide with the different stages of mental and physical development. And Morris, although not able to discern a clear-cut sequential scheme, says that his material supports the general Piagetian view. Finally, Peck and Havighurst make it perfectly clear that their motivational theory of morality supports this view. Behind moral behaviour, consistent though it may appear to be, lies a pattern of sequential development which preserves continuity of conduct as the child grows.

Yet this does not mean either than the findings of Macaulay and Watkins are substantiated or that those of Hartshorne and May are rejected. Many American and British studies indicate that although they support a developmental pattern theory they are also aware of the complexity of moral behaviour and the existence of situational factors. It may be concluded that all these researchers have tried to locate their findings upon a continuum stretching from the extreme specificity of Hartshorne and May and the generalized developmental pattern of Macaulay and Watkins. But on the whole they support the view that a clear scheme of moral development can be traced.

Thus, the basic hypothesis can now be formulated. It is simply that this scheme of moral development is apparent as children grow from childhood to adolescence. There are clearly defined stages in this process. Specific kinds of control are indigenous to each stage. And these controls can be interpreted in terms of moral judgment, social relations, personality structures or moral sanctions.

BIBLIOGRAPHY

Allport, G. W., *Personality*, Constable & Co. Ltd., London, 1959.

Beard, R. M., *An Investigation of Concept Formation Among Infant School Children*, Unpub. Ph.D. Thesis, London, 1957.

Bovet, P., *The Child's Religion*, Dent, London, 1928.

Brennan, W. K., *The Relations of Social Adaptation, Emotional Adjustment and Moral Judgement to Intelligence in Primary School Children*, Unpub. M.Ed., Manchester, 1961.

Brennan, W. K., 'The Foundations For Moral Development', *Special Education*, Spring, 1965, Vol. LIV, No. 1.

Edwards, J. B., *A Study of Certain Moral Attitudes Among Boys in a Secondary Modern School*, Unpub. M.A. Thesis, Birmingham, 1959.

—: 'Some Studies of the Moral Development of Children', *Educational Research*, 1965, Volume VII, No. 3.

Eysenck, H. J., *The Structure of Human Personality*, Methuen, London, 1953.

—: The Development of Moral Values in Children: The Contribution of Learning Theory', *B.J.E.P.*, Feb., 1960.

Flavell, J. H., *The Developmental Psychology of J. Piaget*, Princeton (N.J.); Van Nostrand, 1963, London, 1953.

Fleming, C. M., *Adolescence: Its Social Psychology*, Routledge and Kegan Paul, London, 1955.

—: *Teaching: a Psychological Analysis*, Methuen, London, 1959.

Fleming, C. M., 'Research Evidence and Christian Education', in *Learning for Living*, Sept., 1966.

Fromm, E., *Man for Himself*, Holt, Rinehart and Winston, New York, 1947.

Gesell, A., and Ilg, F. L., *The Child from Five to Ten*, Hamish Hamilton, London, 1965; Harper and Row, New York, 1946.

Gesell, A., Ilg, F. L., and Ames L. B., *Youth: the Years from Ten to Sixteen*, Hamish Hamilton, London, 1965; Harper and Row, New York, 1956.

Goldman, R., *Religious Thinking from Childhood to Adolescence*, Routledge and Kegan Paul, 1964.

Harding, D. W., *Social Psychology and Individual Values*, Hutchinson, London, 1953.

Harrower, M. R., 'Social Status and Moral Development', *B.J.E.P.*, No. 4, 1934.

*Hartshorne, H., May, M.A. and Maller, J. B., *Studies in the Nature of Character:* Vol. 1, *Studies in Deceit*, Hartshorne and May, 1930. Vol. 2, *Studies in Service and Self Control*, Hartshorne, May and Maller. The Macmillan Company, New York, 1929.

Havighurst, R. J., *Human Development and Education*, Longmans, Green and Co., New York, 1953.

Havighurst, R. J. and Taba H., *Adolescent Character and Personality*, John Wiley and Sons, New York, 1949.

Hughes, T., *Tom Brown's Schooldays*, The Macmillan Company, New York, 1898.

Isaacs, S., *Intellectual Growth in Young Children*, Routledge and Kegan Paul, London, 1930; Schocken Books, New York, 1966.
—: *Mind*, Book review pp. 85ff., Macmillan, London, 1934.

Kennedy-Fraser, D., *The Psychology of Education*, Methuen, London, 1944.

Lancaster, J., *The British System of Education*, London, 1810.

Lerner, E., *Constraint Areas and Moral Judgement in Children*, Manasha, Wisconsin, Banta, 1937.

Loughran, R., *A Pattern of Development in Moral Judgements made by Adolescents*, Educational Review, Feb., 1967.

Macaulay, E., and Watkins, S. H., 'An Investigation into the Development of the Moral Conceptions of Children', Parts I and II, *The Forum of Education*, IV, 1925–26.

McDougall, W., *Social Psychology*, Methuen, London, 1924.

* Despite assiduous enquiry it has been impossible to obtain or borrow a copy of Vol. 3. This was produced by Hartshorne and May with the help of F. Shuttleworth and published by the Macmillan Co. in 1930.

McKnight, R. K., *The Moral Sanctions of the Child*, Unpub. B.Ed., Glasgow, 1950.

MacRae, D. Jr., 'A Test of Piaget's Theories of Moral Development', *Journ. Abn. and Soc. Psychology*, 49, 1950.

Morris, J. F., *A Study of Value-Judgements in Adolescents*, Unpub. Ph.D., London, 1955.

—: 'The Development of Adolescent Value-Judgements', *B.J.E.P.*, 1958 Vol. 28. Pt 1.

Neubauer, D., 'The Relation of the Church to Character Formation', in *Adolescent Character and Development*, Havighurst and Taba, John Wiley and Sons, New York, 1949.

Peck, R. F. and Havighurst, R. J., *Educational Research in the Field of Character Development*, Unpub. Manuscript, 1950.

—: *The Psychology of Character Development*, John Wiley and Sons, New York, 1960.

Piaget, J., *The Moral Judgement of the Child*, Routledge and Kegan Paul, London, 1932; Free Press, New York.

—: *The Origins of Intelligence in the Child*, Routledge and Kegan Paul, London, 1953; International Universities Press, New York, 1956.

—: *Logic and Psychology*, Manchester University Press, 1953.

Rowland, B. E., *An Enquiry into the Standards of Behaviour of Boys and Girls Towards Each Other*, Unpub. M.A., London, 1955.

Smith, B. H., *Growing Minds*, University of London Press, 1937.

Stafford-Clark, J., *What Freud Really Said*, McDonald and Co., London, 1965; Schocken Books, New York, 1966.

Swainson, B. M., *The Development of Moral Ideas in Children and Adolescents*, Unpub. D.Phil., Oxford, 1949.

Valentine, C. W., *The Normal Child*, Penguin, London and New York, 1960.

Vernon, P. E., *Personality Tests and Assessments*, Methuen, London, 1953.

Wilson, J., Williams N., and Sugarman, B., *Introduction to Moral Education*, Pelican, London, 1968.

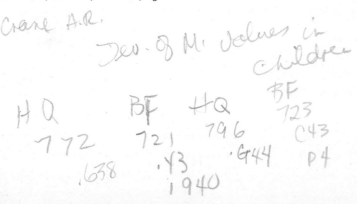

CHAPTER 3

THE THEORY OF RECAPITULATION

INTRODUCTION

The above review indicates that there appear to be clearly defined stages of moral growth in individuals which, occur in a fixed sequence. Now this fact points to an extremely interesting theory which can throw more light on the nature of human moral development. This theory is usually referred to as the theory of recapitulation. It argues that just as the physical growth of an individual passes through all the stages of physical human evolution from a protoplasmic speck onwards,[1] so intellectual growth too recapitulates the mental experiences of the race.

Since a study of an individual's development is referred to as 'ontogeny', and that of a species is called 'phylogeny', this theory is sometimes described in the graphic phrase, 'ontogeny recapitulates phylogeny'.[2] Spinks uses these terms and emphasizes that the thesis may not be so easily dismissed. At one time it was fashionable to do so; but our growing knowledge in both the area of ontogeny and of phylogeny suggest that it is rather precipitate to do this.

As always, vested academic interests are staked on this particular problem. The Piagetian school of thought has so much to gain, and the followers of Isaacs so much to lose, by accepting this theory that it inevitably becomes an area of conflict in which regrettably, the first victim is objective and detached academic judgment. However a review of this theory can throw much light on the problem of human moral growth. It is thus worth a brief mention to help us to understand the nature of moral development.

PRIMITIVE CATEGORIES OF THOUGHT

Lévy Bruhl's researches in Polynesia in the early decades of this century led him to conclude that there were two clearly separate

---

[1] Biologists will recognize this as a gross over-simplification.
[2] G. S. Spinks, *Psychology and Religion*, pp. 201ff.

and defined stages of intellectual evolution. These he called the pre-logical and the logical. Albright has recently confirmed this view. Modern primitives, have clearly emerged from the animal stage but they still think in a way that is alien to modern man. They do not think logically: they think pre-logically. Modern man unquestioningly accepts that Aristotle's laws of thought are axiomatic, and that these logical laws limit, confine and determine the nature of our thinking. For primitives this is not so. Thus one has a simple threefold pattern of development composed of the animal, pre-logical, and logical stages.

This pattern was made more complex by the work of Albright. He argued that one must distinguish sharply between formal logic and empirical logic. Now the pattern becomes clearer. In the intellectual evolution of the race there was firstly the animal stage, then the pre-logical stage, then the stage of empirical logic and finally the stage of formal logic.

This is an inordinately complex line of argument which is based on biblical and anthropological studies, and justice cannot be done to it in a page or two, but already the Piagetian pattern is clear. Moreover, when the characteristics of each of these stages are outlined, it becomes apparent that this anthropological argument is Piaget's psychological argument writ large upon the pages of history.

Little need be said of man living at the animal stage. His manner of life was hardly distinguished from that of the animals. His actions were merely prudent, since by prudence he would survive, and amoral sensori-motor impulses governed his life and thought. At the pre-logical level he lacked any clear understanding of logical principles. He advanced because language developed, but it was a limited step. He still thought ego-centrically. He was still literally the 'measure of all things'.[1] Thus he ascribed his own awareness of personal powers to the inanimate world. Hence arose the logical contradictions. Just as man could experience different and distinct contradictory states within himself so he assumed that the external world would display them. An early Egyptian believed that the sky was a cow, a mother and a sea. These were not possible alternatives. For him the sky was all three. Equally for the early Canaanites the Goddess Anath was both a loving mother and a virgin, destroying avenger. It is

[1] Protagoras quoted by Plato in Theatatus.

argued that just as the development of language enabled man to emerge from the animal stage so the development of art led him out of the pre-logical stage. It is only when one tries to draw an object (i.e. make it real) that one realizes that it cannot be two things at the same time. And before we smile in a superior manner at these ignorant savages we should pause and reflect on the fact that many otherwise competent modern men have booked themselves to be in two places at the same time. They too, like the primitive artist, only recognize the conflict when they attempt to 'realize' the situation.

Thirdly, there was the stage of empirical logic. Here evolving man detached himself a little more from the world of everyday things. He stopped assuming that he was the measure of all and in fact began to decentre his thinking. He could not, however, detach himself from the data of experience. Since much of his mental life was stimulated by sensory awareness his thoughts were inevitably linked to concrete phenomena. For him there was no roundness, or squareness, or sharpness in itself. There were only round things, square things, and sharp things. Boman describes this kind of thought extremely graphically. 'Form without content is simply nothing; for the object is identical with its material.'[1] The arguments of man reflected this. They were compounded both of logic and of observation. It was not so much a logic of propositions as a logic of perceptions.

Even modern man has experiences of this kind. Most adults can remember arguing empirically as a child when they argued on the basis of future events. If one treads on a crack between paving-stones, one will marry a chimney sweep. If one stops biting one's nails one will pass the 'eleven plus'! The most readily available document providing evidence of this kind, is the Old Testament. It is packed with examples of pre-logical and empirical thought. I Samuel 14: 1–13 is a superb illustration of this latter. The behaviour of the guard is built into a logical argument! His action becomes the minor premise of an empirical syllogism.

Finally, there is the logical stage where formal logic is the dominant category of thought. This is where normal European man now stands.

---

[1] T. Boman, *Das Hebräische Denken im Vergleich mit dem Griechischen*, p. 77. (Author's trans.)

The point needs no underlining. This pattern almost exactly coincides with Piaget's description of intellectual ontogeny. Both are sequential processes with qualitatively distinct stages divided by discrete points. From this one may conclude that an infant school child is not just a miniature adult. He is really a modern version of primitive man. And equally the junior school child is more than an imperfect adolescent. He is passing through all the mental experiences of mankind as he approached the logical age and finally had his inarticulate intellectual yearnings satisfied by Aristotle. Indeed the following imaginary conversation between a pre-logical man and a logical man could quite well have taken place between a junior school child and his adult teacher:

Logical man: 'Here we have three kettles, one of iron, one of copper and one made of silver. The material is different but the quality they all have in common is the form of a kettle. A thing is thus an object with content.'

Pre-logical man: 'I don't understand. Take away the material of your kettle and nothing is left. Form without content is simply nothing; for the thing is identical with its material. That which is held in common by these vessels is their function. They are made so that they can function as kettles or to serve as kettles. A tool is therefore matter shaped to be used for a specific purpose.'[1]

It may be said that this is an artificial comparison, and that it is wrong to draw conclusions about man at the pre-logical stage of phylogeny on evidence supplied by modern primitives. That may be so, in which case, one may only comment that it is at least a valuable analogy by which greater understanding of children is reached. Yet this recapitulatory theory cannot be rejected so easily. Piaget himself subscribed to this view. Nowhere has he withdrawn his thirty-seven-year-old observation, 'that the day will come when child thought will be placed on the same level in relation to adult, normal and civilized thought, as primitive mentality as defined by Lévy Bruhl.'[2]

Before leaving this preliminary to the argument it is interesting to note another parallelism between the anthropologist Lévy Bruhl and the psychologist Piaget. Both of them began by talking about pre-logical thought as the precursor of operational think-

[1] *Ibid.* p. 77. (Author's trans.)
[2] J. Piaget, *Judgement and Reasoning in the Child*, p. 256.

ing and both of them had to modify this terminology under pressure from almost identical criticisms. Albright gives the details of Lévy Bruhl's experience and explains why Lévy Bruhl gave up the notion of a simple *prelogique* category of thinking. But he also adds that since 1950 he, Albright, had 'replaced the term "pre-logical" by the much more satisfactory "proto-logical" '.[1]

In his explanation of the changed terminology, Piaget is inordinately gracious. Speaking of the pre-operational category of child thought he acknowledges his indebtedness to Susan Isaacs and admits, 'We once regarded this period as "pre-logical". Mrs Isaacs and many others rightly criticized this view, since some of the early evidence which we thought satisfactory was too verbal in character.'[2] He said this in 1953, and one cannot help wondering how far this is an admission of his earlier defeat, by Susan Isaacs. Twenty-five years previously she had routed him on the evidence of little Dan. Perhaps the memory of that self-assured infant enjoying his discomfiture was a ghost which Piaget had finally to exorcise in this way!

THE STAGES OF MORALITY

In addition to clarifying our understanding of immature thought this recapitulatory theory can help us to understand immature morality, for the pattern of mankind's moral development appears also to be directly recapitulated in the moral evolution of the child. Just as the pattern of intellectual growth can be simply described as passing through the stages of animal behaviour, pre-logical thinking, thought governed by empirical logic and finally by formal logic, so morality can be described as passing through the stages of behaviour controlled firstly by taboo, then by law, thirdly by conscience[3] (i.e. irrational, introjected values) fourthly by reciprocity, fifthly by social concensus and finally by personal moral principles, though not necessarily in that order.

Such a description of the process is naturally liable to be misunderstood. It does not mean that *all* the behaviour of *all* the people at *one* level is controlled by *one* sanction. During the

---

[1] W. F. Albright, *Archaeology and the Religion of Israel*, p. 223.
[2] J. Piaget, *Logic and Psychology*, p. 12.
[3] Acting as a superego.

legalistic period many individuals must have been prompted to behave in ways which resulted from social direction or inner control. In Riesman's language, even during the earlier stages of moral development, the race must have contained some 'other-directed' and some 'inner-directed' men and women. Equally, as he has shown so well, both 'inner' and 'other-directed' men and women exist now side by side in our society.

This will be scrutinized more closely when we come to study the psycho-social development of individual children. For the moment, however, one can say that just as intellectual phylogeny is recapitulated in intellectual ontogeny, so the moral development of the race appears to be repeated in the moral development of each individual.

The Taboo Stage[1]
At the stage where taboo governed human behaviour one can clearly recognize the essence of childlike amoral, prudential conduct. Smith is generally considered to be an authority on this point. His work is extraordinarily erudite and his statements measured and moderate. This is surprising when one realizes that he was fighting Frazer on the one hand and Durkheim on the other. Frazer attacked his view that religion was the primary experience of man and argued that it was not religion but magic which qualified for this distinction; and Durkheim attacked his high view of morality, arguing that morality was nothing more than the expedient behaviour which allowed the tribe to survive. In both of these attacks one finds some implicit recognition of taboo as a prudential form of morality, but Smith makes this quite explicit. He argued that all primitives believed that their conduct was circumscribed by a system of arbitrary penalties, originating in the supernatural world. For this he coined the Polynesian word *taboo*. Thus primitive man's conduct was controlled in an amoral way.

These taboos regulated every facet of life. We would perhaps like to distinguish between the religious, secular, personal and corporate areas of experience, but the primitive will acknowledge none of this. To him life is a unity under compulsion in all its areas from these supernatural, and therefore irrational and amoral, powers. Lévy Bruhl also admits that this is true of modern

[1] *See* J. C. Flugel, *Man, Morals and Society*, pp. 150–75.

primitives. Conduct which did not anger the God, blight the harvest, abort the first-born or disturb the dead, was behaviour that it was prudent to cultivate.

That this is so of modern children there is little doubt. Memories of one's own childhood or close association with infants makes it perfectly clear that their conduct is governed in this way. Anything which does not anger the parent, endanger the regular supply of sweets, abort an expected treat or disturb the sleeping neighbour constitutes behaviour which they deem it wise to cultivate. It is thus not an exaggeration to say that their morality is a morality of taboo. There is a taboo on dirty hands, unnecessary shouting, needless destruction, and illegitimate forages on the biscuit tin.

That is not to say that this stage is harmful and unnecessary. Just as the primitive was able to evolve a moralist religion out of this amoral system, so many unreasonable taboos, to which the English schoolboy is subject, are not without value in the formation of moral character. Taboo is the rather offensive soil in which morality may grow. No normal person would desire to decorate his lounge with stable manure, but the roses which grow so perfectly because of it are given an honoured place. It is the same with morals.

It may be argued that one must distinguish sharply between the sophisticated taboo system of the primitive and the eclectic prudence of a child; but the difference is one of emphasis rather than essence. The taboos growing up around a smoking, latent volcano are only more sophisticated forms of the child's prudential inclination not to be burnt. Equally the primitive's fear of the capricious force which may be unleashed upon him when least expected is only the cultural equivalent of the shock attending a clip on the ear. These, like erupting volcanoes, come when least expected. A shepherd may be tending sheep, a child may be filling the key-hole with plasticine. Then suddenly it happens. There's a whistling sound and a sudden pain: and the troubled primitive or child recognizes a new taboo.

The Legal Stage

Gradually however, the caprice of taboo-type, prudential conduct was eliminated and reasonable and stable laws replaced its regulations. One can easily see how this would take place as man emerged from the more primitive stages of his social development. Taboos may be violated with impunity. Hence such violating conduct can go unpunished. Even the most pernicious and offensive deeds can be done under the aegis of taboo. It only required one tribe to make moral progress. With a high proportion of intelligent and compassionate men they would resist a witch-doctor whose capricious interpretation of taboo was making life intolerable for all except himself. This naturally took time. One can even see in Greek literature that taboo-type, unreasonable and capricious behaviour was acceptable. Agamemnon after violating the taboo on private property had only to say, 'My mind was bewildered'[1] to quieten his own conscience, appease society and even satisfy the injured party. This can surely only be because since conduct was built on a capricious foundation, every human being had a right to be capricious if he so desired.

Thus arose the great systematizers. These men, Hammurabi, Moses and Solon, for example, codified the traditions and customs into laws. Much of what had been inherent in the taboo system of morality was irrelevant and offensive; but much of it was valuable. Taboos could preserve human dignity and the pattern of culture. It was these elements which were codified, and of course since this turn of events was precipitated by outstanding men who were supported by the changing mood of society, society in its turn subscribed to the new system. Man had entered the legal stage. His conduct was no longer prudential; it was authoritarian. He now behaved as he did because the law said he must. Naturally the laws were given impeccable credentials. They either came straight from God or originated in the golden age of antiquity, when all women were fair, and all men were heroes.

Such a brief summary can only violate this concept of law, which is now central in our culture, even though its corrollary, authoritarianism, is being pushed to the edges. One brief point, however, can be made to compensate for this. It is quite clear that laws changed in structure as society progressed. At first they were negative in form and only slowly changed into positive prescriptions. It is possible that the earlier negative forms emerged from taboo because taboos are essentially negative in character. Such laws may then slowly be seen as valuable tools in social

[1] Quoted by J. S. Mackenzie, *A Manual of Ethics*, p. 98.

construction and so their positive nature may then have been emphasized. The earliest laws would have been built around the simple prescriptions. 'Thou shalt not, etc.', and only in course of time would the positive laws emerge in the form 'Thou shalt etc.', Rowley calls these categorical laws and argues that they were characteristic of the early Mediterranean cultures from which the Hebrews emerged. Thus the code of law known best to us— the Laws of Moses—are all in this form.

The more sophisticated form came later. These were the apodeictic laws which were based on the pattern, 'If you do this . . . then so and so will follow'. From what has been said above it is possible to see that this law is virtually the placing of empirical logic upon a legal basis. As far as we know these apodeictic laws were peculiar to Israel. It is thus possible to argue that they were a corollary of Israelite monotheism; a conclusion which can locate this development almost exactly at the point where mankind emerged with a monotheistic faith.

Now all of this can be seen clearly replicated in the moral behaviour of young children. Out of the unsystematic and capricious controls regulating their behaviour, emerges a notion of law as that which must be obeyed. These laws are usually reasonable. Even the most sweet-crazy child can see the sense of the law about not eating a bag of sweets just before lunch. Many of them may still seem unreasonable, like the household law which prohibits the blowing of whistles and banging of drums before parents are awake. Still most of them are reasonable, but even if they were not it is quite clear that at a particular stage in his development a child has an inbuilt positive response to laws. Thus even the laws which they construct themselves, like 'over the garden six and out', which regulated the street cricket of one's youth, are still obeyed implicitly.

Such a parallelism between the morality of children and of early man is even evident in the general development of child authoritarianism. At first children can be heard using negative categorical laws. Regularly throughout the day plaintive soprano voices can be heard proclaiming with mixed feelings, 'No you mustn't do that'. It may be of course, that they are merely echoing their parents. One police station tells a humorous story of the lost child who did not know his own name. 'What does your mother call you?', asked a kindly sergeant. 'Tommy stoppit!' said the boy.

It is only later that the more positive cry of, 'Yes we must do that' is heard.

Piaget has shown too how the apodeictic form of law emerges as the concept of causation becomes amenable to the processes of the young child's thought. Now the more subtle form emerges, which can be twisted into the most complicated and tortuous patterns by a pre-adolescent child. His society virtually becomes a web of apodeictic law. Regularly one finds such children imposing this kind of law with rigid and inflexible authoritarianism. 'If you do this ... then that will happen', they argue. Many adults can remember quite clearly the Chinese burn which followed a violation of the group law; a vicious sequel to a trifling offence. Yet one submitted passively and stoically to it just because it was the law.

At this point in the evolution of moral phylogeny one faces a dilemma. One of the most valuable contributions of Jesus to the social and individual life of man was his vehement affirmation that the legal age was passing. Men should no longer be controlled by law, he argued. Their conduct should be directed by the intelligent application of perpetually valid principles. The unchanging law, he continued, became a prison in which man was incarcerated. It hindered him from releasing his potential. The ideal of the developed life was impossible to realize while law held sway. It is against thinking of this kind that one must assess the liberating quality of his message. This is the truth he proclaimed. And it was this truth which would literally make men free.

But here lies the dilemma. Christ's followers, founded an institution which was anti-legalist in spirit. Yet it soon became apparent that the Church was perpetually attracted to a legal and authoritarian form of organization. Some would even say that this monolithic system dominated in Europe until the Reformation, when once again in all parts of christendom the liberating message of Jesus could be heard. Thus it must reluctantly be concluded that although the end of authoritarian legalism was proclaimed by Jesus two millenia ago, we His followers have on the whole tended to perpetuate the much simpler and safer authoritarian structure.

Again it is possible to see this development in the morality of children. Swainson showed clearly that although they were beginning to grasp the essential personal nature of morality, and were even under pressure from their peer society, the morality of pre-adolescent children is still authoritarian in form.

Before continuing it must be again noted that although legalism can never be a substitute for genuine morality, it is nevertheless not only an essential preliminary, but also a valuable ingredient of it.[1] Our lives must be disciplined. We cannot do just as we please. Even the early Hebrews realized this. In describing one of the worst periods of their history they said, 'Every man did that which was right in his own eyes.'[2] Institutions and societies must have a legal structure. Indeed the nurturing of this quality in junior school children is an essential pre-requisite of moral growth.

It does not take long to realize why this is so. If motorists ignored the highway code mortality rates would rise. Clearly a judiciary and a police force are essential even in the most morally enlightened community.[3]

An interesting illustration of this point occurred recently at Cape Kennedy. There, in an area devoted to the space programme of research, and inhabited by so many Doctors of Philosophy that they have all agreed to forego the title in order to avoid confusion with the medical practitioners, a strange incident occurred. A highly placed scientist was late for his morning conference and seeing that there was no other traffic about on an uninhabited stretch of the road, he exceeded the speed limit. A patrolman immediately stopped him and gave him a ticket. The scientist was furious. He explained who he was. He said all that he dare say about the conference. He gave the poor patrolman a clear indication of his opinion of officious lower-ranking police officers who had nothing better to do than impose stupid laws. Yet the police officer remained adamant. He knew the law; the law had to be obeyed. The law had been broken; it followed

---

[1] Indeed one value of legal authority is that it ensures the perpetuation of sound 'moral' habits, just as the rules of any game ensure that the contestants play habitually in a way which provides pleasure for all concerned.

[2] Judges 17 : 6 et al.

[3] This would presumably also include the School community. But while such a community reflects society by having both a police and a judicial system it differs in one important respect. Its primary task is not to protect its members from aberrant conduct, but to prepare them for moral maturity.

logically and irrefutably that no matter how eminent the scientist, how important the conference, or how isolated and bereft of traffic may be the road, he, the representative of the law insisted on 'booking' the transgressor of the law. But who was right?

This, of course, is a nice point to argue in a seminar. It is very difficult however, to resist the view that this kind of discipline is essential for social security and cohesion. If any doubt this let them try an experiment. If they approach traffic lights which turn red, at a junction where the road is clearly unused by any other cars, possibly at three in the morning, let them try to cross while the light is red. All the heritage of barbarous man emerging into civilization will resist this. Restraint may partly result from the sanctions which accompany the law. The rational will argue that it is not worth spending a morning in a magistrate's court and paying a heavy fine for the sake of the few minutes saved. But even the enlightened, situational moralist cannot break that law with impunity. It is impossible to transgress without the slightest whisper of guilt rustling in the depths of an unused conscience.

Like prudentiality and discipline, authority is a valuable precursor of mature morality and even deserves a place in the most enlightened systems. This may well be simply because it is economical. Instead of having to argue each case on its merits, one can slip the moral sense into neutral and coast along on the demands of authority.

The Reciprocal Stage

The next stage in racial moral development was clearly enunciated by a number of outstanding moral teachers. It still has yet to take root in society but it is probably the most commonly held moral principle of all. It is usually called the 'Golden Rule', and recommends what Piaget called 'moral reciprocity'.[1] Jesus is quoted as saying 'As ye would that men should do unto you, even so do ye also unto them.'[2] An equally well-known variant of this comes from Confucius, 'What you do not like if done to yourself, do not do to others.'[3] Yet it is not realized that many

---

[1] J. Piaget, *The Moral Judgement of the Child.*

[2] Matthew 7 : 12.

[3] J. Hastings, *Encyclopaedia of Religion and Ethics*, vol. 6, London, T. and T. Clark, 1959; New York, Charles Scribner's Sons, 1951.

other enlightened intellects in the ancient world subscribed to this principle. Hillel the famous Rabbi was asked to provide a short summary of law to guide man's conduct and he replied 'Whatsoever thou wouldest that men should not do to thee, do not do that to them.'[1]

As one would expect this restraining principle is found in the writings of classical Greece. Isocrates, Plato and Aristotle all agreed that in human relations one should 'Do not to others that at which you would be angry if you suffered it from others.'[2]

Many would agree that Shaw was being rather more than usually cynical when he said that this was the last consideration that he would use as a guide to his conduct because we are not all alike. One man's meat is another man's poison. But this is clearly a step forward in moral evolution, or rather it is two steps forward. Firstly, all these moral statements enunciate a moral principle and so depart from the *legal* pattern of moral thought. Secondly, they began as negative prescriptions in the pre-Christian era and emerged on Jesus' lips as a positive moral principle. Men began by saying '*Do not* do to others what you *would not* like them to do to you', and were led finally to say '*Do* unto others what you *would* like them to do to you'.

This is self-evidently a moral advance. The first sign of moral autonomy is apparent here. When laws remain outside and rule us by considerations other than our own, we act at the level of heteronomy. But when a principle such as this resides within a man and is made his own, and controls his conduct from within, his behaviour becomes autonomous.

Piaget has shown that this type of morality emerges between the legal and social stages in children. Instead of simply obeying the rules they begin to regulate their conduct with a consideration for the feelings of others. At its lowest level this can produce a rigid legalism when all the rules are applied to all the children without discrimination. This, however, slowly changes. Situational circumstances are given weight and finally, when all the circumstances are considered, autonomy is reached. This will be studied more fully below. For the moment it only needs to be noted that Piaget believed, 'Reciprocity to be the determining factor of autonomy'.[3]

[1] *Ibid.*   [2] Aristotle, *Ethics*, Cap. 9. Sect. 8.
[3] J. Piaget, *The Moral Judgement of the Child*, p. 194.

There is also the further point that some consider moral reciprocity to be the moral equivalent of reversible thinking. Therefore, it can be located at a particular stage of individual development, i.e. when the junior school child can begin to think operationally.

Once again the observant teacher or parent will be able to supply illustrations of this morality in action. 'It's not fair', they cry. 'I wouldn't do that to you'.

Of course it can't always work. Shaw was partly right, as the story of the friends, who had two apples to share, shows. One apple was large and one was small. Boys being what they are, the sharer had the larger. His friend complained, 'If I'd shared them I'd have given you the large one.' 'Well', said his complacent friend, 'I've got it!'

The Social Stage

The next stage in this evolution of morality may be inelegantly called the social phase. Here conduct is determined by society. Even laws can be transgressed with impunity if one's peer group approve of such conduct. Again, like taboo, this is an extra-ordinarily complicated stage in human phylogeny and can there-fore only be discussed superficially. There is however, so much agreement between contemporary anthropologists, sociologists and psychologists that one may deal summarily with this subject without risking being misunderstood.

There is no longer any doubt but that human personality re-flects the society in which the individual is embedded. Karen Horney has confidently argued the thesis that even neuroses are sociological phenomena. But the culture determines not only the abnormal but also the norm in personality and behaviour. Horney as a Freudian sustained this argument with evidence from contemporary Caucasian man. Mead, however, showed that this was equally true of primitive man. Amongst the related Arapesh, Mundugumor and Tchambuli tribes of New Guinea she found clear evidence that the norms of personality and con-duct were imposed by each society.

The most dramatic element in her evidence here is the fact that the deviants in each of these geographically related tribes were only deviants in relation to the group. The deviant Arapesh acted and reacted in a way which was similar to the

Mundugumor norm. And equally the deviant Mundugumor behaved and thought like a normal Arapesh Indian.

Riesman developed this argument still further. He was primarily concerned with the apparent changes in the personality and morality of modern Americans. Since he wished to trace this back at least to the nineteenth century he made a historical survey of the problem. From this study emerged a clear picture of man as an evolving moral being. For Riesman medieval man was under the control of tradition. This was imposed by social approval and disapproval. Therefore, in this early stage, morality resulted from the social control of tradition. The emphasis here, however, is on tradition for taboo and law also belong to this period. He then argued that early industrial man was primarily controlled by conscience or the super-ego. Finally he argued that modern admass man has his morality controlled by public opinion.

From these last two points emerge the terms most associated with Riesman. He concluded that the age of *laissez-faire* in industry and society produced the 'inner-directed' man and the modern mass-age produced the 'other-directed' man. To this we need only add the name of Whyte. In his work the familiar argument, that society produces particular personality types, is sustained with a wealth of evidence. For him the organized society produces the organization man.

We have now it seems, reached the stage of social conformity. Here men are integrated into their communities or industrial organizations. If they resist this their security is at stake. They work together in teams on research projects. The individual, whether he is a genius or a fool, is ruthlessly suppressed. The average, conforming, socially-aware, organization man dominates. He lives in a grey society where all incentive to individual originality is vitiated by the organization. Thus it seems that this is as far as man has progressed. The acme of his progress to date is the social stage of morality.

At this point a confusion has to be dealt with. Many students reading Riesman and finding that they can handle his ideas and use his terminology, make a fundamental mistake. They talk about the 'inner-directed' man of the early industrial era and the 'other-directed' man of today and then assume that this implies a retrograde step in the area of morals. It is wrongly assumed that the 'inner-directed' man has a morality based on personally held moral principles while the 'other-directed' man is the socially malleable moral chameleon. In contemporary society, they argue, we have men who, morally speaking, have regressed to an earlier stage.

Now this is just not so. Such an interpretation is a complete misunderstanding of Riesman's thesis. The man who is controlled by an irrational conscience is not morally superior to the socially orientated personality. Peck and Havighurst have made this quite clear from their research in America.

The morally mature man is the rationally-altruistic person. Morality is no mystery; there is no mystique about it. It is not a vague quality like the *mana* of primitives. Morality is simply the action of the man who having reasoned compassionately, acts on his convictions. Below such a man in the hierarchy of moral maturity stands both the irrational-conscientious and the conforming personality. It is thus reasonably certain that mankind has so far only progressed towards and has not yet reached, racial moral maturity.

Peck and Havighurst have argued that the rational-altruistic personality is still a small minority in Caucasian society. It is therefore perfectly possible to believe Riesman who argues that society today is dominated by 'other-directed' conformists. Thus at this point in history ontogeny and phylogeny[1] meet and merge. At this social stage of racial development it is natural that most individuals should live at the level of social morality.

A full description of its characteristics is unnecessary here. Every reader knows for himself the sophisticated ramifications which he can use to support this morality of 'keeping up with the Jones's'. 'What on earth will the neighbours think?' is a constant worry, for we are a society of conformers. The eccentrics of the 'inner-directed' phase have passed and left us suspicious of the exceptional man. We do not want people to be too clever, or too good, or too kind, or too independent. We suspect any excess, no matter how excellent it may be. Perhaps the most sophisticated insult which can none the less mortally wound is the jibe that a man is 'too clever by half'. The educated support this by quoting Aristotle and his 'Mean' and thereby damn human initiative.

[1] For the technical meanings of these terms see p. 72 above.

The unthinking adolescent may suppose that he is rebelling against authority figures when he dresses like a peacock. Perhaps he is; but even here the tedious conformity of speech, habit and clothing display clearly the fact that even those who strive to escape from the prison of conformity, merely shrug off one kind of enslavement for another. They are like prisoners who tunnel out of their cell only to find that they emerge in the warders' common room!

Yet this kind of immature morality, where one just goes morally limp and floats with the human moral tide, has its value. It is a cohesive social force. It may be that this stage is necessary to help us to achieve the long overdue elimination of social, cultural and ethnic barriers which divide men from each other. But it must never be forgotten that this is not genuine morality. There is nothing moral in the action of a multi-coloured budgerigar which pretends to be a sparrow. It does it merely to evade being pecked to death by his monochromatic peers. Equally, many an apparently upright, honest, industrious pillar of society behaves as such simply because he wishes to evade a particularly painful social death.

Education for autonomy

Man's moral destiny thus hangs in the balance. In his climb out of the nasty and brutish primitive stage he has reached one peak which many are mistakenly calling the summit. Whether he will rest here or reach the highest point depends on education. Our educational task now is to show the next generation that genuine autonomy, in which a man acts on his own moral principles, is not an unscaleable height but an Everest whose summit beckons us. In this case, we do not climb just because it is there, but because the internal drive which brought us from the palaeozoic slime urges us to scale the highest summit of achievement. The danger is that man may tragically lie back upon this lower peak and be complacently content to survey the path which he has thus far climbed.

We now stand at a crisis in our development; and it is a real crisis. It is not a pipe-dream of the disgruntled, noble, animal man. In society today, both amongst adolescents and adults, morally mature individuals can be seen having this personal struggle. It is to aid them that moral education is necessary. And to those who are content to remain embedded in society the vision must be displayed. Thus moral education is not merely a palliative to reduce the incidence of delinquency and its disturbing corollaries. Moral education is an absolute necessity in our society at its present stage of development. It is not because society is less sure of its own moral structure, it is simply because it has little genuine morality. For we have not yet, in the evolution of the species, had an opportunity to be really moral.

In a tribal society conduct was regulated by tradition. In the village society it was regulated by a desire not to antagonize one's neighbours. Some, it is true, moved to the cities in the hope of finding freedom, but even there the rigid social class stratification determined precisely the kind of conduct each individual was expected to display.

Today it is different; for the first time in western civilization we have a chance to be moral. We are detribalized.[1] We are no longer trapped in a programme of morals determined by a small community in which our work, our status, our family and our friends form an impregnable barrier to autonomy. We live in sprawling conurbations. There, very few people know what we do for a living. We go to work in an institution or organization, where, again, hardly any know our family background. We belong to clubs whose members know very little of either our home or our work. For the first time we can be free from social restraint. We can be moral.

In our club we can be either the hearty likeable chap full of bonhomie or the wise sage who knows a thing or two. At work we may be the efficient member of a team, or an 'influence-leader' always expected to produce the brilliant flash of insight. In our homes we may be a loving, devoted spouse and parent, or a bristling, irascible, impatient, emotional tyrant. We can be all things to all men. We can stretch our moral wings and test our moral muscles because we control our own behaviour. Nobody controls us. We are at the driving wheel.

The passing of the tram was an allegory. No longer do we run in the tracks laid down by others. We can go where we like,

[1] This, of course, is an oversimplification. It is more true, as Morris has said, to think of our present society as a system of 'interlocking and overlapping tribal groups'. He develops this argument in *The Naked Ape,* pp. 186ff.

do what we like and be what we like. Autonomous man is coming of age.

Of course there are qualifications, this is why the best of our moral heritage must survive. There are many occasions when we must be prudent. To ensure that a complex technological society runs smoothly regulations must be made and kept; laws must be framed and obeyed; and being social animals, as Aristotle insisted, we must consider the effect of our behaviour on our neighbours. We must be prudential, authoritarian and social in our morality. But these elements must be minimal. The trend towards paternalism in the large organizations of modern industry and commerce, must be resisted. This is why the crisis facing each individual also faces society.

Thus even if moral education becomes a viable subject, it may become a source of social discord. We shall be preparing mature autonomous moral agents for a conforming, heteronomous ad-mass society. This is the central thesis of Hauser. He desires to see a fraternal society made up of independent moral agents acting responsibly and maturely. But he can only see the paternal structure. Why? Because most men find it easier to fit into a welfare state where the faceless 'Them' take all the responsibility.

The final tragedy then could be that moral educators may lose their nerve and argue that they are producing the wrong product for the market. So far as is known, they will say, no commercial venture has yet been launched to make refrigerators for eskimos. They would not want the product and the firm would go bankrupt.

This analogy however, is dangerous and misleading. Moral educators are not analogous to bankrupt refrigerator manufacturers. Their product of autonomous, responsible citizens each with a personal system of moral principles of the highest order, is not only intended to serve the community. Their function, is primarily, to transform it.

CONCLUSION

However, the central argument is clear. In the moral evolution of man one can trace different stages. From control by taboo we passed to control by law. At this point reciprocity emerged as the primary moral principle, but man lapsed into authoritarianism.

More recently the race passed into the age of 'inner-direction', then of 'other-direction' and now stands on the brink of autonomous morality.

This is precisely the picture that modern research has painted, of the development of individual morality. At least in its general features the theory of recapitulation is not discredited.

A final point must be emphasized. The confidence with which we may speak of moral development and the elucidation of its different stages in individuals in no way depends upon the validity of this theory of recapitulation. Whether the theory is valid or not must remain an open question. Its value for us lies in the fact that it can illuminate our understanding of individual moral development. It is for this reason alone that it has been included here.

BIBLIOGRAPHY

Albright, W. F., *From Stone Age to Christianity*, Doubleday, New York, 1957.
—: *Archaeology and the Religion of Israel*, Johns Hopkins Press, Baltimore, 1953.
Aristotle, *Ethics*, trans. J. Warrington, Dent, London, 1963.
Aristotle, For a penetrating analysis of his thought see *The Open Society and its Enemies*, Vols. I and II, K. R. Popper, Routledge and Kegan Paul, London, 1963; Princeton University Press, Princeton (N.J.), 1963.
Boman, Th., *Das Hebräische Denken im Vergleich mit dem Griechischen*, Vandenhoeck and Ruprecht, Gottingen, 1959.
Durkheim, E., *Moral Education*, Free Press, New York, 1961.
Flugel, J. C., *Man, Morals and Society*, Penguin, London, 1955.
Frazer, J., *The Golden Bough*, Macmillan, London and New York, 1954.
Goldman, R., *Religious Thinking from Childhood to Adolescence*, Routledge and Kegan Paul, London, 1964.
Hauser, R. and H., *The Fraternal Society*, Bodley Head, London, 1962.
Horney, K., *The Neurotic Personality of Our Time*, Routledge and Kegan Paul, London, 1958; Norton, New York, 1937.
Isaacs, S., *Intellectual Growth in Young Children*, Routledge and Kegan Paul, London, 1930; Schocken Books, New York, 1966.

Lévy-Bruhl, L., *How Natives Think*, Allen and Unwin, London, 1926; Washington Square Press, New York, 1966.

—: *Primitive Mentality*, Allen and Unwin, London, 1923; Beacon Press, Boston, 1966.

—:*Natives and the Supernatural*, Allen and Unwin, London, 1928.

MacKenzie, J. S., *A Manual of Ethics*, University Tutorial Press Ltd., London, 1948, for refs. to Agamemnon,

Mead, M., *Sex and Temperament in Three Primitive Societies*, Routledge and Kegan Paul, London, 1952.

Morris, D., *The Naked Ape*, Jonathan Cape, London, 1967; McGraw-Hill, New York, 1968.

Peck, R. H., and Havighurst, R. J., *The Psychology of Character Development*, John Wiley and Sons, Inc., New York, 1960.

Piaget, J., *The Language and Thought of the Child*, Routledge and Kegan Paul, London, 1926; Free Press, New York.

—: *Judgement and Reasoning in the Child*, Routledge and Kegan Paul, London, 1928.

—: *The Moral Judgement of the Child*, Routledge and Kegan Paul, London, 1932; Free Press, New York.

—: *The Psychology of Intelligence*, Routledge and Kegan Paul, London, 1950.

—: *Logic and Psychology*, Manchester University Press, 1953.

—: *The Origins of Intelligence in the Child*, Routledge and Kegan Paul, London, 1953; International Universities Press, New York, 1956.

—: *The Growth of Logical Thinking from Childhood to Adolescence*, Routledge and Kegan Paul, London, 1958.

Riesman, D., *The Lonely Crowd*, Yale University Press, New Haven, 1964.

Rowley, H. H., *The Changing Pattern of Old Testament Studies*, Epworth Press, London, 1959.

Smith, W. R., *The Religion of the Semites*, A. and C. Black, London, 1927.

Spinks, G. S., *Psychology and Religion*, Methuen, London, 1963; Beacon Press, Boston, 1965.

Swainson, B. M., *The Development of Moral Ideas in Children and Adolescents*, Unpub. D.Phil., Oxford, 1949.

Whyte, W. H., *The Organization Man*, Jonathan Cape, London, 1957; Simon & Schuster, New York, 1956.

CHAPTER 4

A SUGGESTED ANALYSIS OF MORAL DEVELOPMENT

INTRODUCTION

The argument thus far has established two related facts. First, that educators are increasingly accepting the view that a pattern of development can be discerned in every area of a child's personality; and second, that this leads to the suggestion that 'readiness for learning' should be a principle applied to the practice of moral education. It is therefore necessary now for the developmental scheme of morality to be outlined clearly.

This is not quite so simple as one would expect. Not only is moral conduct extremely complex and often very difficult to analyse with complete certainty, but 'moral development' is itself an omnibus term containing a number of related ideas. It is rather like talking about an 'African' and forgetting that this is about as meaningful as talking about a 'European'. Until the emergence of the new African states, we in the west tended to ignore the ethnic and cultural differences which sharply distinguished the indigenous inhabitants of that continent. We were acutely aware of the differences between a phlegmatic Anglo-Saxon and a voluble Latin but were blind to the equally profound differences to be found amongst the inhabitants of Africa.

This is an almost exact parallel. Many educators would talk about intellectual development and recognize the clearly defined elements within it. Yet until very recently they have been content to speak of moral development without acknowledging that it is as equally complex in a similar way. Nobody today would contest the view that one way of understanding intellectual development more clearly is to reduce it to the growth of conceptual understanding. Nor would they disagree that amongst the basic concepts one would place time, space, number and causation. Therefore one way of trying to understand how an individual child is developing intellectually may be crudely described as an attempt to isolate each element of this growth in conceptual understanding. Not to do this would make the teacher's task more difficult than it already is. If then this attempt to outline the stages of moral development, is to eliminate as much complexity as possible, moral development too must be reduced to its component parts.

Moral philosophers have tried to do this for centuries and have thereby bequeathed a tradition to us in which one talks of the intellectual element consisting of understanding clearly what ought to be done under certain circumstances, and the element of will which determines whether in fact this is done. This analysis which highlights the twin elements of the 'should' and the 'would' of human experience is very valuable in the study of morality where one is concerned with both ethical thought and actual moral behaviour. Moreover, recent research projects have shown that this is a factor which must be borne in mind when discussing moral education. Soon after the Second World War, for example, McPherson made a study of the effects of a course of moral instruction in a Scottish school. He found that although the instruction enabled children to understand more clearly what they *should* do, it was discovered that this had hardly any effect at all on what in fact they *would* do under the same circumstances. This raised the fundamental problem of the nature of the moral dynamic. At some stage the question must be asked 'When children know the right thing to do, what is it that leads them on to actually do it?' This will be examined in the companion volume. For the moment however one must simply note that there is firstly this analysis of moral development which began as a philosophical attempt to understand human conduct and has subsequently received a considerable amount of experimental support.

There is, however, another analysis which originates not in speculation but in actual research work with children. It is rather more complex, but that is an advantage since frequently the more complicated analysis produces elements which in themselves are easier to understand. This second analysis, which is outlined below, does not dispense with the first. It merely enables us to see more clearly exactly what happens as children mature morally.

Here a warning must be added. It must not be thought that the following classification suggests that these elements are mutually exclusive. As will be seen later there is a mutual interaction between them. This obviously results from the fact that one is dealing with artifically abstracted elements from a living whole. Each one is a different, impersonal way of looking at the behaviour of a complex human being; and people are rarely more complex than when involved in a moral dilemma. It must never be forgotten that the unity of behaviour and personal development is the reality. This following bloodless dissection is a device for understanding actual reality with greater comprehension. Nor should one forget that this caveat must not be limited to moral development. Such interactions occur in intellectual development too. There is a stage for example where the concepts of time and space become mingled. If one asks a child how far it is to school, he may very well answer that it is a ten-minute walk. Asked a question about space he will answer in terms of time. And many a vexed motorist finds that on making similar inquiries of adults he has to translate their statements about a ten-minute bus ride or a half-hour walk into actual mileage.

THE DIFFERENT ELEMENTS IN MORAL DEVELOPMENT

Recognizing then that this is an artificial analysis with no one element in it existing independently of the others it can now be clearly presented.

There is firstly the simple view that moral development passes through different stages and that the behaviour characteristic of each stage can be clearly described. Secondly, this development can be understood in terms of the different sanctions which govern moral behaviour. This is rather more complicated and involves one in a study of the varying motives underlying behaviour at different stages of development. Thus we have passed from simple descriptions to a study of the motivational elements in moral conduct. Next comes the study of moral judgment. This is not so much concerned with behaviour and its motivation as with the developing maturity of moral judgment. Obviously actual behaviour and the motives behind it are important too, but the emphasis here is on the intellectual element involved in judgments made concerning moral problems. Finally this development can be viewed in terms of insights provided by psychology. Here the actual personality of the individual is linked with his behaviour and his stage of psycho-social development. The elements of moral development can thus be teased out into the following four categories:

(1) Simple stages of development.
(2) Moral sanctions
(3) Moral judgment.
(4) Psycho-social development.

Those who know anything about the work of Piaget in this field will immediately see that he must be considered under the third heading above since this work was concerned wholly with moral judgment. It could then be argued that since one may assume that readers involved in education are familiar with the general theories of Piaget's developmental psychology, such an analysis should begin with him. This is an attractive argument. Unfortunately it discounts the complexity of Piaget's theories. It has therefore been deemed preferable to begin with the most easily understood element and slowly build upon this.

THE STAGES OF DEVELOPMENT

Bompas Smith

Thirty years ago, Smith published a book called *Growing Minds*. In it he was concerned with bringing the educational relevance of developmental psychology to the attention of practising teachers. Much of what he says is now clearly embedded in a past age, but this is a valuable book for our purposes. In it, he distinguishes three clearly defined stages in moral development. Nowhere does he refer to research evidence nor tighten his argument with age-normative statements. He does not for example say that such and such is the conduct which would be normal for a child of five years and ten years and fifteen years. Yet even in the present more rigorous academic climate this book has great value. He refers to the stages of obedience, legalism and personal morality, and assumes that they will emerge in children in that order.

This is an almost naïvely simplified analysis but, in general, subsequent research has confirmed it. There is firstly the stage of obedience, particularly that of obedience to parents. As the child grows and more people have authority over him, so his number of authority figures grows. But morality is little more than obedience to them. Therefore 'right' and 'wrong' are understood in terms of obedience. When he does what they tell him, he is doing the 'right' thing. When he disobeys he is doing the 'wrong' thing, regardless of the nature of the action itself. Slowly he leaves this stage behind as it becomes clearer that authority figures are only *passing on* these moral requests. He begins to see that behind them stands a higher source of moral command to which even the adults must submit. Thus he develops a notion of laws which regulate human conduct. When therefore he sees that his parents only transmit these requests for obedience, he realizes that morality consists of subscribing to these laws. His sense of right and wrong thus undergoes a subtle change. An action is right now if it follows an accepted *rule*. It is wrong if it does not. So his morality here is characterized by an attempt to so act that each particular situation is brought into conformity with a specific rule. Finally in adolescence he moves away from the ideas of obedience and legalism altogether. His adjustment to society is not achieved either by obedience or subscription to law. It consists of personal adjustment in which the adolescent begins to feel for himself not only the criteria determining what is right and what is wrong, but also the claims of those actions which he believes should characterize his conduct.

Thus here is a simple analysis which exactly follows the findings of Piaget five years earlier. Indeed it is difficult to avoid the conclusion that Smith has presented a simplified version of those theories, which are so ably outlined in Piaget's book *The Moral Judgement of the Child*.

Beatrice Swainson

As was observed earlier the complexity of the Hartshorne and May findings seemed to deter others from working in the field of moral development. Thus one has to wait until the post-war years for work to begin again in Britain. Soon after the war however Beatrice Swainson began her investigations. She accepted from Bompas Smith that there were three clearly defined stages in this process, but her work and conclusions were infinitely more subtle. Her basic assumption was taken over from Martin Buber. He had recently argued that personal relations made up the reality of the life which human beings lead. Thus for him morality emerges from relationships. This is summed up in his use of the 'primary-word I–Thou'.

This is extremely valuable because it emphasizes the important fact that genuine morality can only exist between people in relationships. If one demeans a fellow human being and uses him as a tool for gratification or self-advancement there is no relationship and therefore no morality. Equally if one treats non-human objects as though they were persons, there is again no relationship and therefore no morality. Swainson took her stand on this premise and so argued that the essence of morality consists of relationships. Beyond this one cannot go for 'in the beginning is relation', and 'all real life is meeting'. Thus for her that moral development which can be discerned in the three stages of infancy, childhood and adolescence takes place by means of the creative tension between a morality of being true to oneself and the morality of relating to others.

The stage of infancy lasts from birth until the eighth year. In describing it she has to speak of the primitive sensations and feelings of the young infant in rather sophisticated terms, but the quality of morality native to this stage of development is perfectly clear. For the first five years this is dominated by the tension existing between the need of the individual child to be true to his own nature and also the need to be acceptable to others. Any morning spent in a nursery school will provide scores of illustrations of this morality in action. Each child wishes to express himself with no concern for others. He wishes to play with the best toys, sit on the most comfortable chair, bang the loudest drum and make clamant demands for the satisfaction of his every whim. But this leads to rejection by his peers and the disapproval of his parents and teachers. Hence he makes his first venture into morality. He behaves in a way that will please them. His need to be acceptable to them is greater than his need to display monomania. So he seeks their good. He shares the toys; he co-operates with his friends and teachers; and he tries to help them.

Now this is a spontaneous morality in which actions clearly matter much more than motives. His motive is still basically ego-centric but his actions please others. What may not at first be apparent, however, is the prudential and authoritarian nature of this morality. The child is still satisfying his basic needs but doing it in a prudent manner. It is prudential to seek the welfare of others if this behaviour preserves one's relationships with them. And since this unity with others is the child's first priority he is satisfying his *own* need by seeking *their* welfare. One can see this tension being resolved when small children bribe others with toys or promises on condition that they will be 'best friends'.

But this conduct is also authoritarian. Very often the conflict cannot be resolved and a young child may burst into a paroxysm of grief at his inability to establish relationships with others. He just does not know what to do. He wants his own way but he also wants to retain his friends. Thus more often than not the loud wail of frustration coming from a young child, is a call of help to any adult to resolve this tension. Every young mother knows only too well how often she is called for in this capacity in any one hour of any day. So she with all her superior wisdom and experience restores the relationship. It may require the return of a toy, a word of apology or the keeping of a promise but in essence it restores the relationship in a way which does no damage to the personalities and dignity of the children concerned. In this kind of dilemma, where prudence cannot resolve the issue, children look to adults for guidance and help. Thus although this stage is dominated by tension between the needs of self and society, this tension is reduced by prudential and authoritarian considerations. And since the reduction of tension results in moral conduct, one can say that morality at this level is characterized by prudentiality and authoritarianism.

There is however a third element, which Swainson claims to have discovered. From the evidence she accumulated Swainson argues that very young children hold a conviction which is really a crude metaphysical theory. They believe, she says, that there is a fundamental moral order in life to which they may have access. When this is discovered it will form a basis for their morality for it can guide them so that they behave in such a way that the frustrations and tensions of inter-personal conduct can be resolved. They believe that existing somewhere is a solution to all their moral problems. Their complete trust in the guidance of adults presumably implies that they believe that grown-ups understand the nature of this fundamental order. Thus they willingly subscribe to authority because of this conviction, but equally they will also argue on the basis of their perception of this fundamental moral order by saying that certain things 'aren't fair'.

By continuing into the eighth year this stage contains one of the most crucial experiences of childhood. At five years of age each normal child begins to attend a school. This is a decisive factor affecting the morality of children. Their society is suddenly enormously enlarged. It now consists not merely of siblings and playmates, but hundreds of peers. In addition new authority figures appear who are invested with much more dignity and awe than their parents. And coupled with this is a psychological change which also has far-reaching consequences. The process of introjection[1] approaches its completion. Hitherto the child has been guided by his parents from without. Their personalities and requests helped him to resolve many personal problems. Now these values are absorbed into himself so that he responds to their guidance from within. Thus parents now have an ally planted in the child's personality. And if the teachers and parents are sufficiently similar in character, teachers too can count on the co-operation of this outpost of their authority.

Now two things follow from this. Firstly these introjected values can be looked upon as the seeds which will ultimately flower into moral autonomy. Because this has happened he will finally become an independent moral agent. And secondly, since the voice of authority is now heard from within as well as without, his morality is marked by submission to authority. Swainson believed that this inevitably means that the influence of teachers becomes powerful at this stage. Every parent of a primary school child will surely recognize that this is so. There is a phase during which the teacher of one's child becomes the final authority in every area of knowledge. And the daily litany of 'but Miss says' can at times be very vexing indeed.

Swainson also found that although religion played hardly any part at all in the morality of the pre-school child its influence became apparent during the school years. Whether this is linked with an authoritarian morality with God standing at the apex of a hierarchy of authority figures, or whether it results from the overtly Christian influence of the school, she does not say. But

---

[1] The term 'introjection' is here used in its psychoanalytical sense. It can refer to the total process of absorbing environmental influence, but is usually meant to imply that the agent interiorizes the personal characteristics and values of other persons and then reacts to external events accordingly.

since religion acts as a moral sanction it will be considered in the next chapter.

The next stage of development lasts from the eighth to the twelfth year. This is the stage of childhood. For our purpose it would be accurate to think of them as junior school children. Their infancy is past. It was clearly a turbulent time. Morally speaking the two great crises consisted of finally overcoming self-assertion by relating to people, and then introjecting the values of which adult society approved. Fortunately this second stage is relatively tranquil. It is the latency period spoken of by psycho-analysts. After the storm and stress of infancy, childhood offers a haven.

Those familiar with junior school pupils may object that this is not so. These children are bustling with energy all day. They devour food and information in gargantuan quantities and tumble in and out of trouble like puppies. Their startling physical and intellectual development too, endows them with those quali-ties which are most able to drive parents and teachers to distrac-tion and despair. All this is true. Their moral extraversion and healthy resistance to guilt and remorse lead them into perpetual conflict with authority. But this is all external and uncomplicated. The punishment for coming into conflict with authority may be a swift stinging smack; and unlike the remorse and moral despair of adolescence, soon passes. Or if the school system de-mands that such effusive behaviour is to be punished by detention, there is little venom in the barb. The pockets of these children are filled with such abundant evidence of their hoarding inclina-tions that they can provide either a toy to wile away the time, or a piece of material on which to exercise the imagination.

Such crises as do occur are therefore easily resolved by recourse to a rough and ready justice. There is no inner turmoil. Introjec-tion enables them readily to accept the demands made by justice upon their behaviour. Thus they are still orientated towards authority, and since authority can disperse swift and painful justice of which, despite its form, they approve, they are still pru-dential. They deem it preferable not to be *seen* and not to be *caught* rather than not to *do* anything wrong. Thus they live in a secure framework controlled by adults with whom they have a stable relationship.

Their relation to adults, however, particularly parents, is

ambivalent. Growing friendships, peer relationships and pre-adolescent gangs all combine to make social approval a powerful determinant of conduct. In addition this peer culture tends to stand in opposition to authority figures; hence the ambivalence. Parents are the enemy to be outwitted even while they provide the framework within which the child's every need is satisfied and every tension resolved. Thus in spite of the emerging social sanction, Swainson found that until about the eleventh year morality was still conceived of largely in terms of adult authority.

The third stage is that of adolescence, lasting from the thirteenth until the nineteenth year. After passing through the comparative tranquillity of childhood the adolescent now reaches the most turbulent stage of all. The tension of external relationships, so easily resolved by the child, now becomes an internal problem. The interiorizing of this conflict between self and society means that it now has to be resolved from within; and this is not only a complex but also an acutely painful process. Despair, doubt and depression often accompany the conviction that it cannot be resolved. Hemming presents a vivid picture of the agony through which many girls pass; and this, of course, is equally true of boys, though with them it is not so obvious for they tend to be less willing to discuss their problems with adults. The adolescent is now a moral agent standing alone. Unlike the infant he must look within for the means to resolve the tension which, unlike that of the child, is also within. He thus feels personally responsible for the successful achievement of this task. This is enhanced even more by the growing conviction that he must become fully himself. It is therefore not only a search for true morality, but a search for one's true self. Having now the intellectual power to recognize that behind the law lie moral principles, it is to these that he turns to resolve his dilemma. Firstly he must discover them in order to validate the rules and laws which society bind upon him, and then use these as the criteria for his moral judgements. Indeed it is rare to find an intelligent adolescent who is willing to subscribe blindly to rule and regulation. This probably helps to account for the apparent decline of morality in adolescence, which will be examined below. Wanting to question the relevance of law and the validity of moral judgments based upon it, he may appear in adult eyes as an uncouth, anarchist, barbarian. In fact he may simply be emerging as a moral agent, easing the tensions for himself, by using valid moral criteria to resolve his dilemmas. Seen in this light the adolescent questioning of hallowed tradition, and its impatience with society's sacred cows can be viewed as a thoroughly healthy insistence that moral rules and regulations should be perennially re-appraised.

This discussion has gone rather further than Swainson takes it, but it is clearly relevant since she also observes that in morality, altruism seems to dominate during the period of adolescence. This is not only her deduction from test material. The young people themselves rated the love-motive more highly than any other in their conduct. The point is this. It is not only perfectly consistent to recognize that adolescents in search of meaning in their morality should also display unanimous approval of altruism: they are searching for the principles which give meaning to moral regulations and here is the highest order principle itself. One does not have to say this simply because christianity affirms that 'Love is the fulfilling of the law'. It stands in its own right. Question a law, and if it is a good one behind it stands a principle. Question the principle and one stumbles upon a higher order principle. Do this over and over again with intelligent adolescents and the same conclusion will be reached every time. In the last analysis, they will argue, it is concern for *people* which matters. The good law haltingly and fumblingly expresses this; but its essence is altruism.

Love in adolescence is inevitably associated with physical corollaries since the sexual drives are at their strongest. But if the human relationship is unimpaired and Buber's 'I-Thou' experience remains to validate the relationship then the adolescent slogan 'Make love, not war' and the assertion 'All you need is love' are profound moral statements which jaded adults would do well to heed.

The only final point which needs to be underlined is that there are three different easily identifiable strands woven through this developmental fabric. Two of them, the dominance of a love-morality, and the existence of a religious moral sanction; are dealt with below. The third must be finally emphasized here. Throughout this simple scheme of a three-stage development the central thesis was that morality emerges from the tension between self and society. This is the pre-eminently important point to affirm for it underlines the often overlooked fact that morality is interpersonal and can only exist in human relationships.

Arnold Gesell

The work of Andrew Gesell introduces us to the third clear scheme which assumes that there are three stages in moral development. From their research in America he and his associates have produced a picture of child development which is unique for its meticulous observation and helpful hypotheses. This development is outlined in three publications, *The First Five Years of Life*, *The Child from Five to Ten*, and *Youth, the Years from Ten to Sixteen*. Fascinating though his portrayal of general child development may be, attention can be directed here only to what he has to say about *moral* development.

There are many affinities between this work and that of Swainson and Piaget, but the central theory is sufficiently distinct to show clearly the contribution which Gesell makes to this study. Reference was made earlier to this theory (see pp. 54ff. above). It argues simply that moral development proceeds in cycles. As the titles of his books suggest, each of these lasts for five years. All the basic moral attitudes are created or constructed in the first five years of life. During the second cycle they are developed further and in the third cycle are elaborated still more. Each of them however is characterized by the emergence and development of a consistent value system because the same growth mechanisms are operating from early infancy to adolescence. The inevitable growth in intellectual power, widening personal experience and, increased social sophistication induce moral development without altering the basic pattern established in infancy. Thus it is external relationships which classify the stages, for the internal value-system remains relatively stable. This is made clear when one studies the names given to each phase. There is firstly the intrinsic-self cycle; then the social-reference cycle; and finally the reciprocal-self-and-social cycle.

In the first stage, where the moral attitudes are first constructed, the child, from birth until his fifth year, is essentially egocentric. There are many clues pointing to this. Not only does he begin by refusing to capitulate his independence to any external element in his environment, but he also ascribes personality to inanimate objects. This undiluted, independent egocentricity is evident from his total refusal to accept culpability for anything he has done. Anyone in charge of young children at this stage will recognize the symptoms. With only two children standing aghast before a paint pot spilling its colour over a new carpet, or a roughly pencilled drawing on a recently papered wall, each child will adamantly accuse the other of doing it. They are not lying. They are simply displaying the impregnability of their egocentricity. It is also to this that their excessive competitiveness and flagrantly selfish anti-social attitudes point.

The ascription of personality to inanimate objects is a familiar phenomenon to anthropologists and psychologists.[1] Primitives perpetually do this. For them trees can talk: the sun can join in a battle: mountains can clap their hands. All of this is familiar to readers of the Old Testament, many of whom recognize that this language is not merely an indiscriminate admixture of animism and metaphor. Fairy stories also are crammed with assumptions of this kind and are therefore native to the thinking of young children. This explains why they can be angry with inanimate objects and frightened by things. However it is clear that this egocentricity is slowly eroded and as this happens morality develops. Now the child is no longer beyond the control of social regulations. He must subscribe to them. He cannot be a law to himself. In this way a very crude form of primitive legality emerges. It is still egocentric as the furious cry, 'It's not fair, he's got more than me', shows, but it is an egocentricity which subscribes to the demands of law. This requires also that *others* should submit to its demands and therefore one can often hear another shout, less loudly this time and clearly laced with glee, but he still says, 'It's not fair. I've got more than him, Ha! Ha!' Gesell claims at this point to have recognized an element of altruism and thus here emerges the tension between the self-regard and the love which Swainson saw so clearly. Towards the end of this first cycle, it is clear that morality is emerging. It springs both from the child's recognition of the demands of law and his awareness of a tension between his selfishness and his altruism. But it is *genuine* morality

[1] The technical term 'interjection', in its psychological rather than its psychoanalytical sense, (see p. 100 above) is used to describe this process of ascribing personal characteristics to non-personal objects. To the anthropologist however it is a characteristic of mythopoeic thinking. See Frankfort, *Before Philosophy*.

and now begins to weave a moral pattern into all his actions. He accepts responsibility for his misdeeds and expects retribution to be meted out according to the law.

His passage to the second stage of moral development seems to be characterized by an increasing dependence upon adults. He now begins to consolidate the values and attitudes which have developed in the early years. This of course is not done consciously. He responds to moral dilemmas as he has always responded, and so endorses his values and confirms his attitudes. But the world is a very frightening and mysterious environment for a six-year-old[1] and he perpetually seeks the security which adults can offer him. Thus while his basic morality is being endorsed a subtle change is apparent in his moral judgement. Goodness and badness earlier seen in terms of their effect on him are now viewed differently. No longer are they judged according to their effect on *him* but according to their effect on *his parents*. Thus goodness and badness are equated with adult approval and disapproval. Whereas before he considered cleaning out his toy cupboard and washing his neck, as two thoroughly bad things to do, now when he does them he proclaims that he is 'a good boy'.

Two further changes mark this phase. The child becomes conscious of belonging to a peer group and just as his notion of good became equated with adult approval so also it now becomes equated with his group's standards and norms. If there is a clash between the two, parents inevitably win, but he becomes increasingly conscious of the social pressure inducing him to conform. Finally this growing intellectual power enables him to respond to reason and rational argument. And there the most profound moral transformation occurs. By discussing moral issues independently of parental or peer approval he slowly evaluates his behaviour in specifically moral terms. From now on he increasingly speaks not of 'good' and 'bad', but of 'right' and 'wrong'. As a result of this growth the complex of attitudes and values which have not yet been entirely confirmed, must now be evaluated in *moral* terms. On the whole, however, that of which parents and society approve is thought to be right, and that of which they disapprove is generally deemed to be wrong. Thus the modifications are not so startling unless a sub-cultural conflict exists in which case the child either develops two systems of

---

[1] This, of course, only refers to Caucasian, industrial societies.

morality or makes a choice and so rejects one element in his sub-cultural environment.

Thus the final stage is reached. Again Gesell is insistent on the fact that development through this stage does little more than reinforce the existing moral system. This he argues was clearly prefigured in the first stage, more firmly confirmed in the second, and now so acted upon that it becomes a permanent feature in the personality of each individual. Again, however, there are subtle changes. The adolescent is developing into an autonomous agent. He has left behind his dependence upon law and parental care and wishes to make his own autonomous ventures into society. The adult world is a glittering and attractive society and he wishes to explore it. But he soon feels lost and helpless. He therefore needs a secure base from which to make his ventures. This is provided by his peer group. It can either be a small intimate circle of friends who experience their adventures together, or a large amorphous gang in relation to which he can retain his sense of identity.

He has now substituted a peer society for that of his parents and other adults. But what can take the place of law to help him make moral judgments? Gesell here claims to have found evidence for the fact that 'feeling' enters into ethical judgments. This 'feeling' is probably linked with the notion of 'conscience' but whatever its origins it leads to intuitive ethical judgments which discount the rigid rule of law. Loyalty to friends and group solidarity are valued much more than subscription to an adult code of conduct. Thus he begins to make situational moral judgments in the light of circumstances as they appear to him. But this does not lead to anarchy. Two further elements emerge which prevent this happening. Firstly, he becomes aware of the claims of reason, and secondly of the claims of love. The first demands that even a purely intuitive moral judgment must yet be amenable to rational analysis: it must be seen to be reasonable and sensible. Secondly, this skeletal form of morality has to be clothed with the living flesh of altruism, so finally he reaches the stage where his intuitively discerned moral judgements not only recognize the relevance of the particular circumstances in question and demand that they also be reasonable, but also that they should be characterized by a genuine consideration and concern for others. This is the acme of moral development as Gesell sees it. But again it must be made clear that this may not appear to be so to any adult involved in the situation. Examples of this are not difficult to find. In a secondary school recently the writer was invited to comment on a situation in which four adolescent pupils were accused of disgraceful conduct. Yet gentle probing into the circumstances showed in fact that these adolescents had been prompted to act as they did by a genuine concern for a fellow pupil, and had done so by paying due regard to the circumstances. It is not therefore surprising to learn that these intelligent, young adults who had made a genuinely moral decision were perplexed and hurt by the attitudes of the adults involved, who seemed to do nothing more than quote school rules at them. When later discussing this point with a group of students it was exhilarating to see how they reacted. All of them had a fund of anecdotes which they proceeded to tell with the enthusiasm of people who had made a remarkable discovery. One such story was submitted in writing and is included here. The narrator, it must be remembered, is a teacher in training.

'A fifth-form girl had reported the theft of cash from her desk in my form-room. The matter had been reported to me and passed on to the Headmaster in the usual way because this was the third similar case within a short space of time.

'The Head confronted the whole school and asked the culprit to see him or the matter would be referred to the police. The following day there was great consternation when the senior prefect admitted, to the Head, that he had "taken the money for a lark". He was caned, the money returned immediately and the matter was dismissed. Two days later, another boy in the fifth form was found to be extremely bruised about his face and had cut lips. When asked about this he said that he had fallen over. Tactful, confidential questioning, however, revealed that it was he who had stolen the money to help pay for a bicycle he had bought (through his widowed mother) on hire purchase. It appeared that the prefects knew about this and "drew lots" to see who should "cover" for him because of the harm such a deed would do to his reputation with his mother. Having drawn lots, the prefects then collected between them sufficient cash to repay the amount stolen.

'When asked why the real culprit has been thrashed by the prefects, the reason given was: "Well Sir, he had done wrong and this sort of thing, so we covered up for him, paid the cash and then 'told' him about it."'

Before leaving this scheme of moral development a word must be added about the apparent age-normative statements made by Gesell and his co-workers. Such a rigid definition of the conduct normal at each stage of development opens itself to a serious criticism. It was noted above that one undoubted characteristic of moral conduct was its specificity. A man may be honest in one situation, but not in another. He may conscientiously hand his bus fare to a fellow passenger while the conductor is upstairs and yet deliberately falsify his tax returns. He may be truthful in one situation and not in another; loyal in some circumstances but disloyal in others. How would Gesell meet such criticisms? In addition there is the fact of individual differences. In any classroom covering the same age range, every child is still unique! How would he answer that challenge? In both cases there is no charge to answer. Gesell has guarded against this by speaking of the emergence of an ethical sense as an unquestionable but intangible product of long term growth. He admits that it has perturbations and crises but still affirms that under favourable conditions and in a healthy personality one may see this ethical sense nevertheless gradually emerge. And if one reads his reports with care it soon becomes apparent that he is consciously guarding himself against charges of this kind. Time and time again he uses such careful phrases as 'intangible product of growth', 'orderly trends' and 'steadily takes form'. Clearly these terms are sufficiently elastic to accommodate not only the undoubted specificity of morality but also the existence of profound individual differences.

CONCLUSION

It is clear from this evidence that the majority of children in infant, junior and secondary schools represent three stages of moral development. One may advance subtle theories like Swainson and Gesell to explain both the distinctiveness and interconnectedness of these three phases of morality. But the essence of these theories is that they proclaim that there are three clearly defined levels of moral development which may be roughly located at different stages of a child's general development. To now collate them would only involve one in needless repetition. These three schemes are clearly complementary to one another and when conflated provide a comprehensive picture of this element in moral development.

If we accept this analysis then the implications of this for educational practice are far reaching. Teachers should not only come to expect different kinds of morality from the three different age-groups, but must clearly accommodate their attempts at moral education to the developmental level of these children in our infant, junior and secondary schools respectively.

BIBLIOGRAPHY

Buber, M., *I and Thou*, T. and T. Clark, Edinburgh, 1937; 2nd ed., Charles Scribner's Sons, New York, 1958.

Frankfort, H., *Before Philosophy*, Pelican, London, 1954.

Gesell, A., and Ilg, F. L., *The Child From Five to Ten*, Hamish Hamilton, London, 1946; Harper and Row, New York, 1946.

Gesell, A. (ed.), *The First Five Years of Life*, Methuen, London, 1954; Harper and Row, New York, 1940.

Gesell, A., Ilg, F. L., and Bates, L. B., *Youth; The Years from Ten to Sixteen*, Hamish Hamilton, London, 1956; Harper and Row, New York, 1956.

Hartshorne, H., and May, M. A., *Studies in the Nature of Character*, Vol. I, *Studies in Deceit*, Macmillan Company, New York, 1930.

Hartshorne, H., May, M. A., and Maller, J. B., *Studies in the Nature of Character*, Vol. II, *Studies in Service and Self-Control*, The Macmillan Company, New York, 1929.

Hemming, J., *Problems of Adolescent Girls*, Heinemann, London, 1960.

McPherson, D., *An Investigation Into the System of Moral Instruction*, Unpub. B.Ed., Glasgow, 1949.

Piaget, J., *The Moral Judgement of the Child*, Routledge and Kegan Paul, London, 1932; Free Press, New York.

Smith, H. B., *Growing Minds*, University of London Press, 1937.

Swainson, B. M., *The Development of Moral Ideas in Children and Adolescents*, Unpub. D.Phil., Oxford, 1949.

CHAPTER 5

MORAL DEVELOPMENT IN TERMS OF CHANGING SANCTIONS[1]

INTRODUCTION

From the above simple description of moral development one may now turn to examine a similar yet more complicated analysis. Instead of studying the behaviour of children at different stages of their school life, an examination will be made of the factors which prompt them to behave as they do. Instead of the conduct itself, one studies the motives which account for this conduct. This is what the term 'sanction' implies. Instead of approaching children with the question 'How are they likely to behave?' one asks instead 'Why will they behave in this way?'

There are, in addition, five more points to be made. Firstly, the word 'moral' is used here in a new way. It does not refer to conduct which conforms with the conventions of society; nor does it mean conduct which reflects the moral standards current at any particular time in a specific culture. In fact, it does not refer to conduct at all. It refers to what Vernon describes as the 'system of internalized controls'.[2]

Secondly, it must again be remembered that these conclusions are statistical. They describe groups, not individuals. In the above account of moral development it was only legitimate to conclude

[1] This chapter presents a linguistic problem. The book argues that only autonomous, rational, altruistic and responsible behaviour can be termed *genuine* moral behaviour. Rather than complicate the data by using cumbrous phrases it must be understood that anything less than this although referred to as a 'morality' is technically not so. Thus rather than use inverted commas or speak of early *moralities,* or varying *moral systems,* the child's conduct will be described as moral if it is clearly evaluated in terms of 'right' and 'wrong' or 'good' and 'bad'. But here lies a dilemma. Many would say that action which was 'right' but done from social pressure was not moral action at all since moral action has to be autonomous. Yet in another sense it may be argued that all morality is social since the essence of a 'moral' action is that the doer holds that it should be universally valid i.e. that *all* people *everywhere* should be bound to do it too.

[2] P. E. Vernon. Editorial comment in *The Development of Children's Moral Values.*

that the *majority* of children at any stage of development would display the moral features characteristic of that level of development. Equally one may now only conclude that at any given age the *majoriy* of children will be motivated by the sanctions which are apparently appropriate to that stage.

Thirdly, we may only speak of the *general* nature of those motives which determine the behaviour of most children at a loosely defined stage of development. Fourthly, we must remember that all the sanctions operate throughout the life of a child, but that one of them emerges as dominant in any particular activity.

Finally, we must recognize that these moral controls too will vary with circumstances. In one situation a child may be prompted to act as he does because he fears the consequences. For example he may not steal for fear of being punished. Yet although this may be the most familiar feature of a particular child's morality he may, under different circumstances, act as he does because he respects the law or because he personally considers it to be the right thing to do.

Perhaps the most familiar sanction for children's conduct is the desire both to be socially acceptable to their peers and also to display their concern for them. Every playground is an arena in which this last sanction can be seen to operate. Any teacher on playground duty, alerted for signs of this, will find many examples of unsung bravery occurring under his supervision.

Indeed it is always advisable to discover why boys are fighting in school, before bustling across in the role of indignant peacemaker or law-enforcer. That which so often passes for hooliganism can often be a desperate act of moral courage prompted by genuine concern for friends and siblings. Many acts of high moral worth are concealed from our eyes because all that we see is a coldly furious child with clenched fists and grim face.

WILLIAM MCDOUGALL

The first reference to these internalized controls appeared early in this century. In *Social Psychology*, William McDougall had discussed four levels of moral sanctions. His outline is rather vague and has to be read against the background of his general psychological theories, but he does make two things clear. He is quite precise in his definition of the moral controls which dominate at each of the four levels of development; and he is equally certain that they emerge in the order followed below.

There is the first stage in which conduct is characterized by its spontaneity. Here, the only modification in behaviour emerges as a result of natural consequences. He describes this graphically as 'instinctive behaviour modified only by the influence of the pains and pleasures incidentally experienced'.[1]

Then follows the second stage in which the pains and pleasures conferred by natural consequences are replaced by artificially constructed consequences. Conduct is still spontaneous and unrestrained, but it is now 'modified by the influence of rewards and punishments administered by the social environment'.[2]

Thirdly there is the stage at which each individual becomes more acutely conscious of his status in society. At this level conduct is less spontaneous and much more controlled. The consequences of actions are now seen to be more remote and complex than those imposed by nature of authority. Thus conduct becomes infinitely more subtle and is consciously manipulated to meet the demands of different social environments. Its essence however, lies in the fact that it is 'controlled in the main by anticipation of social praise and blame'.[3]

Finally, the last stage is reached when an individual conducts himself with little reference to external factors. If he deems an action to be right, then he will pursue it despite any painful consequences or social disapproval. Literature abounds with illustrations of this morality, where courageous men set their face against social disapproval and painful consequences in order to do what they deem to be right. Socrates and Christ immediately spring to mind as examples of such morality. Ibsen's *An Enemy of the People* deals with this problem in a way which highlights the opposition which even well-meaning and good people can generate against such a person. Of this level of moral behaviour McDougall wrote, it is 'the highest stage in which conduct is regulated by an ideal of conduct'.[4]

D. KENNEDY-FRASER

Little more was heard of this analysis of moral development until the passing of the 1944 Act, which drew specific attention to

[1] W. McDougall, *Social Psychology*, p. 156.   [2] *Ibid.*   [3] *Ibid.*   [4] *Ibid.*

moral and religious education. In that year Kennedy-Fraser published his book, *The Psychology of Education*, in which he applied McDougal's theory of moral development to the problem of school discipline.

Much of what he writes is now less relevant than when first published, for our knowledge of moral development has increased enormously. However the chapter, in which he argued that classroom discipline can be helped by an understanding of McDougall's theory, is extremely important for at least two reasons.

Firstly, he accepted McDougall's position without qualification but refined the concept. Admitting that McDougall's theory 'seems to agree best with the observed conditions',[1] he went on to argue that an individual passing through these various levels need not at the same time cease to be controlled by considerations more appropriate to an earlier stage of development. Writing from the seclusion of his study, an eminent psychologist like McDougall may be forgiven for wanting to have a neat and concise theory, but the practising teacher can see where a theory is inadequate to meet the observed facts. Every teacher knows that even the most morally mature pupil will sometimes be guided in his actions by prudence, or respect for authority, or concern for the opinions of his peers.

Therefore, on passing through these stages of development each individual does not inevitably leave behind his ability to behave in a way which is more appropriate to an earlier level. Kennedy-Fraser makes this quite clear, 'The individual attains these various levels without at the same time ceasing to be controlled by the lower levels'.[2]

Secondly, he appears to be the first British writer to coin the terminology which is now the common currency of discussions referring to moral sanctions. He believed that these four levels can best be described as the stages of prudential, authoritarian, social and personal morality. As will be seen below, it is this terminology which was used by McKnight when studying the moral sanctions of children.

[1] D. Kennedy-Fraser, *The Psychology of Education*, p. 168.
[2] *Ibid.* p. 169.

BEATRICE SWAINSON

In her research Swainson also dealt with moral sanctions, but reference to them has been deferred until now because it is more appropriate to discuss them in this chapter. It is clear that her emphasis on a love-orientated morality is intrinsic to this pattern of moral sanctions. Therefore, this reference to moral sanctions must be recognized as an essential element in her work.

She found that there were five primary sanctions which operated as effective motives in child morality. These were self-regard, law, love, religion and fear. Thus the conduct of children could be explained by reference to any one of these. When asked, for example, why they did or did not behave in a particular way, children could reply, 'What and get hurt?' or, 'You've got to, that's the rule', or 'I had to, he's my friend', or, 'If I did, I wouldn't go to heaven'.

These first four sanctions are perfectly clear, it is the fifth which is difficult to understand. Swainson herself nowhere specified precisely what she meant by referring to 'fear' as a motive for moral conduct. Yet a study of her work suggests what is meant. Children prompted to act from the motive of 'fear' may do so because they fear the consequences of their action. These consequences may be natural, like getting burnt or falling from a window. They may refer to adult disapproval so that the feared consequence here is punishment. Or they may refer to society, in which case the consequence to be feared is disapproval by one's peers. 'Fear' is therefore a very unsatisfactory term for a sanction since it spreads itself over so many areas each of which, as will be seen below, constitutes a valid sanction in itself.

One further point needs to be made. These motives are not mutually exclusive. It is perfectly feasible, as Swainson shows, for a child to list more than one of them in an order of priority. He may, for example, refrain from stealing, firstly because he knows it is against the law, secondly because he likes the shop-keeper, and thirdly because he really believes that he will not go to heaven if he does. In this respect, the most important fact discovered by Swainson was that the order of priority in the sanctions changed as children passed through each stage of development.

In the stage of infancy, Swainson found that the most powerful sanctions were love and self-regard. This is not unexpected. They represent the twin elements in the tension between self and society from which morality emerges. Then followed law and fear, as equally powerful sanctions. Again this is entirely predictable. The fear of consequences is a prudent attitude and respect for law reveals the authoritarian orientation of infant morality. Lastly, came religion, but it will be remembered that this remained in the background until children began to attend school and only then emerged as a feature of infant morality.

In the second stage of childhood there is an almost complete reversal of the order of these sanctions. Religion now dominates. This is the stage at which children at play may admonish one another with such threats as 'Jesus will punish you', or 'You wicked girl, you'll go to hell'. But following hard upon this comes law as a real sanction for conduct. Again this is predictable since children at that age are essentially authoritarian in their moral thinking, and indeed remain so throughout this stage. Here they constantly think of morality largely in terms of adult authority. Then follows 'love', or a concern and compassion for people. It will be seen that this motive continues to dominate until it emerges as the primary sanction of late adolescence. Right at the end of the list now comes 'fear' and 'self-regard', both of which are inappropriate to the conduct of a healthy child whose extraverted courage and sense of adventure leave little place for fear or personal prudence.

It is interesting to observe here that other psychologists consider this to be the stage at which children become acutely conscious of the opinions of their fellows. Yet these two sanctions which come last in Swainson's order of priority, are the only two which could refer to a social control of conduct. Presumably, children sensitive to the opinions of their peers would fear social rejection and be careful to ensure that they retained some secure membership in a peer society. However, since Swainson did not find this to be so, one may only conclude that the dominance of 'love' as a sanction met these two needs. After all, one who expresses genuine concern for people has no need to fear their disapproval.

During the stage of adolescence the changes are sufficiently radical to warrant a dividing of this period into two sub-stages. During the first three years of adolescence, religion still dominates as a sanction; but the authoritarian attitude which looks to laws and regulations to guide moral conduct, is now superseded by a concern for people. For the first time since infancy people again matter more than regulations. These young adolescents are still sufficiently authoritarian to recognize that law can control their conduct, but they have now left behind the fear and prudent self-regard of their infancy.

Again it must be observed with some surprise that a social sanction does not emerge with more force. At this stage it is clear that the opinions of their fellows begin to carry much more weight with them than those of their parents. One can only conclude that love and concern for peers and fear of their disapproval are the obverse and reverse side of the same coin. Therefore, the slow emergence of love as the dominant factor may point to the domination of the hidden social sanction.

Finally, during the last years of adolescence, love emerges as the dominant motive for moral conduct. This is confirmed by many researchers. According to Peck and Havighurst the altruistic person stands at the highest point of moral development. Piaget admits that the highest level of morality, which he designates as 'equity', is little more than the demand for reciprocal morality softened and informed by genuine concern for the needs of others. A further confirmation of the dominance of this moral sanction can now be added. The children tested by Swainson were also asked to name any other sanctions which were not listed. A large number spoke of 'sympathy for others'. It is interesting to note this further reinforcement of the notion of a 'love-morality'.

The most obvious features in this process of moral development are quite clear. It is a process in which prudential self-regard and authoritarian legalism slowly wane while the personal sanctions of love and religion become more and more prominent. Nevertheless it contains two unique features. At no point does the social sanction gain any real force. Nowhere does the negative need to be acceptable to one's peers emerge with the power usually associated with it. And finally the much derided religious sanction emerges as valid for each stage of development.

These two features which do not easily fit into our picture of children today may be explained by the fact that this research is now nearly twenty years old. We, today, are dealing with another generation entirely. It is the sons and daughters of Swainson's children who are now being studied today and we must expect to find many changes.

ROBERT MCKNIGHT

In the following year, the conclusions of McDougall and Kennedy-Fraser were empirically tested by Robert McKnight. His work on *The Moral Sanctions of the Child*, is a succinct report almost exclusively concerned to discover just how far McDougall's sanctions are effective.

He consciously accepted the terminology bequeathed by Kennedy-Fraser and studied the force and sequence of the prudential, authoritarian, social and personal controls in the morality of school-children. His research confirmed that McDougall was right in arguing that these stages were sequential, for he found that in all cases this was the order in which these moral controls emerged.

He also confirmed that Kennedy-Fraser was right in insisting that the power of earlier sanctions persisted in the morally mature. He claimed emphatically that, 'It does not follow that the earlier stages disappear on the emergence of a higher'.[1]

It thus becomes more and more evident that as a child grows the number of 'moralities' accessible to him at any one time continues to increase. This is important because it means not only that the specificity of moral conduct can be explained as resulting from this, but also that one need not suppose that a child must 'regress' to an earlier stage of development in order to display more primitive forms of moral behaviour.

It is, however, very easy to conclude from McKnight that there are four stages in moral development each of which can be described only in terms of the sanction which controls the behaviour characteristic of each stage.

The evidence of Swainson should prevent one from falling into this error. She showed how all the sanctions are operative throughout the life of each child. When therefore one speaks of moral development in these terms one is simply describing the nature of the sanction which appears to dominate at each stage.

A close study of McKnight's findings reveals that he too must

[1] R. K. McKnight, *The Moral Sanctions of the Child*, 1950, pp. 15–16.

be understood in this way. He found that all the sanctions operated throughout the complete age-range of the children studied. But instead of describing their order of importance at each stage he preferred to emphasize the dominant sanction. Therefore, he describes each stage in terms of that one dominant sanction.

Finally, it must be made perfectly clear that when one speaks of a dominant sanction it means not merely that it dominates in the majority of pupils but also that it only dominates in the majority of moral dilemmas facing each individual child. Even where a child is so representative of his stage of moral development that his conduct bears all the marks of either prudentiality, or authoritarianism, he may yet still be controlled by the influence of his peers or his personal moral ideals in some isolated moral dilemma. With these qualifications in mind one may thus turn to the four levels of morality described by McKnight.

At the level of prudential morality it is the fear of natural and perhaps painful consequences which controls moral behaviour. Children learn not to play with fire because they can be burnt. They can be prevented from harming animals because they know that animals can scratch and bite. Sometimes these natural consequences can be engineered. The writer knows of one family who raised three delightfully mature and moral children by such means. In the early years there was no moral training as such. If one of the children hit either parent they were immediately hit back. When any damage was done, the culprit had to repair it himself.

It seems a rather unloving and cruel technique, but by being completely impersonal and thus having nothing to do with the personal relationships of parent and child it seemed to work. Its gravest shortcoming seems to be the inherent assumption that conduct which produces beneficial results is good conduct, while behaviour whose results are injurious is bad conduct. However, every parent and teacher can recognize this moral sanction operating in young children. And if they wish to argue that in this natural morality of a young child one may find a guide for moral education, they will find support in Rousseau. He argued that 'nature illustrates to us in the simplest way the true theory and practice of discipline'.[1] This point is discussed fully below.

---

[1] J. J. Rousseau, *Emile*, p. 90.

The second stage of development is one in which the authoritarian control determines the nature of the child's morality. This is very similar to the moral control of the first stage, but it differs from it in three important respects. Although adults may manipulate the natural consequences in order to induce moral behaviour in children at the first stage of development, this stage is marked by three new factors.

Firstly, the child refers to the consequences determined by authority, rather than those determined by nature. Washed, dressed and waiting to go to a party, even an adventurous child will refrain from climbing a tree, not because he may fall and break a leg, but because his parents will punish him if he does.

Secondly, rewards as well as punishments emerge as a consequence of conduct. Natural consequences are invariably harmful. If a child plays in the road he may be knocked down; if he strays from a cliff-top path he can fall to his death. Obedience merely avoids these painful consequences. But if he obeys his parents and teachers then he can invariably be assured that some pleasant consequences will follow, not because they are *naturally* associated with his conduct, but because those in authority choose to associate his good conduct with a pleasant reward. Thus parents perpetually say, 'If you are a good boy . . .' and complete the sentence by describing some pleasant consequences for the child. Teachers too have a ready supply of stars or house points to dispense as rewards under exactly the same moral system. All this of course, is now familiar to educators as a result of Skinner's work.

He calls such behaviour 'positive reinforcement'. Speaking of this control he writes, 'When he behaves as we want him to behave we simply create a situation he likes. As a result the probability that he will behave that way again, goes up.'[1] Thus a much more sophisticated terminology can describe the difference between these two sanctions. Nature tends to use the inefficient technique of 'negative reinforcement', while authority tends more and more to use the highly efficient techniques of 'positive reinforcement'.

All this, of course, ignores the more subtle rewards which accompany good behaviour. These can range from the respect and admiration which follows good conduct to the inner serenity

[1] B. F. Skinner, *Walden Two*, pp. 259ff.

which accompanies it. As wise moralists through the ages have said, 'The reward of being a good man is that one is a good man'.

The third difference is that whereas the consequences in the first stage of development follow a breach of natural law, in this stage it is a breach of man-made law. The Highway Code, for example, does not reflect natural law. There is nothing natural about driving on the left-hand side of the road in England or on the right-hand side in France, but those who break this law are punished, even if no disastrous natural consequences follow. Those who are seen to be pre-eminent in their observation of the highway code are given car badges which proclaim their excellence to the world. But even such commendable qualities cannot enhance what is little more than legalism veneered with moral bribes. As McDougall sourly observes 'It can hardly be called moral even if the laws are never broken'.[1]

Easy though it is to thus dismiss so-called moral conduct of this kind, children at this stage of development look naturally to authority to guide them and many teachers claim that this lays upon them obligations to moralize. Often a perplexed child who has nibbled at a moral problem for hours can be completely satisfied by an adult he trusts who says to him, 'I know that you can't understand it but that is what we have to do. It's like a law that must be obeyed.' And, as tea-time approaches in any area where children are playing, one may observe even the most recalcitrant child submitting to the final force of his sibling's cry, 'You've got to come, mummy said so!'

At the third stage of moral development, where the social control begins to operate with increasing power, it is apparent that a radical change has affected the child's general thinking as well as his moral assumptions. His thoughts are marked by reciprocity. Since this is central to Piaget's theory, a full discussion of it can be left until later. It is quite clear however, that this happens. Children seem suddenly to be assailed by the humbling thought that the condition of being themselves does not confer upon them any privileges which it does not at the same time confer upon their friends, since they are also in the state of being themselves. This is clearly a stage in intellectual development since this new factor is produced by the process of operational reasoning.

[1] W. McDougall, *Social Psychology*, p. 162.

But the realization that one's personal relations must all be reciprocal has a profound effect upon morality. Now for the first time children make a moral response to their peers and become extremely sensitive to the ethical code of this society. They slowly develop the conviction that the right thing to do is not only that of which authority approves; it is also that of which their own peer community approve. Thus an ethical code springs up which can be in sharp opposition to that of adult society.

In this process children slowly detach themselves from parents and attach themselves to peer groups. This is an acutely painful phase for loving parents, especially the mother, but it must be remembered that this is a necessary interim stage between moral dependence upon parents and that moral independence which marks the mature adult.

As a moral system it obviously has many deficiencies. Often the truly moral man or child must swim against the tide of public opinion. But perhaps the gravest deficiency here is the necessarily cyclical value judgment which is involved. If a child seeking to know the right thing to do is told that conduct of which the community approves is necessarily right conduct, he will have been guided in a circle. Conduct which is stimulated by social consensus cannot help but be acceptable to that society and therefore the problem of moral values has been shelved. But this, say the pragmatists, need not be a bad result. It may not produce any unchanging absolute moral values, but at least it works. For this reason, Dewey argues that 'the moral and the social quality of conduct are, in the last analysis, identical with each other'.[1]

The last stage of moral development is one in which the personal moral control is exercised. It will be seen below just how complex is an analysis of personal morality. For the purpose of this chapter however, it only needs to be emphasized at this stage that the moral sanction resides within each individual and is based upon personal moral principles. This is the highest level of all, and can be described in a number of different ways. It is most obviously a move away from the morality which springs from obedience to external commands to that which originates in the possession of a series of inwardly accepted regulating moral principles. In a word, it is marked by the transition from moral heteronomy to moral autonomy.

[1] J. Dewey, *Democracy and Education*, p. 358.

Equally important is the fact that this development has been accompanied in most cases by a growing refusal to follow the selfish impulses which originate in one's own self-regard, and an increasing recognition of the rights and needs of others. This can therefore, be described very succinctly as the movement away from egocentricity towards moral altruism.

J. F. MORRIS

A further development in this analysis appears in the work of Morris. He also reports that moral actions could be classified according to their motives or sanctions. Since he deliberately took up the problem of moral development where Piaget had left it, his conclusions have a Piagetian flavour, but they are remarkably close to McKnight's findings too.

His evidence suggests that adolescent behaviour is controlled by five moral sanctions. These are self-interest, authoritarianism, reciprocity, conformity to friends, and moral independence. Although he was not concerned to show where these could be placed in a scheme of moral development it is clear from his report that the above order is deemed to be the one in which these motives make their appearance. The most morally immature of these children are prompted by self-regard; the most morally mature tend to act from the vantage point of moral independence.

F. H. HILLIARD

At this point the reader may be wondering about the fate of Swainson's religious sanction, and perhaps pondering too on the absence of any reference to conscience. In the public mind both of these concepts are central to morality. It is almost impossible to discuss morality for very long with either children or adults without finding that the conversation turns to consider religion and conscience. This omission can now be made good.

The evidence for the operation of a religious sanction comes from Hilliard. In his publication *The Influence of Religious Education upon the Development of Children's Moral Ideas*, he examines the effect of a religious sanction on moral behaviour. His work is interesting not only because of its important conclusions but also because he reviews the history of this alleged relationship between the two.

He begins by showing that the findings of early studies in child psychology are relevant here. He agrees with Bovet, for example, who in *The Child's Religion*, argued that children deify their parents and parentalize the deity. Thus it can be argued that since the influence of parents is essential for the moral development of every normal child this deifying of the parent endorses and perpetuates an equation of religious sentiment and moral perfection. Hilliard also demonstrates how Piaget's acknowledged dependence upon Bovet led to his acceptance and development of this idea.

This relationship between religion and morality in children was also confirmed by a series of research projects which followed hard upon the passing of the 1944 Education Act. Given government approval as it were, to the view that religious education would inculcate moral growth, a number of researchers were stimulated to investigate this assumption. During the forties it seemed that, as an assumption, it was well founded. One researcher discovered that nearly three-quarters of his 500 respondents believed explicitly that God upheld the moral law. Again during the fifties it was found that the religious sanction operated as a moral control. As children matured its force declined but it never finally disappeared.

It can thus be seen that Hilliard's findings were almost predictable. He worked with students studying in establishments of higher education where it would be expected that the religious sanction had ceased to operate as an active dominant force in morality: yet he found that almost all the students believed that the Christian Gospel was a satisfactory moral guide, and an overwhelming majority considered that belief in God was intimately related to moral uprightness.

Such bald conclusions as these need to be discussed at length for they contain all sorts of ambiguities and misconceptions. Obviously a religious sanction depends very much upon the religious maturity of the individual. Unfortunately, for those who seek clear guidance on this central issue of moral education, a pernicious and unworthy argument seems to be gaining currency. It is argued that such a linking of morality and religion is based on the view that we are only good because the Almighty will

punish us if we are bad. Every transgression it seems is meticu-
lously noted and reserved for an indictment at the last judgment.
The Humanist, like Lionel Elvin, quite rightly dismisses this as
nonsense and says simply that if anyone says, 'You will steal from
Woolworth's if you don't believe in a God who tells you, you
mustn't, I can only ask him not to be silly.'[1] For the Christian
there is, however, a very real and inherent connection between
religion and morality which can be illustrated by far more
weighty considerations than these.

It is clear then that a religious sanction can operate at the prudential or the personal level, according to the maturity of the
believer. That it can also operate at the interim stages there is no
doubt, for religion in the west has been characterized by its imposition of authority and its demand for conformity with the
ecclesiastical group. However, Hilliard's finding that 'the
majority believe that God upholds the moral law',[2] and that
students 'continue to look to religious education and religion to
assist in the development and maintenance of moral standards'[3]
makes it clear that his work at least confirms that Swainson's
religious sanction still operates.

CONSCIENCE

Now it only remains to rescue 'conscience' from the obscurity
into which the foregoing writers appear to have forced it. During
her work Swainson discovered that about 3 per cent of her respondents referred to conscience as an active moral control, but
she considered this too insignificant to be worth pursuing.[4] Perhaps it is the complexity of the idea[5] which leads researchers to
avoid it for the various interpretations of its meaning make it a
very slippery concept to handle.

[1] L. Elvin, 'Moral Values in a Mixed Society', in *Aspects of Education:
One. Morality and Education,* p. 15.

[2] F. H. Hilliard, 'The Influence of Religious Education Upon the
Development of Children's Moral Ideas,' pp. 51ff. [3] *Ibid.* p. 54.

[4] In her research report, however, Bradburn notes that, 'After making
detailed studies of many problem children, Redl and Wineman said that
whilst the strength of the conscience may vary from individual to individual, they had never seen a child in whom it was totally absent.
Educational Research, June 1967 p. 207.

[5] In addition, contemporary research is showing the wide variety of ways
in which conscience functions as a moral control.

It can, for example, be understood in the Freudian sense of an internalizing of parental authority. The voice which spoke to us as infants from without, now speaks to us as children and adults from within. Or a behavioural psychologist like Eysenck can argue that it is an accumulation of conditioned responses to moral stimuli. As we grow we respond to moral stimuli in ways which produce both comfort and anxiety. The well regulated life in which we are admired and respected produces pleasure, therefore conduct which is prejudicial to this produces the pains of conscience.

Yet again it can be understood in religious terms. It is the 'light which lightens every man coming into the world'. It is placed there in our personality by the Creator who leaves it so that we shall have something to guide our conduct. Here it acts not only as a moral compass and ethical director but as a goad which keeps man on the path of doing God's will. Finally, the Thomist philosopher might say it is that aspect of man's mind which is specifically concerned with determining his moral decisions and actions. It thus looks as though it is the ambiguity to which this brief discussion points, which has led to its neglect. However, this can now be partially remedied.

Norman Williams places it firmly in its moral context. Even here however, it is not referred to as 'conscience'. He prefers to speak of 'introjected, irrational values'. It will be seen later that Peck and Havighurst do something very similar when they refer to one of the personality types studied as the 'irrational-conscientious' person.

Williams bases his scheme of sanctions on active observations of children in their natural surroundings.[1] He thus employed the technique which Susan Isaacs commended as suitable since in this way 'the behaviour which is recorded is that which occurs naturally'.[2]

---

[1] Williams carefully emphasizes that 'The development stages given below may look as though they are intended as a firm scheme. This is not the intention; they are offered merely as *examples* of the *kind* of distinction I have in mind' (*The Moral Development of Children*, para 2). Since then we have had a protracted correspondence on this point and he has been kind enough to point out two important developments. Firstly, that his use of a much larger classification scheme has enabled him to think of ordering the material in a different way. Secondly, that he is reluctant to correlate his categories with motivational elements, as I have in this chapter.

[2] S. Isaacs, *Social Development in Young Children*, Introduction.

The natural surroundings in this case were a boarding-school for maladjusted children and the natural behaviour was the conduct of children conspiring to raid the school larder. He is careful to point out that the children were thus involved in a moral dilemma which was real to them; that they were unaware of being observed or overheard; and that they were children with retarded rather than distorted personalities.

He records how in this dilemma a number of children flatly refused to be involved in theft. Thus all of these acted in an identical way; they withdrew from the planned raid. Yet they gave many reasons for this decision, revealing that different sanctions were operative. Thus one would argue, 'I'm not going to do it because the teacher says it's wrong.' Another argued, 'I'm not joining in, I can't explain why, I just know that it's wrong.' Older children would explain, 'We don't do that sort of thing in our group now', and assume that this closed the matter. Then there were those who expressed concern for their fellow pupils. These would say, 'No I won't do it, it isn't fair on John, if I came he would want to come and it would only make him cry.' Then finally, there were those who simply dismissed the idea. 'What do you take me for?' they would ask, 'I'm a senior now and don't do things like that.'

This was the furthest that such retarded children could go. In addition to this it is worth noting that there was no evidence of prudential morality. This is surprising. It is difficult to believe that none of the children refused to join in a raid on the school larder by saying, 'No fear, you might get caught.'

These standard responses point at least to a series of stages in development, each of which is characterized by the dominant motive or sanction. These can be listed in what seems to be the natural order of emergence in an individual.

There is firstly the stage of obedience in which morality consists of a natural compliance with external restraints. Then follows the stage of introjected irrational values. This appears to be characterized by conduct which would normally be described as dictated by conscience.[1] After this, comes the level of group-

---

[1] Anyone interested in the nature and evolution of the human conscience should read Stephenson's *The Development of Conscience*. For a wider view of the meaning of 'conscience' the reader is referred to J. G. McKenzie's *Guilt*, where its legal and ethical implications are examined.

orientated morality in which the values and standards of the peer society dominate in the life of each individual. At this point an empathic morality emerges where moral conduct displays altruism and concern for people, without necessarily being based on reciprocity. An individual child, for example, does not argue 'I expect him to do this to me therefore I'll do it for him'. He seems to be driven to act as he does by natural compassion for for others. Before mature morality emerges the child has yet to pass through a further stage in which an ego-ideal controls his behaviour. It could be argued that this is personal morality, but since his 'self-picture' may be partly produced by society, it is more accurate not to think of this as an autonomous stage of development. He is here guided by the picture he has of his ideal self, and so behaves only in those ways which are consistent with this ideal. Finally, the personal sanction presumably emerges in a fully developed form when reasonable, personal moral principles control the individual's behaviour.

A CURRENT RESEARCH PROJECT

To conclude this section, reference can be made to research conducted by the writer. In an attempt to discover the moral sanctions which operate amongst children in the seven to sixteen year age range, a long term project was initiated. The first step was an attempt to disclose the various moral motives of school-children and discover whether these sanctions could be related to the general moral maturity of each child.

In order not to impose any pattern of moral thinking on to the children an incomplete sentence test was given to 300 pupils, a further 150 children writing free essays on such subjects as 'Why be Good?', 'Myself', 'Why is it wrong to Steal?', 'Why it is Wrong to Lie', and 'The Ways of Telling Right from Wrong'. And 100 more completed an open-ended moral-situations test.

This project is not yet complete. It must therefore, for the moment, be sufficient to say that this material was carefully analysed and found to produce eight moral sanctions[1] which

[1] There were in fact fifteen different motivational factors in the material but this was reduced to eight for two reasons. Firstly, as was noted above, moral development is both quantitative and qualitative. On the basis of

operated over the whole age range. The next stage was then relatively easy. Out of this material a closed-ended test paper was compiled in which each item consisted of a moral dilemma in which a specified character behaved in a particular way. Then followed the eight sanctions with the children being required to tick those which they thought controlled the behaviour of the person in the test item. Younger children in the primary school had the test administered verbally.

A pilot survey using these tests, as well as interviews moulded from the same material, showed that these moral sanctions dominated in roughly the following chronological order.

In terms of the sanctions governing their moral behaviour children are firstly prudential and authoritarian. They then begin to apply the principle of reciprocity and so become amenable to the control of a social sanction. Thus the next sanctions are reciprocal expectations and social approval. At this point it was clear that the influence of their own self-concept became apparent and so they emerged finally at the level of personal morality where the sanction is clearly personal. It was equally clear that conscience was a moral control throughout this whole age-range, as indeed was the religious sanction. The latter however, was only effective amongst about a quarter of the primary school children and was much less apparent with the secondary school pupils.[1]

this distinction it was decided to syphon off those items which could be regarded as moral attitudes which developed quantitatively. This left a developmental list of eleven which was then reduced to eight because some of them were closely related. These are representative of different stages of development.

Thus the original list of fifteen items, i.e. prudential, egocentric, amoral, hedonist, authoritarian, social, reciprocal, religious, ego-idealist, conscience-derived, autonomous, altruistic, rational, independent and responsible considerations all together produced four tests. The first two tested for moral maturity and by conflating the egocentric, amoral and hedonist elements with the prudential, produced tests with eight stages of moral maturity.

The four elements which were then left, i.e. the altruistic, independent, rational and responsible considerations, were then moulded into two attitude tests of the kind proposed by Likert.

[1] It should be noted that religious sanctions may also be classified under most of the other headings. They can, for example be catalogued as prudential, social, authoritarian, or personal in nature. In addition to this fact it is extremely difficult to decide how much weight to place upon such an overt relationship between religion and morality. In the pilot test,

The validity of this list of sanctions can be seen from the following material. In the first place it was elicited from the pupils by means of essays, and by the moral-situations test, and since the children's own responses were used, this produced two sets of two tests; one appropriate for primary and one suitable for secondary pupils. Each test consisted of twenty-four items but for the purposes of this argument only one test item is used here. In this a hungry child refrains from taking any food from the larder at home. This is not only a common uncomplicated moral situation, but is sufficiently close to the planned raid of Williams's boys to make comparison more rewarding.

In response to this test item the total range of moral reactions to the situation described was covered by the following examples. In explaining why the child took no food from the larder the secondary school pupils answered variously:

1. She might get caught doing it. (Prudential).
2. Her mother said she must not take food from the larder. (Authoritarian).
3. Her mother would not take anything from her without asking. (Reciprocal).
4. Her friends would call her a thief if they knew. (Peer society).

conducted by the author, using the above material, religious sanctions were cited by 27 per cent of the primary school children and 17 per cent of the secondary school children. This seemed to follow Hilliard's findings. Yet the reduction correlating with increased maturity indicates that this sanction loses its force. This is confirmed by Cox. He discovered that with different moral issues between 1.2 per cent and 19.8 per cent of the boys, and between 1.6 per cent and 30.3 per cent of the girls in sixth forms cited religious sanctions for their moral affirmations. But the figures are low for central moral issues, e.g. 3.6 per cent of boys and 5 per cent of girls gave religious sanctions to disapprove of lying; 8 per cent of the boys and 13.3 per cent of the girls considered stealing to be wrong on religious grounds; and 5.8 per cent of the boys and 17.6 per cent of the girls considered that pre-marital sexual intercourse was wrong for religious reasons. (See Cox *Sixth Form Religion* pp. 150–68.) This trend seems to be supported by the Eppels in their study of adolescents and morality. Amongst 230 essays dealing with moral values 'There are only four references to faith or religion' (p. 153). But even in these, two comments merely thank God for making the particular boy and the particular girl as they are, and one links the Archbishop of Canterbury with Krushchev as admirable people who 'have found loyalty and faith' (p. 153).

5. She was not the sort of girl that took things without asking. (Ideal-self).[1]
6. There might not be enough left for tea if she did. (Personal).
7. Stealing is a sin against God. (Religious).
8. Although she was hungry she still knew it was wrong. (Conscience).

In almost exactly the same way the responses of the primary school-children fell into this pattern with the following as typical answers referring to each sanction:

1. She would get into trouble. (Prudential).
2. She should ask somebody first to get permission. (Authoritarian.
3. She did not like other people taking her things. (Reciprocal).
4. She would get a bad name amongst her friends. (Peer society).
5. She was not a thief. (Ideal-self).
6. She might not leave enough for tea. (Personal).
7. God does not like girls who steal. (Religious).
8. She just felt it was wrong. (Conscience).

Further research indicated that these tests were both reliable and valid. Indeed the Spearman Rank Correlation Test revealed a high degree of reliability.[2] Validity was then confirmed by testing 30 more children and comparing the results with teacher-ratings, and also with moral tests given verbally in unstructured interviews. In addition this further research confirmed that apart from religion and conscience (which deserve special study) these moral sanctions seemed to emerge chronologically in the order listed above. This only means that it is usual for the majority of children in the majority of instances to be guided by the sanctions appropriate to their stage of development.

[1] The moral element here referred to is almost identical with the notion of a child's self-concept. Thus it may be related to the 'self-picture' of the pupil which Staines considers to be so important as a factor in the classroom.

[2] With a sample of fifty children ranging from 7 to 16 years of age the following results were obtained. Using the standard formula $r = 1 - \dfrac{6 \Sigma \delta^2}{N^3 - N}$ the coefficient of correlation for the four tests was as follows:
0.8723 : 0.8138 : 0.6619 : and 0.6012 where the significance level is 0.475 at 0.01.

In addition to these eight moral sanctions it was also discovered that four others emerged. These are rationality, altruism, responsibility and moral independence. It will be argued in Chapter 9 that these are best treated as attitudes. There the structure of moral development in terms of attitudes is then presented in detail. For the moment it is sufficient to observe that these four primary moral attitudes are all part of the 'personal' sanction. Thus, although Swainson speaks of altruism, Morris refers to moral independence and Williams includes rationality in their lists of sanctions, they do not appear in the list proposed by the writer.

The Implications for Education

This analysis of moral development in terms of changing sanctions seems to be the one most readily accepted by parents and teachers. After delivering a course of lectures on the subject of moral education the writer found that it was this one element which remained most vividly in the minds of students.

One can see why this is so. Once the initial conceptual difficulty is overcome this system is easily understood, particularly in its four-fold form as advanced by McKnight. It is simple to remember. It explains much of the moral conduct observed amongst children. It seems to conform to the evidence supplied by any group of children at work or at play.

For these reasons it is valuable to pause for a moment and briefly review our educational practice in the light of this analysis.

When this is done a most disturbing conclusion is reached. Much of our educational endeavour seems to be dedicated to both preventing children from reaching the highest level of personal morality and also to perpetuating the lower authoritarian forms of morality. That many children will fit snugly into our authoritarian system, there is no doubt at all. Adorno has shown that many members of our society have an 'authoritarian personality', and will thus take to this environment like a fish to water.

Obviously there must be noteworthy exceptions, but on the whole schools do not approve of children whose moral control is personal. These can be awkward and difficult pupils since they tend perpetually to question the established system. They are critical of the quality of life inculcated by the school as an institution and invariably disapprove of the school regulations and general educational practice.

Older pupils may be encouraged to give honest opinions on matters relating to school life, but when they do so, and it is at variance with the school tradition and ethos, the intelligent and outspoken young man or woman may be told that he has now gone too far. Bound thus by a complicated and rigid system of authoritarian regulations even the most intelligent pupils tend to be prevented from making very much progress in moral growth.

One may perhaps argue that the present constitution of schools cannot cater for a community in which personal moral principles are allowed full expression. Schools are authoritarian systems. Such a system may be undesirable but it works. Therefore, it may be argued that personal morality, although desirable, has no place in it.[1] The fact that it is less arduous to control a society by authoritarian means, is a practical argument to which many teachers subscribe by their conduct in the classroom. Indeed some teachers have asked for more authority to help them cope with increasing difficulties. In America, for example, teachers are now asking for greater power to help them to control vicious and violent teen-age pupils. In this case, they argue, let us have a fence at the top of the cliff, not an ambulance at the bottom. Yet there are many others who see clearly the deficiences of an authoritarian system. It is not only now completely out of phase with the development of society at large, but it prevents further moral growth. In addition Moore has recently argued that authoritarian infliction of pain on children, for example, need not be punishment in any legitimate sense and may in fact be downright immoral. Unfortunately the fear that moral anarchy might be introduced by a genuine desire to help advance the moral development of their pupils may prevent them from doing anything about it.

But moral development proceeds by stages! There is also the interim stage of social morality, where the social sanction operates. Yet even this moral advance may be prevented.

Such a charge can be levelled at schools which disapprove of too strong a peer culture. Young adolescents are at that stage of development in which their conduct and attitudes tend to be

[1] For those who may be attracted to this view Spiel's book would make salutary reading.

reinforced largely by the society to which they naturally belong. The group exerts an enormous influence over the individuals, and the individuals in turn look instinctively to the group for guidance. Yet very few schools use this powerful social tool which is actually placed in their hands.

It is possible to see why this happens. These peer values are often directly opposed to those of the school. Sometimes of course, they are not. It is possible for a particular peer group to subscribe to the value-system embedded in the adult community of that school. In this case, the pupils are encouraged to continue their association with it, and the 'influence leaders' of such groups often become the prefects and house captains; but more often than not a peer society stands in opposition to the adult society of the school. Then instead of using this social tool the authorities try to blunt it. This can be done in a number of ways. The staff may undermine loyalty to peers by emphasizing that their values conflict with the school tradition. Or the techniques may be crude and ruthless. Authority is imposed and children are forced to revert to a morality out of which they have recently grown. As a result there appears to be a general tendency in British education to compel children to remain at an immature moral level.

This would be unacceptable in any other school subject. The malicious stupidity of forcing children to think with the conceptual understanding of infants would be immediately apparent. Yet in morality this is not so. Authoritarian and even prudential morality is endorsed and supported by our educational system. Because this is unfortunately so this fact will be discussed more fully.[1]

---

[1] A legitimate argument to use against the subsequent discussion could consist simply of saying that since children pass through both prudential and authoritarian forms of morality the schools must cater for this by being authoritarian and prudential at the appropriate stages. This is a nice point. On the basis of the evidence supplied in chapter 3 above and chapter 10 below it is clear that teachers must use authoritarian or prudential techniques in order to facilitate the development of children at those moral stages. But this is a rather different proposition to what actually appears to happen in unenlightened schools. There authority and prudence may be inculcated as *values possessing moral worth,* and not regarded as dispensable aids to moral progress. It is this elevation of immature morality to the status of socially desirable conduct which the following discussion attempts to criticize.

Authoritarian Morality in Schools

If it is true that schools tend to create an authoritarian frame of mind then some further comments are needed on this point. This is the kind of moral preparation which sends young men and women into the adult world with the minimum of preparation for life's challenge. At its best, such education produces law-abiding but uncritical and unthinking citizens who can only work to rule and whose behaviour is best controlled by reference to the laws of a trade union, a church or the state. At its worst, such a system may produce citizens who are unable to resist even the most pernicious propaganda so long as it is disseminated with sufficient authority. That such a population is also ripe for the demagogue and dictator was clearly shown in the history of Nazi Germany. So when thoroughly abused such a technique may create criminals like those tried at Nuremburg, whose only explanation of their bestial behaviour was that they were told to do it. As Deighton has said, 'A man doesn't obey without question, or he's not a man any more'.[1]

It could be argued that many institutions today demand this kind of morality from their members. In the armed forces the highest excellence is that of immediate and unquestioning obedience: and a whole system of conditioning on the parade ground is employed to ensure that every soldier approximates more and more to this ideal.[2]

Industrial organizations too are beginning to expect this kind of behaviour and demand that personal morality should be subordinated to obedient execution of the corporation's demands. Even Trade Unions are making the same demands on their members, and the individual who refuses to subscribe to what he believes is a wrong and stupid policy, faces social ostracism from his workmates and even the possibility of physical assault from the union's 'loyal' members.

All this is true. The flaw in such an argument however, lies here. Schools may at this moment be preparing pupils for life in

[1] L. Deighton, *An Expensive Place to Die*, p. 246.

[2] This is not intended to deny the value of good habits and habitual conduct. In many of our social relations we respond by habit, just as we tie our shoes by habitual patterns of behaviour. If we had consciously to think about the morality of everything we did, or even think about how we tied our ties or shoes, we would have little time for the more important things in life.

a society moulded by hard political, social, economic and industrial facts, but they are not thereby committed to perpetuating imperfect moral values. It is true that the schools have a responsibility to serve society and so reflect its legal structure but equally they must act as agents of social change. Given the opportunity our schools could present a generation of morally mature adults to society. In this way the social health of our community could be transformed in a generation, and many of its apparently endemic social ills would slowly disappear.

Authoritarian means can never cure these ills. As Manson argues, 'The attempt by rules and regulations to mend the manners of mankind is to treat symptoms instead of disease'.[1] This social disease can only be cured by an injection of healthy, morally mature, young people, and this, it seems, is the task of the schools today. Contemporary totalitarian attempts at such social transformation have not been entirely successful. Reports from Russia, Cuba and China, however, make it quite clear just how much power is held by the educators of the next generation, and although only a work of fiction B. F. Skinner's Utopian novel *Walden Two* contains many valuable insights provided by this eminent behavioural psychologist. There he shows with consummate skill how our present knowledge of the behavioural sciences can assist in the creation of such people who will then inevitably transform society for the better.

There appears therefore, to be no justification for perpetuating the authoritarian system of control in our schools. Obviously, there must be a system of regulations, but these should be formulated by the society which will subscribe to them. They should not be imposed in an authoritarian manner upon the young by command of the old. This at least was the opinion of the Spens Report. It advocated that 'the function of the staff in the corporate life of a school is one of guidance, not one of control'.[2] This policy is even more urgently required today. An emerging 'youth-culture' with what Acland has argued is a peer-orientated resistance to authority will inevitably become an increasingly implacable enemy of those schools in which this maxim is ignored.

[1] T. W. Manson, *The Teaching of Jesus,* chapter IX on Religion and Morals, pp. 285ff.

[2] Spens Report, *The School as a Society,* pp. 197–205. Clearly this moral principle should be unequivocally accepted in colleges too.

This aspect of school life will be discussed more fully in the companion volume when attention is directed to the influence of school organization on moral development. For the moment it only needs to be observed that with the raising of the school leaving age this problem is likely to become more serious than it is now. Young adults will increasingly demand the right to question cherished beliefs, hallowed traditions and revered practices. In such a situation tradition-orientated teachers will presumably be in danger of becoming more insecure and therefore more rigid in their imposition of a safe authoritarianism.

Prudential Morality in Schools[1]

It is even more surprising to find that some educators have argued that the prudential control should be used as a technique for moral education. This theory is referred to as 'naturalism'.

Rousseau, it will be remembered, argued that 'nature illustrates to us in the simplest way the true theory and practice of moral discipline'.[2] As a consequence he argued that if Emile—the boy he is educating—should misbehave and break a window in his bedroom, he should not be punished for that misconduct since nature herself will punish him. He should be made to continue sleeping in that room and if as a consequence of sleeping in a cold and damp atmosphere he catches a cold, it is the wind and the rain which discipline him. Only in this way will he learn how to behave properly.

A more developed form of this theory can be found in the writings of Herbert Spencer. When it was pointed out to him that his theory of moral discipline was very close to Rousseau's he denied ever having read the *Emile*. However, the similarity is immediately apparent. In his essay on 'Moral Education' he argued that the natural consequences of any misconduct should be employed as a disciplinary device. If children leave their rooms in disorder, then says Spencer the disorder should be left for the children to tidy since 'The labour of puttings things in order is the true consequence of putting them in disorder'.[3] Equally, he

---

[1] My philosopher colleague, T.W.Moore, has pointed out that many would wish to insist that 'prudential morality' *is* a contradiction in terms. Here the linguistic problem referred to on page 111 cannot be ignored; but rather than enter into a Kantian disquisition on the categorical imperative I must ask philosophers to remember that this is essentially a psychological study.

[2] J. J. Rousseau, *Emile*, pp. 90–1. [3] H. Spencer, *Essays on Education*, p. 95.

continues, if a child does not wash and dress himself in readiness for an outing he should be left behind. Only in this way can moral education proceed.

Many criticisms can be directed at this theory. It is ruthless and undiscriminating, for ignorance is punished as violently as wilful disobedience. It is prohibitive and therefore negative in form. It can produce disproportionate consequences. Finally, it is hedonistic, and this has never been a satisfactory theory since it is not only impossible to define the nature of pleasure, but it would be impossible to measure it if one could.

The exponents of this theory too, can argue cogently for its retention in schools. In adult life, we must be responsible both for our actions and their consequences. If by being dilatory or lazy we miss a train or fail to qualify in an examination we have nobody to blame but ourselves. If then, schools are educating children for real life, they should build this system of discipline into their educational techniques. Such measures are far more effective, they argue, than constant nagging or social pressure or reasoned discussion. Having missed something that had long been anticipated with pleasure the child soon learns to pay due regard to the natural consequences of his actions.

When expressed in this way, it is a very attractive theory and being based on the natural morality of children seems to have much to commend it. The danger seems to lie here. One is not really discussing morality. The subject under discussion is a moral sanction, not morality itself, and this attractive and easily applied theory must be recognized not as a moral theory but as an amoral discussion about natural law. Its final disqualification however, seems to lie here. It reduces morality to little more than the negative evasion of inevitable consequences. Once again this can be resolved down to the naïve equation of legalism and morals. Authoritarianism, it was seen, is the positive side of this equation. Prudentiality is the negative side. Thus, if the schools perpetuate prudential and authoritarian morality a legal interpretation of virtue will inevitably be endorsed in our society. In this case our culture will undoubtedly become completely amoral. Virtue will then consist of a negative evasion of moral consequences and a positive overt subscription to a legal code. In this situation the proclamation of individual virtue will be achieved by making a non-moral claim. The assertion that one is a law-abiding citizen

may provide some justification for pride, but it says hardly anything about morality.

CONCLUSION

To focus attention in this way upon the four stages of morality as
defined in terms of these four moral sanctions is not intended to
enhance the status of this element in our discussion. Attention
needed to be drawn to these deficiencies in our educational system
and it was deemed wise to do this where the analysis was
clearest. This, however, is only one small uncomplicated constituent element of a complex whole. McKnight's work was undertaken almost twenty years ago. Since then the researchers referred
to above have learnt much more about this subject and have
thereby made it infinitely more complex.

The present analysis can now be added to that of the preceding
chapter. In addition to understanding moral development in
terms of different stages with each displaying moral behaviour
appropriate to that level of development, one can now also understand moral development in terms of a sequence of maturing
moral sanctions.

Apart from providing the parent and teacher with new insights into the conduct of his children this analysis has a very
satisfying academic quality. It not only illuminates many observable features of child morality but is at the same time a coherent
system of analysis. Each list of sanctions blends with the others
into a unified whole and such a consensus of agreement amongst
the researchers in this field suggests that their conclusions are
valid. Figure 1 not only shows how this may be done, but by list-
ing each series of sanctions in the order suggested by the researchers' findings, it presents a simple visual picture of the
pattern of this dimension of moral development.

This material can then be moulded into a simpler schema
which reveals the close relationship existing between the material
of this and the preceding chapter. If one uses a similar classification to Kohlberg these elements may be presented as belonging to
three stages of moral development, i.e. the amoral, the pre-moral
and the moral. This would then appear as:

The amoral stage; egocentric, hedonist and prudential considerations.

FIG. I. THE PATTERN OF MORAL SANCTIONS

McKNIGHT	SWAINSON	MORRIS	HILLIARD	WILLIAMS	KAY
PRUDENTIAL ⟷	SELF-REGARD ⟷	SELF-INTEREST ⟷			→ PRUDENTIAL
AUTHORITARIAN →	LAW ⟷	AUTHORITY ⟷		OBEDIENCE ⟷	→ AUTHORITARIAN
		RECIPROCITY ⟷			→ RECIPROCITY
				IRRATIONAL ⟷	→ CONSCIENCE
SOCIAL ⟷		→ CONFORMITY TO FRIENDS ⟷		GROUP-ORIENTED ⟷	→ SOCIAL
	*FEAR				
	LOVE ⟷			→ EMPATHY	
				EGO-IDEAL ⟷	→ SELF-CONCEPT
PERSONAL ⟷		→ INDEPENDENCE ⟷		RATIONALITY ⟷	→ PERSONAL
	RELIGION ⟷		→ RELIGION ⟷		→ RELIGION

* Swainson's FEAR is the only non-integrated sanction but since this could refer to a fear of consequences, or of authority or society, etc., it is easily integrated into the above system.

The pre-moral stage: authoritarian, ego-idealist social and reciprocal considerations.

The moral stage: personal, autonomous, altruistic, rational, independent and responsible considerations.

It is wise not to insert either religious or conscience-derived factors since they appear at every stage and in forms appropriate to that level of development.

BIBLIOGRAPHY

Acland, R., *We Teach Them Wrong*, Gollancz, London, 1963.

Adorno, T. W., *et al.*, *The Authoritarian Personality*, Harper and Row, New York, 1950.

Bovet, P., *The Child's Religion*, Dent, London, 1928. Trans. from the French version.

Bradburn, E., 'Children's Moral Knowledge', *Educational Research*, June, 1967.

Cox, E., *Sixth Form Religion*, S.C.M. Press, London, 1967.

Deighton, L., *An Expensive Place to Die*, Jonathan Cape, London, 1967; Putnam, New York, 1967.

Dewey, J., *Democracy and Education*, Macmillan, New York, 1961.

Elvin, L., *Education and Contemporary Society*, Watts and Co., London, 1965.

—: Moral Values in a Mixed Society', in *Aspects of Education*, University of Hull Institute of Education Press, July, 1964.

Eppel, E. M. and E., *Adolescents and Morality*, Routledge and Kegan Paul, 1966.

Eysenck, H. J., 'The Development of Moral Values in Children', *B.J.E.P.*, February, 1960.

Hemming, J., 'The Development of Children's Moral Values', *B.J.E.P.*, June, 1957.

Hilliard, F. H., 'The Influence of Religious Education Upon the Development of Moral Ideas' *B.J.E.P.*, February, 1959.

Ibsen, H., *An Enemy of the People*, Oxford University Press, 1960.

Isaacs, S., *Social Development in Young Children*, Routledge and Kegan Paul, London, 1951.

Kennedy-Fraser, D., *The Psychology of Education*, Methuen, London, 1944.

Kohlberg, L., 'The Development of Children's Orientations Towards a Moral Order', *Vita Humana*, Vol. 6, Nos. 1–2, 1963.

Likert, R., *A Technique for the Measurement of Attitudes*, 1932.

McDougall, W., *Social Psychology*, Methuen, London, 1936.

McKenzie, J. G., *Guilt: Its Meaning and Significance*, Allen and Unwin, 1962.

McKnight, R. K., *The Moral Sanctions of the Child*, Unpub. B.Ed., Glasgow, 1950.

Manson, T. W., *The Teaching of Jesus*, Cambridge University Press, 1948.

Moore, T. W., 'Punishment and Education', in *Proceedings of the Philosophy of Education Society of Great Britain*, December, 1966.

Morris, J. F., *A Study of Value Judgements in Adolescents*, Unpub. Ph.D. Thesis, London, 1955.

Peck, R. H., and Havighurst, R. J., *The Psychology of Character Development*, John Wiley and Sons, New York, 1960.

Piaget, J., *The Moral Judgement of the Child*, Routledge and Kegan Paul, London, 1932; Free Press, New York.

Rousseau, J. J., *Emile*, trans. B. Foxley, Everyman, 1957.

Spiel, O., *Discipline without Punishment*, trans. E. Fitzgerald, Faber, London, 1962.

Staines, J. W., 'The Self-Picture as a Factor in the Classroom', *B.J.E.P.*, June, 1958.

Skinner, B. F., and Holland, J. G., *An Analysis of Behaviour*, McGraw-Hill, New York, 1961.

Skinner, B. F., *Walden Two*, Macmillan, London, 1962.

Spencer, H., *Essays on Education*, Dent, New York, 1924.

Spens Report, H.M.S.O., *The School as a Society*, reprinted 1959.

Stephenson, G. M., *The Development of Conscience*, Routledge and Kegan Paul, London, 1966.

Swainson, B. M., *The Development of Moral Ideas in Children and Adolescents*, Unpub. D.Phil. Thesis, Oxford, 1949.

Williams, N., *The Moral Development of Children*, Farmington Trust Research Unit, Oxford, 1965.

Vernon, P. E., Editorial Comment in 'Development of Children's Moral Values', by J. Hemming, *B.J.E.P.*, June, 1957.

APPENDIX

The completed first stage of the author's research project, with 400 midland school-children, now confirms the conclusions of this chapter; but the stages appear as follows:

Prudential: Characteristic of nursery and infant but not junior and secondary school-children.

Authoritarian: Dominates in the Junior School but also emerges as a religious sanction.

Social: Typifies morality in the Secondary School but operates in a subtle way. With girls it is an *ideal self-concept*; with boys a *reciprocal mode of moral thinking*.

Personal: Slowly emerges but does not dominate at any stage.

In addition it is relevant to note that regardless of the dominant moral control, conscience occupies a position of near dominance at every stage.

CHAPTER 6

THE DEVELOPMENT OF MORAL JUDGMENT—PIAGET

INTRODUCTION

In turning from a study of moral sanctions to a consideration of moral judgment we pass from what at first sight would appear to be a complex dimension of human personality to one which is relatively simple. Moral sanctions are necessarily conative, that is, they are involved in the striving and forward-reaching activity of the human personality.

Moral judgment on the other hand is presumably cognitive in form, that is, it is an aspect of intellectual activity.[1] Thus whereas a consideration of moral sanctions leads one into the complex and comparatively incomprehensible area of human motivation, the study of moral judgment inevitably leads one to consider the relatively clear and comprehensible activity of human thought. It could thus look as if we are leaving behind the tangle of human intentions and entering the ordered area of logical thinking.

This is a natural conclusion to reach. We do not expect human motives to be amenable to logical analysis. We accept without question that ordinary people every day of their lives are prompted to act morally without at the same time feeling it incumbent upon them either to explain the reason for their behaviour or to supply a logical explanation of their conduct. 'I just felt that I had to do it', they say, and the normal person accepts this without question since it echoes his own moral experience.

It does not seem to be so with moral judgment. Here the individual is primarily involved in cognitive activity. He is applying his mind to a moral problem. Just as he would solve a logical

---

[1] The philosopher may wish at this point to argue that a consideration of moral judgment must necessarily lead to a discussion of ethics. It is rather cavalier to refer to the cognitive element of morality and omit any mention of millenia of ethical controversy. This is true, but it would be inappropriate to discuss the philosophy of morals in a psychological study.

problem and reach a decision by purely intellectual means, so he applies the same mental apparatus to a moral problem and reaches a decision by almost exactly the same process.

Yet this would be a superficial view. We are passing now into an area fraught with difficulties and dangers.

There is firstly the problem of normal human experience. Moral judgments are rarely made without emotional involvement of some kind. They extend beyond the realm of detached and objective logical considerations and become inextricably involved with human feelings. There is in addition the further complicating fact that except where such judgements are made as decisions about hypothetical situations, they invariably lead to action of some kind. The moral judgment is usually accompanied by adjectives describing human states, and verbs describing human behaviour. Thus it is often accompanied by some such phrase as 'I just felt that I had to do something'. The expressions 'felt' and 'had to do', both show clearly that the discussion has left impersonal and uninvolved logical considerations behind.

There is secondly the semantic problem of deciding precisely what one is talking about when discussing moral judgment. Is there a specific and identifiable aspect of human ability which can be termed 'moral judgment'? Or should we speak of moral judgments, i.e. about separate and identifiable critical judgments which are all related to a moral topic?

This is an area of discussion in which neither the philosophers nor the psychologists have yet erected their signposts. We can all agree on the area defined by this term, but we are then all left to wander around in it. By doing this it is possible to learn a little more about moral experience but until these semantic and psychological signposts are erected we shall be on a ramble through the subject rather than on a hike to a clearly defined goal. It was while discussing the characteristics of the growth of moral judgment that Johnson referred to this second problem. 'Whether there is such a thing as moral judgment as such', he writes 'or whether moral judgments merely consist of a number of specific areas of response that are essentially unrelated to one another, seems an even more basic question that has not yet been answered satisfactorily.'[1] Thus, there are at least these two difficulties to

[1] R. C. Johnson, 'A Study of Children's Moral Judgements', p. 329.

negotiate before assuming that the matter of moral judgment is uncomplicated and amenable to sweet reason.

Yet with these two qualifications held in mind, it is still possible to plunge in and discuss the development of moral judgment. We do know what we are diving into for many others have taken the plunge and reported what they have found. Perhaps Piaget's report is the most well known. It would therefore be natural to start with him, but he in turn depended on the reports of others; in particular the theories of Kant, Durkheim and Bovet.

As our main concern is neither philosophy nor religion both Kant and Bovet can be bowed off the stage. We cannot however, do this with Durkheim. Piaget was so indebted to the sociological theories of his fellow countryman that any attempt to understand Piaget must begin with a review of Durkheim's theories in moral education.

DURKHEIM

It will be remembered that Harding criticized Piaget for his apparent oscillation between sociology and psychology. At times, he complained, one is not sure whether the psychologist Piaget is using concepts native to his own subject or poaching them from the field of sociology. This criticism loses some of its force when it is realized how deeply dependent Piaget was upon the sociological theories of Durkheim.

It must therefore firstly be emphasized that Durkheim introduced the social dimension to discussions on moral development. All his arguments, whether they concern rewards and punishments in school, or the rights and duties of pupils and teachers, are viewed from the vantage point of a systematic social theory of education. It is this which makes Durkheim both valued and devalued by many students. The practical nature of his discussions attracts them. But after reading him it is common for students to dismiss his contribution as common sense clothed in technical jargon. We are so familiar with the social relationships and processes which Durkheim elucidates that there is an almost inevitable tendency to be blind to the value of his theories. Thus his penetrating analyses tend to be dismissed.

Perhaps the time has now come to help bring him from relative obscurity and apply his sociological concepts to the current problem of morally educating the young. This is precisely where his value lies. He not only argues most persuasively for secular schools to accept this responsibility but he also provides a framework within which to do it. This framework is easily described. It is an analysis of the elements which go to make up morality, followed by a discussion of the most effective means which may be employed to develop them.

Perhaps the most important part of this educational project is the identification of those qualities which moral education should be intended to develop in individual children. By studying these against their social background Durkheim makes a most valuable contribution here. This is not only because his analysis is acute, but also because it is made in a social context; for morality has no meaning unless it is embedded in that system of personal relationships which forms the essence of a social unit. This is the most fundamental of all his views about morality. Every social system, he argues, has a morality appropriate to it. Therefore, any discussion of morality must acknowledge that it is intrinsically related to the social structure within which it operates.

The importance of this principle will have to be re-examined later. For the moment it must be accompanied by a caveat. Since it is axiomatic to this study that morality is indissolubly linked with the social system, all Durkheim's comments must be seen against the background of a French society. Here one has a social system built upon a constitution which specified clearly the separation of Church and State. It is inevitable then that the morality of this society should be avowedly secular in form. Though it must quickly be added that one essential element in it is the apotheosis of the state.

God is excluded so the State takes over. Perhaps it would be uncharitable to say that this is metaphysical sleight of hand. But it is very difficult not to avoid the conclusion that 'God' is an offensive term while 'State' is an acceptable one. Therefore, the secular structure of morality is merely the religious one billed under a different name. Durkheim admitted this and in concluding triumphantly that he had replaced a religious morality with a secular system, admitted, 'All that we needed was to substitute for the conception of a supernatural being the empirical idea of a directly observable being which is society'.[1]

[1] E.Durkheim, *Moral Education*, p. xxvi.

However, the analysis is crystal clear from his writings. Morality consists of these three essential elements:

(1) Discipline   (2) Attachment   (3) Autonomy.

These terms are likely to be misunderstood unless the sociological orientation of such an analysis is kept firmly in mind. Discipline must be understood in this sense. It is not merely an individual regimen of self-imposed regulations and restraints. It takes its quality from society. It is a regularly ordered response to society as well as a consistent submission to the demands of society. It is therefore not personal but social. 'The domain of the genuinely moral life', argued Durkheim, 'only begins where the collective life begins—or in other words, that we are moral beings only to the extent that we are social beings.'[1]

Attachment is equally social in form. It consists simply of an identification of oneself with the social group. One may argue that this is simply the other side of the coin. Morality consists of social relationships. These relationships are maintained by bonds between the individual and society. Discipline is merely the name given to the relationship when society takes the initiative; and attachment is the name given when the individual establishes the bond. Of this second element Durkheim adds 'Morality begins, accordingly, only in so far as we belong to a human group, whatever it may be'.[2] These two elements are felicitously joined when speaking of the state as a family. In discipline the state as father makes demands upon us. In attachment it functions as a mother, eliciting our devotion. He does not pursue the analogy but it looks very much as though this is fertile imagery.

It does not appear to be entirely coincidental that those nations who speak of the fatherland tend to emphasize discipline as the prime good, and those who refer to the motherland look upon social integration as the ideal. There is moreover, further interesting evidence from the field of religious activity. European protestants, who emphasize the fatherhood of God, tend on the whole to subscribe to a puritanical view of religion in which they emphasize duty. European catholics on the other hand respond to the Virgin Mary as the mother of God. This induces them to emphasize the motherhood of God and so they are characterized by a permissive view of religion as a life of devotion.

[1] *Ibid.* p. 64.　　　　　　　　[2] *Ibid.* p. 80.

However, these are only two of the elements in Durkheim's analysis. The third is entirely predictable, for morality must be autonomous. Behaviour which is regulated by external compulsion cannot, in any sense, be described as moral conduct. Durkheim now saves his theory from disappearing in an amorphous sludge of heteronomous social conduct. The state may be the focal point in this kingdom of right relationships, but these relationships can only be moral when they are the autonomous. This conclusion fortunately resolves all the tensions which are likely to destroy this moral theory.

One does not act morally when under the restraint of group discipline, nor when one is committed to the group. As we have seen above, these two forms of conduct—the authoritarian and the social—are both elements in heteronomous behaviour. One only acts morally when the compulsion comes from within and is illuminated by understanding. Thus, this third element, autonomy, implies that each individual acts as he does in an enlightened and uncoerced manner. He both freely accepts group discipline and willingly attaches himself to the group because he understands both what he is doing and why he is doing it. Hence, as Durkheim concludes, 'we can say that the third element in morality is the understanding of it'.[1] It is this understanding which makes social conduct autonomous.

All this theorizing is reflected in Piaget's work. For this reason it is important to have at least a rough idea of what Durkheim said about morality. But its value extends beyond this. It will be seen below that the system of moral education advocated in this present work emphasizes that there are certain moral attitudes which must be inculcated in each individual child. Already the review of Durkheim's theories has made clear what these are. In order to respond in a spirit of social discipline one must have a sense of responsibility. The attachment of oneself to the social group to promote the good of society clearly implies the need to be prompted by altruism. The transformation of discipline and attachment into genuinely moral activities is achieved by an understanding of all that is involved in this relationship. This thus imposes upon each individual the obligation to be rational. And since the aim of moral education in France was to be the creation of autonomous individuals, the fourth and last moral

[1] *Ibid.* p. 120.

attitude is clearly defined. Thus throughout Durkheim's work it is possible to see an alternative analysis which finally emerges.[1] This was not made explicit, but is clearly implicit in all that he said on the subject. Moral education can also be viewed as the process which is intended to produce citizens in whom there are four fully developed moral attitudes, namely:

(1) Responsibility (2) Altruism (3) Rationality (4) Autonomy.

Although all of these moral attitudes are essential, Durkheim seems to emphasize 'responsibility' as the *sine qua non* of morality. 'When the moral forces of a society remain unemployed, when they are not engaged in some work to accomplish, they deviate from their moral sense and are used up in a morbid and harmful manner. Just as work is the more necessary to man as he is more civilized, similarly, the more the intellectual and moral organization of societies becomes elevated and complex, the more it is necessary that they furnish new nourishment for their increased activity. A society like ours cannot therefore, content itself with a complacent possession of moral results that have been handed down to it. It must go on to new conquests; it is necessary that the teacher prepares the children who are in his trust for these necessary advances. He must be on his guard against transmitting the moral gospel of our elders as a sort of closed book. On the contrary he must excite in them a desire to add a few lines of their own and give them the tools to satisfy this legitimate ambition.'[2]

PIAGET

The present chapter, however, is primarily concerned to show that the process of moral maturation can be understood in terms of the evolution of moral judgment. Here Piaget is extremely important for he concludes that it is possible to see a pattern in this development. Although he confined his interest in morality to this one thirty-five-year-old research project, his conclusions have been steadily endorsed by a series of subsequent researchers who were all stimulated into activity by his controversial and

[1] This alternative analysis is the central thesis of the present study, i.e. that morality in essence consists of behaviour resulting from the possession of responsible, altruistic, rational and autonomous attitudes.

[2] E. Durkheim, *Moral Education*, pp. 13–14.

provocative conclusions. During the years since he first investigated the development of moral judgment in children, his conclusions have gained wider and wider acceptance. Thus it is now axiomatic that a child's moral judgment changes as he grows older.

Almost every reputable developmental psychologist would now agree with his general proposition that as a child matures the basis of his moral judgments change. He begins with a morality of constraint in which moral judgments are based on external authority and a rigid interpretation of rules and regulations, and passes finally to a morality of co-operation in which judgments are based on social considerations and a flexible interpretation of what had previously been inflexible rules.

Unfortunately, such a simple analysis conceals the complexity of Piaget's findings. It is certainly true that this development follows a clearly defined path but in order to trace this journey more accurately it is necessary to break this concept down into its component parts. It is only when this has been done that one is in a position to provide a final and definitive description of the stages in this growth.

There appear to be four elements which can be abstracted from Piaget's conclusions. It is these which will enable us to trace the development of moral judgment with greater certainty.

There is firstly the changing attitude of children to the rules which govern their conduct and upon which they base their moral judgments. Secondly it is possible to see that this changing attitude reflects the changing social relations of children. This growth can then thirdly be understood as a sequence of qualitatively different moralities. And finally, it can be viewed as a growth from heteronomous to autonomous conduct.

A Changing Attitude to Moral Rules

In this moral theory Piaget is undoubtedly indebted to Durkheim, for he says quite specifically, 'It is this consciousness of obligation which seems to us, as to Durkheim, to distinguish a rule in the true sense from mere regularity'.[1] It is this system of rules and the attendant feeling of an obligation to obey them which Piaget deems to be the essence of morality. On this point there can be no doubt at all since he begins his report by affirming this prin-

[1] J. Piaget, *The Moral Judgement of The Child*, p. 23.

ciple. 'All morality consists in a system of rules and the essence of all morality is to be sought in the respect which an individual requires for these rules.'[1]

At first it is thought that these rules are eternal and unchanging. One finds here a faint echo of Swainson's view that young children build their morality on the basis of this crude metaphysic. Then it is realized that rules are imposed by adults and finally it is seen that they are created by consenting social equals. Thus the development of moral judgment can be looked at in terms of a changing attitude to rules. The rule perpetually imposes some constraint on the child, but the reason for accepting this limitation changes as the child develops.

Here there are three clearly defined stages each of which is characterized by a growing concept of 'this consciousness of obligation'.

Stages in Social Relationships

But these three stages can be viewed in another way. Each of these attitudes to moral regulations reflects a child's relationship with the other people in his social environment.

In early childhood it is perfectly clear to Piaget that children base their judgments on a unilateral respect for authority figures. Thus one finds here a concept of restraint as the limiting factor. Moral judgments are made in the light of what each child would deem to be the demands of his immediate moral authority. Whatever this authority requires him to do, is, he judges, the right thing to do. One cannot yet use moral terms like 'good' and 'bad' for these judgments are made under compulsion from non-moral considerations.

Then secondly, there is a change in middle childhood where judgments are made on the basis of the concept of 'equality justice'. This phrase of Piaget's merely means that a child's moral judgments are now rooted in his social experience. In playing with his peers he assumes that the basis of his relationship with them is the mutual respect which they all contribute and receive in the group. Thus the ethical concept has moved from obligation to co-operation. It is no longer unilateral but multi-lateral.

Finally, Piaget sees this conceptual development reaching its climax in late childhood where the concept of equity dominates.

[1] *Ibid.* p. 1.

Now moral judgments are made not merely on the basis of socially reciprocal equality but on the basis of moral equity. This means simply that instead of applying a rigid yardstick with which to measure the conduct under consideration, the individual child, impelled by altruism, considers all the possible factors which both prompted and justified the action concerned. This means that a rigid and inflexible concept of equality is replaced by a pliable and flexible concern for people.

One can see this kind of moral judgment being exercised in the upper forms of the primary school. When called upon to make a moral judgment children do not merely ask 'What did he do?' Once having established this fact they then go on to ask, 'Why did he do it?' 'Did he really intend to do what he did?' Instead of considering the particular circumstances of an action they tend to inquire about motives and intentions and relate these to moral principles. In Piaget's graphic phrase 'equity is nothing but a development of equalitarianism in the direction of relativity'.[1] And with this erosion of the notion of moral absolutes the way is opened for each child to consider moral principles rather than moral regulations.

A Sequence of Different Moralities[2]

The slow evolution of moral concepts which thereby change the basis of moral judgment can also be looked upon as a sequence of different moralities. Prior to reaching the stage of moral equity there are two clear moralities displayed by young children. This naturally involves them in two qualitatively different kinds of moral judgment in their personal relationships.

There is firstly the morality of restraint. This is the morality which springs spontaneously amongst egocentric infants who can only be restrained because they have a natural and healthy respect for the authority and power of their elders. Here blind prudential subscription to law is apparent from many aspects of infant behaviour. Piaget, for example claimed that amongst these children the rule was the 'be all and end all' of morality and moral judgment. At no point in his researches did he find any evidence either that a young child would alter a rule or that he would consider the needs of the children compelled to obey it. Central to this morality stands the immutable law. Indeed its

[1] *Ibid.* p. 316. [2] See footnote on p. 111.

basic assumption is the opposite of Christ's dictum concerning the Sabbath and Man. A child at this level argues unconsciously that, 'The child was made for the law and not the law for the child', and all his moral judgments are based on this moral axiom.

Then secondly there is the morality of co-operation. As the term suggests its basis is a concern for people rather than for rules. As a natural consequence, if the rule is seen not to be working to the advantage of those concerned then the rule is changed. Here clearly one is dealing with a morality described by Jesus as that in which the rule was made for man and not man for the rule.

The intellectual basis for this form of judgment seems to be the emergence of reciprocal thinking, which is necessarily associated with operational thinking in which reversible thought is possible. Here the moral judgment is based firstly on the conviction that rules must be subordinated to human needs and secondly that human needs must be met in terms of strict equality. In the words of Jesus again, this is the morality in which children do to others what they would have others do to them. The final stage of moral equity is then reached when morality, characterized by an uncomplicated insistence on equality of treatment, is replaced by the equity mentioned above.

To complete this analysis in terms of different moralities, each with its inherent form of moral judgment, one is led to a very interesting consideration. The stage at which an individual makes his judgments on the basis of equity not only points to the emergence of moral autonomy but also the emergence of moral creativity. Here moral judgments are based not on conformity either to an immutable moral code or a social consensus, but upon an individual's consideration of the claims, needs, motives, intentions and ideals displayed by the moral agent. In a word his morality is no longer conformist, it is creative. Thus one important aspect of moral autonomy is its moral creativity.

This is an extremely interesting conclusion. Just how far moral maturity depends upon moral creativity is not known.[1] At the moment there do not appear to be any current research projects associated with this hypothesis. Undoubtedly researchers will eventually turn to this, for one of the most fascinating areas of current educational research is that which is attempting to lay bare the nature of creative thinking in children.

[1] This is expanded in the companion volume *Moral Education*, A. W. Kay.

From Heteronomy to Autonomy

However, the reference to moral autonomy leads naturally to another method of analysing the research data reported by Piaget. It must be remembered that we are still dealing with the pattern of developing moral judgment which was Piaget's primary concern. It is merely that the focus shifts and thus requires different terminology to describe what is now disclosed.

These different moralities may be classified as either heteronomous or autonomous. Sometimes the terms objective and subjective are used respectively to describe these two stages. The moral judgment exercised in the first is objective in character, while that exercised in the second is subjective in form.

At the heteronomous stage, moral judgment is based on objective rules, i.e. rules which exist outside the moral agent and are objects to which he can refer. It has already been noted that the morality of this level is based on the child's unilateral respect for adults. His judgments are thus dominated by 'moral realism'. He is exclusively concerned with adult demands, as expressed through the rules he meets, and so focuses all his moral attention on the outward and visible results of an action. He is accordingly unconcerned with intention or motive. Piaget describes the children at this stage. 'The little one's society constitutes an amorphous and unorganized whole in which all individuals are alike ... it ... is a sort of communion (i.e. community) of submission to seniors and to the dictates of adults.'[1]

It is interesting to note at this stage that the absence of any sense of moral solidarity leads to a scrupulous avoidance of lying. Children here do not only refrain from lying because adults demand the truth, but also because the absence of moral solidarity means that none of them would lie to protect their peers. This is a salutary conclusion which both parents and teachers should note. One's treatment of lying amongst primary school children should be cautious. It is perhaps rather too glib to say so but the truth seems to be that the imposition of adult moral judgment here actually reverses the moral realities. Young children clearly tell the truth for other than moral reasons, while older children may often lie for a genuinely moral purpose. The former display a total disregard for their peers. The latter show a genuine concern for their welfare. Thus probably the most im-

[1] J. Piaget, *The Moral Judgement of the Child*, p. 319.

portant point to make here is that at this stage all the moral values originate from outside the child and are thus imposed upon him as heteronomous imperatives. This is a valuable insight to add to those provided in the previous chapter on moral sanctions or motives, for at this stage moral motivation originates from outside the child. It is not simply that a young child naturally does what he is told to do. The more profound moral truth is that he *only* does what he is told to do. Genuine, creative, spontaneous morality is not only incomprehensible to him, it is also alien to his moral nature.[1]

At the second stage of development moral judgment becomes autonomous and is regulated by values which originate within the child. Hence this phase can be described as subjective. One can now see the child making a *volte face* in almost every moral characteristic. Instead of being prompted to act by moral constraint he is moved by his own inner conviction that conduct must be regulated in such a way that it results in moral reciprocity. Instead of remaining morally dependent upon an adult in a relationship of unilateral respect he finds himself in a peer society where relationships are maintained by mutual respect between all the members of the group. Thus the morality of constraint is transformed into the morality of co-operation.

In these new relationships rules are no longer viewed as unchangeable absolutes but are now accepted as the regulations devised by groups and freely accepted by them as a means of controlling their corporate life for the common good. This new emphasis on human relationships now produces a sense of group solidarity and although these children will now lie in order to preserve peer relationships, they are able to see clearly that truthtelling is an essential quality which must be sustained if social relationships are to be based on mutual trust and respect.

Finally, the moral motivation of this stage comes from *within* each child. There is now a certain moral integrity about him, for this dependence upon subjectively determined values means that he can comprehend the moral ideals which originate in his own

---

[1] There is, however, a paradox here. Swainson refers to the natural altruism of young children and McDougall speaks of a gregarious impulse. Thus spontaneous morality may appear to be both natural and yet unnatural for the very young. This explains the moral ambivalence of a very young child.

thinking. Hence the moral judgment of this stage is not only more complex; it is infinitely more moral. Indeed some would say that it is only at this stage that genuine morality becomes a possibility in the life of each child.

This system of clarification is extremely valuable if one is to understand Piaget's theories concerning the development of moral judgment. However, they leave out of account the extremely important question, 'How do children proceed through these stages of development'? Thus finally this secondary system of analysis must try to isolate the factors which affect the growth of moral judgment.

Factors Affecting the Growth of Moral Judgment

Despite the apparent complexity of the above theory it is possible to see how each child moves from the earlier to the later stage of moral development. Firstly his egocentricity is eroded as he begins to distinguish clearly between himself and his environment. In this development stable peer groups and spontaneous social groupings play an important part. Now for the first time in a genuine social relationship with other children, he finds himself either co-operating or conflicting with them.

He finds that he must come to terms with the rights and obligations of his equals. Since this occurs at a stage in his intellectual development where he is able to think operationally this social awakening of his empathy with others leads naturally to reciprocal moral thinking. Of the society formed by these autonomous moral agents Piaget writes, 'the society of the older children achieves an organic unity, with laws and regulations and often even a division of social work (leaders, referees, etc.). Older children ban lies among themselves, cheating and everything that compromises solidarity. The group feeling is therefore more direct and more consciously cultivated.'[1]

The Common Features in the Present Analysis

From the above attempt to analyse Piaget's conclusions it can be seen that any attempt to review this work meets an insoluble difficulty. Throughout the course of this report we find him expressing his conclusions at different levels and in different contexts. Perhaps this was to have been expected after the analysis of

[1] *Ibid.* pp. 319–20.

his work in Chapter 2 above. Yet although this present survey has referred to the growth of moral judgment in many different contexts it is still possible to reach a final clear analysis. Thus from analysis we may turn to synthesis and show that when collated these different elements have much in common.

One thing is certainly clear. They all agree that there is a change in moral judgment as children grow and that Piaget attributes this development to three factors. Firstly, the increase in peer group co-operation in the life of children. Secondly, in the decrease of adult constraint which earlier carries weight with them. And thirdly, in the intellectual changes which occur as the child matures. From this apparently confusing welter of theory one may continue to draw order, for it is now possible to reduce his research findings to a series of simple propositions about the moral lives of children.

(1) Human beings develop an intelligent and informed respect for law by experiencing genuine social relationships.

(2) These social relationships are found in two basic forms. They are firstly characterized by child subordination and adult supremacy and then slowly change until the relationship is reciprocal. In this case it can either be based on equality or equity.

(3) These social relationships are functionally linked with a system of moral judgment. When the relationship is one of subordination and supremacy then the moral judgment exercised is based on authoritarian considerations which are objective and heteronomous. And equally when the relationship is reciprocal moral judgments are autonomous and reflect the subjective system of morality which now activates the child from within.

(4) Judgment and conduct at the final stage of moral development is based not on subscription to an external code of law nor even in the regulation of rigid reciprocity in human relationship. It consists of the recognition of the rights and needs of all individuals with due regard paid to the situational circumstances and the moral principles expressed in them.

(5) Then finally, it is possible to conflate all the above analyses which were based on Piaget's interviews and observations and produce four clear stages of development. For convenience these can be called the egocentric stage, the authoritarian stage, the stage of reciprocity and the stage of equity.

Four Stages of Development

Such a systemization as is contained in the fifth proposition above is extremely convenient. Not only does it echo Piaget's general view of intellectual development but it also reflects the analysis of development presented in the previous chapter.

In the former case it is perfectly clear that once egocentricity has been left behind, the stage of moral reciprocity emerges concurrently with the development of operational thought. By definition, operational thought is neither egocentric nor irreversible. Thus the way is opened for behaviour which is built upon both an ability to see the other person's point of view and also the recognition of reciprocal claims. In the latter case it can be seen that the moral sanctions discussed above are all appropriate to each particular stage of moral judgment. Prudential sanctions would be most powerful with a child at the egocentric stage. Authority would be the sanction most influential during the authoritarian stage. Social sanctions would operate most effectively at the level of reciprocity. And finally personal sanctions of any kind would be most appropriate to the morality of a child at the stage of moral equity, for whom it is essential that personal value judgments should be made on the basis of personal moral principles.

The Egocentric Stage: In discussing this stage Piaget is slightly obscure. Sometimes he calls it the second stage of development and at other times makes it clear that he deems it to be the first stage. This is only an apparent contradiction. Although he does say quite explicitly 'The second stage is the stage of egocentricism',[1] this is obviously only to be understood in relation to the first most primitive stage of development. This latter is the sensori-motor stage of which he says that it is the 'first stage of a purely motor and individual character' in which 'each child acts at the dictation of his desires and motor habits'.[2] Thus for the purposes of this analysis the first stage is the egocentric stage.

The quality of each child's moral judgment at this level is characterized by his basic egocentricity. He views his environment as an extension of himself and so assumes that it will occupy the role assigned to his body. This provides him with pleasurable sensations, therefore, the environment must do the same. Hence

[1] *Ibid.* p. 26.   [2] *Ibid.* p. 16.

it is thought to be available for, and at the service of, his every whim. Because of this it is understood solely in terms of his own demands.

At this stage one finds a dual moral inadequacy which we all seem to take for granted. Firstly the child is unable to distinguish clearly between objective and subjective phenomena. This is normally found to emerge in the social tension of which Swainson spoke. Thus it results in both social *and* anti-social behaviour.[1] The first of these invariably takes the form of moral conformity since such a child has no defences against anyone older than himself. He hears their authoritative demands and acts as though they expressed his own will. Or it can emerge as moral non-conformity, which is merely the other side of the same coin. Instead of conforming to the voice of authority he resists it and so *opposes* the will of others. Thus one comes to the second deficiency. The ability to co-operate is completely absent at this stage. Both his conformity and his non-conformity are essentially egocentric activities. Piaget brings these two notions together. 'Egocentricism in so far as it means confusion of the ego and the external world, and egocentricism in so far as it means lack of co-operation, constitute one and the same phenomenon.'[2] Perhaps the most important conclusion to make concerning this stage is that its characteristic features preclude children from behaving in any way which could be described as moral. They are prudent and no more. Indeed this is displayed by the intuitively appropriate approach of parents and teachers to children of this kind. Instead of becoming more and more inarticulate as they try to explain; or becoming more and more irate as they increasingly insist on being obeyed; they say quietly and most effectively, 'If you do that, you will get hurt'.

There is a humorous story which exactly illustrates this point. A small boy was left in the play-room of a large London departmental store and refused to leave the rocking-horse when his mother had finished her shopping. The manager finally decided to intervene. He whispered in the child's ear and to the mother's amazement her son meekly climbed down from the horse, slipped his hand in hers and walked quietly out of the store. Hoping to get some valuable advice for future occasions she picked up her son and said winningly 'What did the nice man say to you

[1] *cf*. p. 155n. above. [2] *Ibid*. p. 87.

darling'? With a crestfallen and submissive mien the boy replied, 'He said "If you don't get off that horse I'll smack your bottom".'

The Authoritarian Stage: The moral life of children at this stage is characterized by an almost total submission to authority. Although these rules and regulations can now be seen to originate outside himself and be located in an external source, he still feels obliged to obey them. Thus although he knows that they remain outside himself he still respects them in a way which suggests that they are the demands of his own nature. He thus appears to live under the conviction that an absolutist type of authority is invested in these external regulations.

This of course only serves to underline that his relationship with others is characterized by unilateral respect—or rather that the only social relations that have real meaning for him are those based on dependence and submission to authority figures. The moral judgments made at this level reflect these characteristics of his social life.

All moral judgments are now made in relation to the view that rules are virtually unbreakable. Piaget calls this kind of moral judgment 'immanent justice'. This is simply because the child judges morality to exist solely in relation to the rules. Justice is therefore immanent in this activity. Each child judges explicitly in terms of the breaking or keeping of authoritarian rules. To be good one has to be obedient. To be bad implies that one is disobedient. The right thing to do is to obey the order of an adult. The wrong thing to do is to assert one's own will.

Justice, too, is challenged by a breach of the established regulations. Therefore, punishment is inevitable in society's attempt to heal this breach. As a natural consequence of this thinking, punishment is deemed to be right if it is exactly proportionate to the consequences of disobedience. Equally it is judged to be wrong if it is not. There cannot therefore in the nature of things be any concession made to motive or intention. These have no place in the system at all.

Almost all parents manipulate the child at this level, possibly without even realizing it. Because this is the quality of the moral judgment exercised when a child responds to a request by saying 'Why should I?', the adult replies simply 'Because I say so'. This is not just an example of the parental attitude which argues explicitly, 'I'm bigger than you and I can hit hard, so if you don't do what I say you'll regret it.' It is simply an unconscious employment of the child's own moral judgment in a specific moral situation. Of this stage Piaget says 'The obligation to speak the truth, not to steal, etc., are all so many duties which the child feels deeply although they do not emanate from his own mind. They are commands coming from the adult and accepted by the child. Originally, therefore, the morality of duty is essentially heteronomous. Right is to obey the will of the adult. Wrong is to have a will of one's own.'[1]

Finally, it must be added that the moral judgments made on the basis of authority do not only refer to adults. Anybody who is older or more mature or who is deemed to occupy a position of authority evokes this kind of amenable response in young children. Piaget uses an example which is useful since it clearly divides children into these three levels of moral judgment.

In this instance Piaget attempts to discover the basis of moral judgment upon which a child would reach a decision about sharing some food. The situation is described thus—'Two boys, a little one and a big one once went for a long walk in the mountains. When lunchtime came they were hungry and took their food out of their bags, but they found that there was not enough for both of them, what should have been done? Give all the food to the big boy or to the little one, or the same to both.'

The children are then questioned to discover the basis of their moral judgment in this case. What does emerge with startling clarity is the fact that even here where animal appetites are at their strongest, children at this level of morality make unequivocable concessions to the older. Typical of such answers are: 'The big boys should have most (Why?), Because they're bigger.' 'The big boy should have had most. (Why?) Because he's the eldest.' 'A little more to the big one. (Why?) Because he is older.'[2]

This is clearly a concession to authority, not because authority demands a specific response, but because children at this stage naturally and spontaneously make their judgments on this basis. It is, of course, possible to abuse this characteristic of thought. Dictators, demagogues and authority figures can be guilty of this without realizing it. Because many people remained fixated at this stage of moral thinking, those who issue commands and

[1] *Ibid.* p. 193.   [2] *Ibid.* pp. 309–10.

authoritative statements often do not realize that they are only guarded from having to justify them by the passivity of those who blindly obey.

There are of course adult institutions which depend upon the fact that many adults can be made to base their moral judgments on this criterion. Industry and the armed forces are classic examples. Hence tragic, immoral and inhuman results can accrue. This is how one may view the charge of the Light Brigade at Balaclava. All of those involved in this tragedy based their judgment on the maxim, 'Their's not to reason why, their's but to do and die'. Thus the saga of this annihilation tells little of human bravery or courage. It merely records the fact that at this level of human activity man's dignity can be reduced by turning him into a moral child implicitly obeying the first authority figure which issues a command. After all, they did know that 'someone had blundered'. Why then did they fail to stop and query the order? Simply because like young children it never occurred to them to question it. Their infantile authoritarianism had been reinforced by military training, and so English military history is marred by this sad record of moral infants being butchered to little purpose.

The Reciprocal Stage: At this level the basis of moral judgment undergoes a subtle change. Rules are no longer considered to be the unchanging absolutes which exist independently of children. Hence unquestioning obedience no longer characterizes the conduct natural at this level. Rules are now seen to be creations of society which are worthy of respect because their function is to safeguard society.

It is the changed attitude to others which brings about this transition. Society now gains status in the eyes of these children. Therefore, it must be preserved. This however, is still considered within a legal framework for it is concluded that there is need for such a framework in order to live securely. Hence rules are now judged to be worthy of acceptance because they represent the social 'will' in its search for stability and security.

All of this can be expressed succinctly in Piaget's terminology. Rules are now accepted because they emerge as the expression of reciprocity amongst social equals. Hence this is described as the reciprocal stage.

If the earlier stage represented an ethic of authority, characterized by duty and obedience, this stage can be described as an
ethic of mutual respect. Hence comes the reciprocity, for mutual
respect must inevitably issue in social equality. But although this
stage is still essentially legal, it nevertheless qualifies for inclusion
in the autonomous phase of development. Granted that mutual
respect issues in social equality each child has then necessarily to
be involved in moral judgments which require him to make an
evaluation. It is no longer sufficient simply to know the requirements of the rules and fulfil them. He must now evaluate the
situation and reach a decision concerning the best way to act in
order to preserve equality between social equals.

Therefore, moral terminology too changes radically. Whereas
previously children thought that the good or bad was determined
by the criteria of obedience or disobedience, here a new criterion
emerges. An action is now deemed to be good if it is socially fair.
Equally, an action is judged to be bad if it is palpably socially un-
fair. Thus the *social* experience of co-operation issues in moral
judgments based on equality.

Of this stage Piaget says, 'Solidarity between equals appears
once more as the source of a whole set of complementary and coherent moral ideas which characterize the rational mentality.'[1]
This means that children are less vulnerable to the manipulations
of adults and older children. That is why the note of rationality
enters. Now instead of simply saying, 'You must do it because I
said so', a far more sophisticated approach is needed. One can
begin to reason with children. This rational approach must still
be accommodated to their level of development, but it begins to
have some influence if this accommodation is made.

A delightful illustration of the point in question occurred
recently. A small girl persisted in destroying a house of cards
which her older brother was patiently building and rebuilding.
Each time it was built she knocked it down. Sometimes this was
done openly: sometimes slyly. She would either approach silently
and hit it with her hand, or she would run past the table and
nudge it with sufficient force to send the structure tumbling
down. At last the older child's patience was exhausted and he
appealed to the mother. She first threatened to smack the girl if it
happened again. Even repeated warnings and increasingly violent

[1] *Ibid.* p. 324.

smacks had no effect. The mother then used her authority and issued her demands as forcefully as she could. This too had no effect even though the child could be seen fighting against her own innate desire to respond with obedience. Finally, the father joined in and simply said quietly, 'If you built one, you wouldn't like him to knock your building down, would you?' The effect was astonishing. This simple approach succeeded where threats and demands had failed. It exactly met that child's moral need. It awoke a chord in her which responded to this refrain. Her own judgments were based on this kind of consideration. Therefore, when it was presented she could only respond. It was against her nature not to do so.

That this inherent basis of moral judgment operates under all conditions is shown clearly by Piaget in the example quoted earlier. When asked how the food should be shared, children at this stage of development answer always in terms of equality and parity. Both boys must be treated the same despite the difference in size and age. The following are typical of the responses made. 'They ought to have gone shares.' 'They each ought to have taken the same amount.' 'It would still be more fair both to be given the same.' And finally, 'Each must be given the same.'[1]

The importance of this stage in the development of moral judgment depends on more than the sudden appearance of rational considerations. The ingredient of autonomy, no matter how diluted, marks the emergence of genuine morality. This point is emphasized by Crane who in studying the influence of pre-adolescent gangs on the moral development of children reached this conclusion. 'The important fact is that the child enters the gang voluntarily and the rules, norms and codes of behaviour have either been freely determined by the gang members themselves, or, at the very least, have been fully accepted by the members. In voluntarily accepting restrictions the child begins to become a truly moral being.'[2]

Crane goes on to argue that this is essentially the position held by Piaget. Morality is only possible where there is co-operation between equals leading to voluntary restraint on their behaviour.

---

[1] *Ibid.* pp. 310–11.
[2] A. R. Crane, *The Development of Moral Values in Children*, Pt. IV, 'Pre-Adolescent Gangs and the Moral Development of Children'. *British Journal of Educational Psychology*, November 1958, Vol. 28. Pt. III.

Mead too reached a similar conclusion, though with her this conclusion is placed in a sociological setting. The moral child must be a social child. Thus she argues, 'In so far as the child does take the attitude of the other and allows that attitude of the other to determine the thing he is going to do with reference to a common end, he is becoming an organic member of society.'[1]

The Stage of Equity: Just as the reciprocal stage emerged from the idea of authority, so the stage of equity emerges from the reciprocal concept. Thus there is another change in the nature of moral judgment.

The factors which result in each successive stage emerging are easily identifiable. When a sense of social solidarity is allied with growing intellectual power (particularly the ability to think operationally), authority gives way to reciprocity in human relationships. Equally it is the emergence of a single factor which results in the transition from reciprocal to equitable considerations. What this factor is, Piaget makes perfectly clear. It is the emergence of altruism or the social love of which Swainson spoke. Thus when reciprocity is informed by altruistic concern it issues in equity. This then is not a legal relationship based on considerations of justice and equity, but a human and moral relationship based on concern and compassion. Now instead of rigidly applying the rules which resulted from some social consensus of agreement, situational factors are noted. Hence by this route the child reaches the goal of moral maturity. He now no longer makes his judgments by a consideration of the rules which should regulate the particular situation in question. Instead he considers the attenuating circumstances and reaches a judgment on this basis. That is, he moves from considering the claims of the rule to a consideration of the needs of the person involved. Hence although some moral regulation may still be a factor in his judgment he recognizes that there are personal circumstances to be considered before this rule is applied. Of this kind of judgment Piaget writes, 'Instead of looking for equality in identity, the child no longer thinks of the equal rights of individuals except in relation to the particular situation of each'.[2]

---

[1] G. H. Mead, *Mind, Self and Society,* University of Chicago Press, 1934, p. 160.

[2] J. Piaget, *The Moral Judgement of the Child,* p. 316.

Examples of this judgment in action can be seen in every school playground. In a game controlled by rigid rules, advantageous concessions are made to the young, the disabled or the sick. Frequently, in a game normally governed by the strictest rules of equality one will hear evidence of equitable moral judgments. 'Let him have another go', a child will shout, 'He's only a nipper.' Piaget supplies plenty of evidence to support this contention. In the case of the two boys who had to share an inadequate supply of food, moral judgments show a crude form of equity in such responses as 'They should have given more to the little boy because he was smaller'.[1] The fact that this appears to be illogical will be considered below.

A far more profitable illustration however, is found elsewhere in Piaget. Another situation which called for moral judgments to be made, and which also divided children into these three groups, concerned a stereotyped game. Piaget sets the scene as follows. 'Two boys were running races (or playing marbles etc.). One was big, the other little. Should they both have started from the same place or should the little one have started nearer.'[2] Here the moral judgments based on equity had to take account of situational factors. Responses of this kind took the following form. 'The little boy must have a start because the big boy can run faster.' 'In running races one must put the smallest boy a little farther forward.' 'In races the little ones must have a start.'[3]

It can be seen that whereas earlier these judgments were made legally and logically, they are now made compassionately. One thus has to return to the question raised earlier. Does this mean that when compassion enters as a factor, reason no longer has a place in moral judgment? The answer clearly must be that this does not follow at all. The distinctiveness of moral judgments at this stage lies in two qualities possessed by them. Firstly, they are evidently examples of compassionate, reciprocal reasoning. Secondly they take some note of ideal rules.

On this first point it must be emphasized that reciprocity is still a factor. Thus reason and logic retain their place in this system of moral judgment. The difference appears to be that whereas previously reciprocity was demanded by an external law it is now acknowledged as an internal moral imperative. On this point Piaget is lucidly clear. 'The child begins by simply practis-

[1] *Ibid.* p. 311.   [2] *Ibid.* p. 310.   [3] *Ibid.* pp. 311–12.

ing reciprocity, in itself not so easy a thing as one might think. Then once he has grown accustomed to this form of equilibrium in his actions, his behaviour is altered from within, its form reacting, as it were, upon its contents. What is regarded as just, is no longer merely reciprocal action, but primarily behaviour that admits of indefinitely sustained reciprocity.'[1]

The second consideration, that of ideal rules, is central to morality. Unfortunately Piaget does not pursue this point. He assumes simply that in passing from the stage of equality to that of equity the child passes from a consideration of the 'is' of moral experience, to the 'ought' of moral intention. Thus in judgments based on equity children recognize the limitations of the given regulations and give expression to their view of what an ideal moral situation would require. He likens these ideals to spiritual realities presumably because such realities have physical counterparts, hence he concludes, 'Like all spiritual realities which are the result not of external constraint but of autonomous development, reciprocity has two aspects; reciprocity as a fact, and reciprocity as an ideal, as something which ought to be.'[2]

In this way Piaget evades resolving a problem which must face us later. By neatly linking together the twin ideas of moral conduct, first as a fact and second as an ideal, he has no need to concern himself with the problem of resolving the 'would' and the 'should' of moral experience.

This now enables attention to be turned to the question of moral motivation. This problem will recur again in the following pages. Indeed it might be argued that excessive attention is drawn to it. But this is a crucial issue. How can the 'should' of human experience become the 'would' of human conduct? Here lies the heart of the problem and any attempt to morally educate the young must include some means of ensuring that the ideals of human conduct become the realities of human behaviour.

The solution proposed in this work will be outlined below. The traditional Christian solution however is well known; he looks to divine power for help. St Paul cried, 'The good which I want to do, I fail to do.'[3] and then claimed to have found a moral dynamic in faith. Thus for him the answer was commitment to Christ who would impart the power to strengthen his will.

At this point the discussion could become clouded. Ideolo-

[1] *Ibid.* p. 323.　[2] *Ibid.*　[3] *The New English Bible,* Romans 7: 18–19.

gical convictions can enter to confuse the issue. Christians testify that for them this is the answer and we must accept their word that this is so. Unfortunately Christianity is a diminishing minority religion (at the moment) and even amongst its adherents not all would claim to experience this vivifying power. What then of the rest of mankind? There are hints in Christian theology that secular techniques fulfil God's will when they help His purpose to be achieved. Can we not say that a secular solution need not be at variance with Christian belief?

We are convinced that this is so; that modern psychological insights and techniques will help solve this problem. As a result moral education might produce citizens who not only know what they *should* do, in any moral crisis, but will *also be able to do it.* St Paul's cry will not then haunt our children. Desiring to do the good they will be helped to do it. This plea from adolescents is recorded clearly by that doomed but highly sensitive child Anne Frank. Her diary closes with words which must echo in the ears of every parent and teacher. 'A voice sobs within me "There you are, that's what's become of you, people dislike you because you won't listen to the advice given by your better half." I twist my heart round again so that the bad is on the outside and the good is on the inside, and keep on trying to find a way of *becoming what I would so like to be, and what I could be.*'[1] Surely we can help children like this. Then the frustration and inner conflict of our young people may no longer become sour and ferment into delinquent behaviour. More of their energy would then be turned to positive, creative activities for the good of society. What higher aim could any teacher have for his pupils and the society to which they belong?

Moral Attitudes

This review of Piaget's conclusions concerning the growth of moral judgment in children provides exactly the same kind of information as Durkheim. There it will be remembered, one could trace the development of certain basic moral attitudes. It was argued that such an implicit analysis is as legitimate as that which is made explicitly by Durkheim himself. This is equally true of Piaget's findings. It is possible to take a cross section of these and find exactly the same pattern or structure as that displayed by his

[1] *The Diary of Anne Frank*, pp. 221–2.

predecessor. When this is done the same four moral attitudes appear. The only difference is a matter of degree.

Whereas Durkheim appeared to give pre-eminence to the inculation of responsibility,[1] Piaget appears to emphasize autonomy. This moral independence, for him, marks the morally mature child. Yet the emphasis is placed here not only because this attitude is the culmination of the whole process, but also because it is an essential ingredient of morality. Indeed Piaget frequently makes it perfectly clear that moral judgments are only really morally valid when they are made from a position of moral independence.

Then secondly, it is possible to see that a rational attitude is central to mature moral judgments. At the stage of equality both logical and legal processes are involved in the judgments made. Later, at the stage of equity, due regard has to be paid to the abstract moral principles and 'ideal rules' which are used as a basis of judgment. In both instances formal logic is required if the child's judgments are to be valid. That the whole process is clearly cognitive in form is revealed by a consideration of the origin as well as the evolution of moral judgment. Operational thinking is essential for its existence: then an ability to handle abstract ideas assures its development.

Thirdly, the place of an altruistic attitude is also assured by a consideration of the characteristics of equity. It is this quality which clearly divides judgments based on equality and those that are based on equity. When the demands of justice are modified by concern for people, that is, when legalism gives way to altruism, children enter the last stage of moral judgment. This is the level of equity. Therefore, it is altruism which marks the quality of moral judgments made at the stage of equity.

Finally the existence of a sense of responsibility is affirmed throughout the research report. Moral development depends upon the possession of this attitude. All Piaget's tests assume that children have a sense of responsibility. Otherwise there would be no point in producing test items which depend upon the acceptance of moral responsibility for any relevant moral judgment to be made. Indeed one of Piaget's theses is that as children grow they move from the notion of objective responsibility to that of subjective responsibility. They turn from calculating blame in

[1] As did Swainson. See p. 56 above.

terms of external factors (i.e. the amount of damage done) and proceed to calculate it in terms of internal factors (i.e. the motives and intentions of the children concerned). Brennan adds point to this contention by arguing that children must experience moral responsibility in a peer group to ensure that moral growth takes place. He concludes that 'through the skilful use of specific and limited responsibility he may be provided with experience which will foster his growth'.[1]

Therefore, as with Durkheim, one finds that an analysis of Piaget's work in terms of moral attitudes leaves a simple list of attitudes which have to be inculcated in children if their moral development is to be assured. These attitudes are identical to those found in Durkheim, namely moral independence, rationality, altruism and responsibility.

BIBLIOGRAPHY

Bovet, P., *The Child's Religion*, Dent, London, 1928.

Brennan, W. K., *The Relation of Social Adaptation, Emotional Adjustment and Moral Judgement to Intelligence in Primary School Children*, Unpub. M.Ed. Thesis, Manchester, 1961.

—: 'The Foundations for Moral Development', *Special Education*, Vol. LIV, No. 1, Spring, 1965.

Crane, A. R., 'The Development of Moral Values in Children', Pt. IV 'Pre-Adolescent Gangs and the Moral Development of Children', *B.J.E.P.*, November, 1958. Vol. 28. Pt. III.

Durkheim, E., *Moral Education*, Free Press, New York, 1960.

Durkin, D., 'Children's Concept of Justice—a Further Comparison with Piaget's Data', *Journal Educ. Res.*, 1959.

Frank, A., *The Diary of Anne Frank*, Great Pan Books, London, 1962; Doubleday, New York, 1952.

Harding, D. W., *Social Psychology and Individual Values*, Hutchinson, London, 1953.

Havighurst, R. J. and Taba, H., *Adolescent Character and Personality*, John Wiley and Sons, New York and London, 1949.

Johnson, R. C., 'A Study of Children's Moral Judgements', *Child Development*, Vol. 33. No. 2., 1962.

Kant, I., *Critique of Pure Reason*.

—: *Critique of Practical Reason*.

[1] W. K. Brennan, *The Foundations for Moral Development*, p. 7.

Lerner, E., *Constraint Areas and Moral Judgement in Children*, Manasha, Wisconsin, Banta, 1937.

MacRae, D. Jnr., *The Development of Moral Judgement in Children*, Unpub. Ph.D., Harvard, U.S.A., 1950.

—: 'A Test of Piaget's Theories of Moral Development', *Journal Abn. and Soc. Psychology*, 49, 1954.

Mead, G. H., *Mind, Self and Society*, Univ. of Chicago Press, 1934.

Morris, J. F., *A Study of Value Judgements in Adolescents*, Unpub. Ph.D. Thesis, London, 1955.

Piaget, J., *The Moral Judgement of the Child*, Routledge and Kegan Paul, London, 1932; Free Press, New York.

Swainson, B. M., *The Development of Moral Ideas in Children and Adolescents*, Unpub. D.Phil. Thesis, Oxford, 1949.

CHAPTER 7

MORAL JUDGMENT—RECENT WORK
FOLLOWING PIAGET

AN EVALUATION OF PIAGET'S CONCLUSIONS

Although the work reviewed above represents Piaget's only venture into the field of moral studies, it precipitated a constant succession of related research projects. His conclusions were apparently so fertile that other researchers could not refrain from attempting to harvest a crop of educational conclusions from them. These subsequent studies have shown that Piaget's conclusions are still valid although somewhat over-simplified.

Some concession was made to this complexity in the previous chapter. There it was argued that his report provides sufficient material for a more complicated analysis to be made. Instead of speaking simply of a growth in moral judgment from an early morality of constraint to a later morality of co-operation, it was argued that more dimensions of this development can be discerned. One may speak of this growth in terms of a changing attitude to rules; or to changing social relations; or as the corollary to a sequence of qualitatively different 'moralities'; or as a growth from heteronomous to autonomous moral judgments. But even this further complexity cannot cater for the research findings which followed.

It is a notorious fact that every publication of Piaget's work immediately stimulates a psychologist somewhere to test Piaget's conclusions. Tedious though this may be, such activities have done two valuable things. They have firstly tended to confirm the general outline of Piaget's theories; and secondly they have shown that moral judgments are more complex than Piaget then realized.

Before proceeding to show how firmly entrenched Piaget's conclusions have become in this field of inquiry it must be admitted that his research report has been legitimately criticized in a number of ways. Much of the subsequent confirmation still contained reservations and so did not support Piaget's views in their entirety. Morris, for example, although assenting generally to the Piagetian view warns readers, who are looking for a developmental scheme in his work, that they will 'find little comfort in the data we have presented'.[1]

Again McRae decided to test two theses which are central to Piaget's findings. The first argues that apart from age there is only a single entity which affects moral judgments. The second is that this dimension of moral judgment is a corollary of the authority relationships a child has with adults.[2] In his report McRae is quite explicit. He concludes simply 'Neither hypothesis was confirmed.'[3]

Havighurst and Taba were convinced that very few of the children they studied had actually reached the level of moral autonomy. This is surprising when one realizes that many of the individuals tested were in their sixteenth year. But the most astonishing concomitant of this was their conclusion that few of these children could actually apply moral principles when involved in a moral dilemma.

Finally Durkin reports the disquieting fact that amongst his sample of adolescents he found even seventeen-year-olds making moral judgments more appropriate to infants. This apparently ineradicable tendency for earlier moralities to survive in adult life will be discussed in a later chapter. For the moment however, it is sufficient to note that even young adults can base their moral judgments on considerations which are natural to very young children. Therefore, the supposed inevitability of moral development, which is implied in Piaget's report, needs to be more firmly grounded in research conclusions before it is blithely accepted by teachers and parents.

Apart from criticisms of this kind there has not been any massive opposition to Piaget's general conclusions. Indeed the reverse is true. It would be tedious to recite the list of those who have confirmed Piaget's findings, by means of their own researches, in morality. Those who wish to follow this line of inquiry could do so easily enough. The bibliography appended to this chapter contains references to the work of Lerner, Johnson, Morris, Kohlberg, Brennan and Loughran, who each in their specific ways confirmed some aspect of Piaget's general conclusions.

---

[1] J. F. Morris, *A Study of Value-Judgements in Adolescents*, p. 368.

[2] D. MacRae Jr., *A Test of Piaget's Theories of Moral Development*, p. 14. This 'single entity' is moral judgment itself.

[3] *Ibid.* p. 18.

The Moral Judgment of Adolescents

The reference to McRae and Havighurst and Taba raises an interesting point. Both researches were concerned with teenagers as well as pre-pubescent children. McRae's sample was taken from the five to fourteen year age range and Havighurst and Taba studied children in the ten to sixteen year age range. This is extremely important for very few researchers make a point of emphasizing that the gravest deficiency of Piaget's work was his exclusive concern with children under the age of twelve. Indeed since children appear now to be maturing earlier and earlier, it is clear that Piaget's conclusions may have only a limited application.

Morris appears to have been prompted to work in this area of value-judgements as a direct result of this deficiency. He begins by noting that 'there has been a marked lack of field studies tracing this development particularly in the period of adolescence'.[1] Therefore in order to discover the nature of children's moral judgments during adolescence one must turn to his report. He actually refers to value-judgments rather than to moral judgments, but this makes no difference. He is basically concerned with the development of adolescent moral judgments. Thus although his general conclusions were included in an earlier chapter to help our understanding of the development of moral sanctions, they can equally well be inserted here to assist us in this attempt to understand the development of moral judgment.

There is, however, a clear distinction between those elements in his conclusions which qualify as moral sanctions, and those referred to here which are equally obviously bases for moral judgment. The origin of this lies in his discovery that there was a marked difference between what children said they *should* do and what in fact they *would* do. Here we are dealing with the former, i.e. the moral judgments, not the conduct, precipitated by the moral problem situation.

To obtain his information Morris presented 14 of these problem-situations to over 300 secondary school children and then analysed the nature of the moral judgments which were made by them. Although it is a complex and sophisticated report Morris

---

[1] J. F. Morris *The Development of Moral Values in Children*, Pt. II, 'The Development of Adolescent Value-Judgements', *B.J.E.P.*, Vol. XXVIII, Pt. 1, Feb. 1958, pp. 1–13.

himself distils its essence for the interested reader. He shows that his analysis revealed six categories of value-judgments. Although he speaks of 'actions' this equally well applies to the considerations which should lead to action. These are : (a) Action based on normative considerations, i.e. considerations of accepted principles of conduct. (b) Action based on considerations of self-respect. (c) Action based upon considerations of respect for authority. (d) Action based on conformity to beliefs or behaviour of others of the same age, i.e. actions based on considerations of reciprocity. (e) Action based on claims to independence.[1]

Here one has a pattern of moral judgment which reflects that of Piaget. However, it is when he continues the analysis that this becomes even clearer. He suggests further that this classification can lead to a systematization of the considerations which would lead to actions, i.e. the sanctions, as distinct from the moral judgments made. Here his list is almost pure Piagetianism. He refers to self-interested, authoritarian, reciprocal, normative, independent and conforming trends.[2]

Perhaps it was in order not to be misunderstood that he qualified this conclusion. It was too close to a Piagetian scheme for his liking. Hence he later emphasized that Piaget's 'use of "egocentricity" to describe the social world of the young child distinguishes it from our broader use of "self-interest". Again Piaget's use of "equity" to refer to a balanced concern for the needs of others is not co-terminous with our use of "normative".'[3]

He found in addition that secondary modern school pupils were much more conformist in their moral judgments than grammar school children. That, however, may refer to the social class differences which will be discussed in the companion volume to the present work. In general, therefore, he supported Piaget's conclusions even though he worked with adolescents. Thus he found, 'A move away from the directions of choice which are supported by persons of authority; a concomitant rise in the proportion of relatively indeterminate responses such as "make my own decision"; marked situational difference in the distribution of value-judgments, and the increased complexity of value judgments'.[4]

Before leaving Morris one extraordinarily provocative observa-

[1] J. F. Morris, *A Study of Value-Judgements in Adolescents*, p. 171.
[2] *Ibid.* pp. 174–8.   [3] *Ibid.* p. 9.   [4] *Ibid.* pp. 207–8.

tion of his must be noted. He contended that very often behaviour which appeared to be objective and autonomous in form was very often prompted by considerations of a very different kind. Many of his boys seemed to be mature in their moral judgments, but closer study revealed that they were simply displaying anti-authoritarian attitudes. Just as one may easily underestimate the level of a child's morality, it is equally easy to over-estimate it. In this case one does little to help an adolescent caught in anti-authoritarian postures which may well be his only means of crying to the adult world for help. How far the adolescent C.N.D. activities and anti-Polaris submarine demonstrations of the sixties are thus explained is problematic. It will at least help our understanding of such activities if they can be sympathetically explained in similar terms. To realize that these activities are moral proclamations, may enable us to be of more help to our younger citizens. It should certainly make us less likely to stigmatize this as the undesirable conduct of long-haired, promiscuous lay-abouts.

Johnson was much more avowedly Piagetian in his research. He admits to using test material based on Piaget's original work, but preferring a pen and paper test to an interview, he worked with older children. He explains this himself quite frankly. 'Piaget's questions were generally quite simple, since they were designed for use with six to twelve year olds. The writer wished to use an older sample so that a moral judgment test could be administered as a paper and pencil test.'[1] Yet whatever reasons may have prompted Johnson to act in this way his work presents us with an account of the moral judgments of adolescents.

His research was actually more subtle than this account would imply. He was primarily concerned to discover the consistency of an adolescent's moral judgments when made in different areas of experience. This work emerged as a further confirmation of Piaget's conclusions. Johnson believed that, 'Most findings having to do with the correlation of responses to moral judgment questions were in the direction suggested by Piaget.'[2]

Kohlberg too used adolescents in his research and confirmed Piaget's conclusions while doing so. His terms of reference were much wider than a simple consideration of moral judgment. He hoped to lay bare the sequential stages of moral thought and

[1] R. C. Johnson, *A Study of Children's Moral Judgements*, p. 330.
[2] *Ibid.* p. 353.

show how social forces and experiences affected these. Despite these complexities he was explicitly concerned with moral judgment. Here he hoped not only to trace its emergence but also relate this to other factors. He outlined his aims thus: 'The study of the relation of the development of moral thought to moral conduct and emotion. The application of a stage analysis of moral judgment to subcultural differences as well as pathological deviance in moral orientations.'[1] In order to discover what he calls 'our development analysis of moral judgment';[2] he interviewed seventy-two children aged from ten to sixteen years. His material and technique were Piagetian in form. And he admits himself that, 'Both the content and method of the interviews was inspired by the work of Piaget.'[3]

As the aims already outlined above have indicated, this is an extraordinarily complicated research project. Yet it is possible to draw some clear general conclusions. Kohlberg deduced that there were six stages of development, each of which depended upon the level to which the individual child's moral judgment had matured.[4] He calls this a motivational aspect of morality and thus his conclusions could have been included under our heading of moral sanctions. But because he focuses interest on the development of moral judgment they are more relevant and appropriate here. He relates these value orientations to social class differences believing that these reflect the various views of people located at different points in the hierarchical social scale. He argues that there are clearly defined stages in this development which exactly reflect the list of emerging sanctions referred to above. 'In an initial study,' he says, 'six types of moral judgment were defined after extensive case study. They fell into three major levels of development as follows:

Level I. Premoral.

    Type 1. Punishment and obedience orientation.

    Type 2. Naïve instrumental hedonism.

Level II

    Type 3. Good-boy morality of maintaining good relations,
      approval of others.

---

[1] L. Kohlberg, 'The Development of Children's Orientations Toward a Moral Order,' p. 12. See Addendum p. 190 below.   [2] *Ibid.*   [3] *Ibid.*
[4] *cf.* 'We have spoken of our six types of moral judgment as stages.' *Moral Education in the Schools*, p. 9.

Type 4. Authority maintaining morality.
Level III.
Type 5. Morality of contract, of individual rights, and of
democratically accepted law.
Type 6. Morality of individual principles of conscience.'[1]

Thus despite the many qualifications contained in his research reports he tends in the main to support the Piagetian scheme of development in terms of moral judgment.

Perhaps the most valuable of all the researches recently concluded is that of Loughran. He deliberately set out to discover the pattern of moral judgments made by adolescents and admits that his work was based on Piaget's researches into the nature of moral judgments amongst children. His sample consisted of sixty-eight adolescents aged eleven to eighteen years, who were specifically chosen to represent a cross section of personality and subcultural types. These were tested by interview techniques for which Piaget-like moral situation stories were compiled by the author. With Piaget he concludes that there are three levels of moral judgment. That based on authority; that based on equality; and that which is based on equity.

Perhaps the most surprising conclusion of all is that even adolescents still make their judgments under the moral constraint of authority figures. Of this he writes, 'Although the incidence of judgment by constraint is small it is interesting to find it at all, for if we were to accept Piaget's findings as definitive conclusions we would expect children to be entirely free from constraint by authority as early as nine years of age'.[2]

However, although some of his sample made moral judgments of this kind the number who did so was small and in addition decreased with increasing age. The one thing which did emerge with clarity was that both the intellectually inferior as well as the young judged the right thing to do in terms of what authority figures demanded.

When testing to discover how far his sample based their moral judgments on considerations of equality, i.e. equal rights between peers, Loughran found that once again many of his sample

[1] L. Kohlberg, *Development of Moral Character and Ideology*, p. 400.
[2] R. Loughran, *A Pattern of Development in Moral Judgements Made By Adolescents Derived from Piaget's Schema of its Development in Childhood*, p. 87.

were immature. Only about half of them made moral judgments of this kind. He concluded from his results that 'Adolescents arrive at the level of mature autonomous judgment between 12 and 17 years, not between 11 and 12 as Piaget says.'[1] He then continued to search for evidence of moral judgments based on equity. He refers to this as the emergence of subjective responsibility and explains, 'This concept takes account of the motive and intention behind any moral action; it is characteristic of autonomous judgment'.[2] These are actions which consider all the related factors which would qualify a judgment based on equality. Such factors would be motive and intention, age and intelligence and the degree of provocation. Even considerations of mental health were accepted as relevant factors by some of his sample.

Here two important discoveries were made. Firstly, that nearly two-thirds of his adolescents made moral judgments based on equity; secondly, that objective thinking, i.e. considerations of authority and equality, were not confined to childhood.

Three further very important conclusions emerged. Prejudice was correlated with poor moral judgment. Children with high personality ratings as assessed by I.P.A.T. tests[3] made better moral judgments. Finally there was no correlation between moral judgment and gender.

These studies by Morris, Johnson, Kohlberg and Loughran show that Piaget's general conclusions concerning the development of moral judgment in children, can be applied to adolescents as well. There are qualifications to add before accepting this conclusion in its entirety, but none of these make any radical difference. Children and adolescents make moral judgments based firstly on authority, then on considerations of equality and finally by the principle of equity.

Social Class Differences

Having now established a simple pattern in this development, it is possible to explore all the fascinating byways and detours which subsequent researchers have mapped for us. The temptation to

---

[1] *Ibid.* p. 89.   [2] *Ibid.* p. 95.
[3] I.P.A.T. Personality Tests (H.S.P.Q. and 16 P.F.) National Foundation for Educational Research, London, 1963.

do this must be resisted otherwise the whole book would need to be devoted to this subject. Those psychologists who have indulged in this intellectual luxury have shown a number of tantalizing views, but instead of scanning them we can only afford a passing glance.

Some have questioned whether age is the only factor in this development. Others have argued that moral judgment like moral behaviour, is specific to situations. Yet again a number of studies have shown that moral judgment forms in clusters about related moral situations. Children may make mature judgments in all things relating to money, but immature judgments in matters pertaining to telling the truth. Yet again some have suggested that children do not always think efficiently when their attention is turned to matters of morality. Many more workers in this field have suggested that the pattern of this growth is multi-dimensional. As was suggested at the beginning of this chapter, there may not in fact be an entity which we can call 'moral judgment'.

Others have shown that moral judgment is correlated with intelligence.[1] Perhaps this may be dismissed as a rather obvious point to make, but it is surprising how many think of morals as an area in which intuitive and emotional factors dominate. Finally the fact that moral judgment is itself a cognitive activity has been emphasized by a number of workers in this field of inquiry.

Each of these points could be traced through a series of research publications. Then an inner pattern of confirmation and contradiction could be woven with their evidence. But the urgency of this whole study as an educational priority demands that such satisfying indulgences should be kept to a minimum. There is, however, one final qualification which must be emphasized. Moral judgment depends not only on the individual's age and personality, but also upon his social status. Thus whereas we have hitherto been discussing this in psychological terms, the problem must now be approached as a sociological study.

Moral Judgment and Social Class

It is now generally agreed that the moral judgment exercised by an individual is closely related to his sub-cultural experiences. Clearly this apparent further complication could be avoided by

[1] See pp. 184ff. below.

proceeding to a consideration of the social class pattern of intelligence. From this one may argue that as an aspect of intellectual activity the act of making moral judgments would naturally reflect social class differences. Yet these cultural differences just cannot be ignored, despite the attractions of such a smooth and facile argument.

The history of this evidence can be clearly traced. Harrower was the first of these subsequent researchers. She believed that Piaget had ignored the social influences affecting moral judgment. As a natural sequel to this she tested his results in these terms. She took children from different social classes and tested their moral judgment with Piaget-type tests. Her conclusions were interesting although mildly disappointing. She concluded that the social environment had such a profound effect on the moral judgments made by children that Piaget's conclusions could not be applied indiscriminately to different classes of children. Still she did show conclusively within two years of Piaget's publication that social class differences must be accepted as relevant in the evolution of a child's moral judgment.

Soon after this Lerner turned to the problem. He was convinced that not enough attention had been directed to the quality of parental authority exercised. Then basing his researches on Harrower's conclusions he studied the importance of social class differences in terms of the different kinds of parental pressure which constitute the essence of adult restraint. In general he confirmed Piaget's developmental conclusions, with the proviso that moral judgments should be deemed to form clusters, and therefore that any conclusions must be related not to a generalized entity called moral judgment but to a specific cluster of such judgments.

His most important conclusion in the present context was that social status and moral judgment are correlated. Children from high-status homes tend to display a much more mature form of moral judgment than children from low-status homes. Having carefully matched his samples he was quite adamant about his conclusions. This difference in judgment, he insisted, depended upon social class factors and not on any hidden factors associated with intelligence.

He further found that higher-status children displayed moral judgment which was more sensitive to the circumstantial and motivational aspects of the situation; that this resulted from the fact that adult constraint for them was less compulsive; and finally that egocentricity was overcome so that the reciprocal relationship, which produces more mature moral judgments, was established much earlier.

Such general conclusions were also confirmed by Barkley, who discovered that moral judgment was undoubtedly associated with socio-economic status; and by Hollingshead who in his report on Elmtown found sharp social class difference in moral judgment amongst the teenagers studied. Such also was the passing conclusion of McKnight in his study of the moral sanctions accepted by children. McRae too confirmed this hypothesis in an oblique way. In the first of his publications he studied moral development in the context of parent-child relations and showed the clear influence of socio-economic factors.

When one turns to study urban children these differences appear to be more pronounced, and reference has already been made to Kohlberg's views. Kerr found many deviations in the moral judgment of her lower-status referents in Liverpool, and in that same city Mays had deemed such deviations to be sufficiently constant to allow them to be categorized as a delinquency sub-culture. This is in fact what Peck and Havighurst concluded in their American studies. They recognized that there were sections of urban society which had to be classified in this way. Such a sub-culture had sufficiently identifiable moral characteristics to identify and describe it. Speaking therefore from the vantage point of a middle-class norm of moral judgment they concluded that, 'The great city presents the disturbing phenomenon of "disorganized areas" in which social values have gone awry. In these it is normal for a child to steal, to lie to the authorities and to be sexually delinquent.'[1]

More recent evidence has been supplied by the Newsoms. In their report they discuss 'the class difference in the moral attitudes expressed by mothers in the handling of their children',[2] and observe, 'As we have seen, the infant's behaviour, even in the first few months is frequently evaluated in moral terms, babies who demand a lot of attention often seem to be regarded

[1] R. F. Peck and R. J. Havighurst, *The Psychology of Character Development*, p. 27.
[2] J. and E. Newsom, *Infant Care in an Urban Community*, p. 177.

as little tyrants, passive babies are held up as models of perfection and natural goodness.'[1]

Finally Sugarman confirmed this general thesis. He studied over five hundred London schoolboys and found that moral conduct correlated with socio-economic status. As the social class of the family rose, so did the teacher's conduct rating of the son. This, it must be admitted, is only parallel evidence. He did not study the moral judgment so much as the quality of character displayed by these boys, but at least this total weight of evidence underlines the fact that moral judgment is affected by social class. In the succinct phrases of Peck and Havighurst 'various social classes have different ideas of what is right and wrong'[2] and again 'The various social classes have somewhat different sets of values'.[3]

The final picture of developing moral judgment can now be painted. There are at least three major types of moral judgment, based respectively on considerations of authority, equality and equity. In general the path of development passes consecutively through these three stages, but these need not be mutually exclusive in an individual, in addition other factors may determine the rate of this development. Thus because of personal and social factors it is possible to find all three kinds of moral judgment displayed not only by children but also by adolescents.

CONCLUSIONS

The educational implications of these results are obvious. Firstly it indicates that it is possible to improve the quality of moral judgment by normal educational techniques. This is simply because it is essentially cognitive in form. Secondly a positive practical plan of moral education can be evolved as a natural consequence of this knowledge. Thirdly the area which will present the gravest educational difficulties is that which is concerned with helping children to translate the 'should' of moral judgment into the 'would' of moral behaviour. It is this dichotomy between the 'should' and the 'would' of moral experience which constitutes the real problem.

[1] *Ibid.* p. 176.
[2] R. F. Peck and R. J. Havighurst, *The Psychology of Character Development,* p. 26.   [3] *Ibid.* p. 22.

The first point is the one which must immediately be emphasized. When we are dealing with this dimension of moral development it is perfectly clear that we are dealing with morality as it impinges on the cognitive area of human activity. This conclusion does not merely depend upon the linguistic assumption that any kind of judgment must be a function of the intellect, nor is it based simply on the fact that since moral judgment is concerned with potential conduct and not actual conduct, it must be intellectual and not behavioural in form. It depends upon the findings of research into this field. McRae, for example, concludes from his work that both Piaget and Lerner were 'more concerned with boys' cognitive moral development'.[1] This can be supported by the evidence of McPherson. He investigated the system of moral instruction in Scottish schools and concluded that this work could be conducted as an intellectual activity. Again Kohlberg was able to conceptualize his work. He investigated the emergence of a moral order in terms of what he called 'A more cognitive aspect of morality', and it is under this heading that his material relating to moral judgment appears. So the list could be indefinitely prolonged.

It must not be thought, however, that this is an established and unchallenged fact. It must perpetually be borne in mind that any aspect of human morality is infinitely more complex than one would normally suppose. Thus it should be no surprise to learn that Durkin found hardly any evidence at all that a child's intelligence was correlated with the level of his moral judgment. Nor could Kohlberg or Goldman find anything to substantiate the claims of those who would oppose Durkin's conclusions. Williams found some evidence confirming this[2] in his interviews with children. On one occasion a highly intelligent boy provided research data which suggested that his moral judgments were mature. Yet at the end of the interview it suddenly became apparent that he was essentially egocentric and made moral judgments on that basis, i.e. at the first level elucidated by Piaget.

But we may not leave this denial of any correlation between intelligence and moral judgment without questioning it again. Some interesting evidence to the contrary may be found in testing

[1] D. MacRae Jr., *A Test of Piaget's Theories of Moral Development*, p. 18.

[2] Described in private conversation with the author.

manuals. Terman and Merrill contain standardized comprehension intelligence tests which record such questions as 'What is the thing for you to do when you have broken something which belongs to someone else?'[1] 'What should you do if you found on the streets of a town a three-year-old baby that was lost?'[2] These do not only require intelligence on the part of the child being tested: he must make moral judgments too. The authors clearly assume that one cannot entirely separate out intelligence and moral judgment. And again the Wechsler Intelligence Scale for Children includes such questions as 'What is the thing to do if you lose one of your friend's balls (dolls)?' 'What is the thing to do if a fellow (girl) much smaller than yourself starts to fight with you?'[3] These cannot be other than tests of moral judgment; yet they are now accepted as valid and reliable tests for general comprehension.

Perhaps a partial solution to this apparent inconsistency is that this failure to find any significant correlation underlines a deeper truth. This truth must be that when one describes moral judgment as a cognitive activity one is referring to the *mode* of activity, not to its intellectual *level*. Thus a stupid boy who is willing to reason about moral problems is involved in cognitive activity of a kind which cannot be found in an infinitely more intelligent boy who only makes intuitive or authoritarian judgments. Thus, despite the level of a particular child's intelligence, teachers may still enable him to develop more mature forms of moral judgment.

Even though this may be an academic strain for the very dull child it at least means that every child can be helped to become more rational in this area of his life. It may be extraordinarily difficult to change a child's moral mode of life, but one may at least start with this limited objective. After all, if he is helped to make sound moral judgments the job is partly done.[4] The next limited objective is to find some way of helping him to act upon these decisions.

[1] L. M. Terman and M. A. Merrill. *Measuring Intelligence*, p. 98.
[2] *Ibid.* p. 102.
[3] D. Wechsler, *WISC Manual*, p. 63.
[4] Kohlberg supports this view. He sees, 'The stimulation of the development of the individual child's moral judgment as a goal in moral education'. *Moral Education in the School*, p. 9.

The second implication of this clear developmental outline is equally important. It looks as though the ground plan can be laid upon which to erect a course in moral instruction. Brennan quite deliberately set out to thus relate theory to practice. He worked for four years in a Residential School for educationally subnormal and maladjusted children. His children were aged eleven to sixteen years and came from lower-status homes. Presumably this project was launched since the moral and social education of such children is high on the list of educational priorities. His aim was simple. He constructed an educational environment which was based on our knowledge of moral development. He is quite clear on this point. 'The theoretical frame of reference was derived from the work of J. Piaget.'[1] He then applied a moral judgment test to the children at the beginning and at the end of the course.

He naturally recognized that many factors may have been involved. A course in human relationships would inevitably affect human relationships simply because concern had been shown for them. Yet his findings are sufficiently impressive to warrant a lengthy quotation from his report. Brennan concluded that, 'Senior boys do seem to operate more consistently at the autonomous stage than did their predecessors of four years ago. As a group they also seem more tolerant, relaxed and helpful in their attitudes to younger boys. There is overall much increased respect for personal and communal property. In addition anti-social behaviour amongst boys after leaving school tends to be below the average for the school as a whole.'[2] If this can be done with educationally subnormal and maladjusted children it suggests rather strongly that it can be successful in a normal state school where one finds children equally hampered by social disabilities. The only difference is that they are not sufficiently *outré* in behaviour to bring them to the attention of those concerned with maladjusted children. Yet they still infect the body of the state and direct attention away from themselves by insidiously poisoning society from within. It is possible that an effective system of moral education could cleanse our society in a generation. We now suffer from social septicaemia. Who can tell what unimaginable social benefits may be derived from curing this ill?

Thus, one is led to face the final conclusion. All the prospects

[1] W. K. Brennan, *The Foundations for Moral Development*, p. 6.
[2] *Ibid.* p. 8.

of life in a morally healthy society are reduced to pipe-dreams till this problem can be solved. We may be able to influence a child's moral judgment, but it seems that this has little effect on actual behaviour. Children may know the moral thing to do, but this in no way indicates that they will do it. So we come to the question again which must be answered if moral education is to be effective. How can we get children not only to think morally, but also to act morally? This problem of moral motivation must be solved, before we can assume that any headway is being made in moral education. A solution to this will be suggested in the concluding chapter. For the present it is enough to recognize this incontrovertible fact.

This difficulty is as firmly established as any other fact which meets one in this area of inquiry. Piaget pointed to it clearly. In autonomous development he finds two aspects. He sees moral development 'as a *fact* and as an *ideal*, as something which ought to be'.[1] Beller continued the investigation into this problem by asking her respondents firstly how they *ought* to behave, and then discovering in fact how they *would actually* behave. As was mentioned above, McPherson investigated the effects of a course of moral instruction and concluded that although boys could be taught how to make more mature *moral judgments*, this would have hardly any influence at all on their *actual behaviour*. But the most impressive confirmation of this difficulty comes from Morris. He began his study by noting that while the behaviour of children had often been studied, 'There has been a marked lack of studies of the views of children and adolescents on what "should" be done in a wide range of situations'.[2] After his research had been completed he noted that, 'Discrepancies between what "should" be done and what actually "would" be done are shown.'[3]

Perhaps it may be said without exaggeration that if this difficulty can be overcome then the prospect of introducing effective moral education in our schools comes closer to realization. It will

---

[1] J. Piaget, *The Moral Judgement of the Child,*' p. 323.

[2] J. F. Morris, *The Development of Moral Values in Children,* Pt. II. 'The Development of Adolescent Value-Judgements' *B.J.E.P.* Vol. XXVIII, Pt. 1, February 1958, pp. 1–13.

[3] *A Study of Value-Judgements in Adolescents,* Unpub. Ph.D., London 1955, Abstract of thesis.

be seen below how this problem will be faced. For the moment one can say that the problem of moral motivation should be approached in the light of our current knowledge concerning attitudes and behaviour. It is now known that conduct follows as a result of possessing specific attitudes: and it is equally firmly established that attitudes can be modified or formed. If then the right moral attitudes can be created there is every possibility that the right conduct will follow.

This chapter thus emphasizes the cognitive element in morality and so establishes the principles upon which the cognitive element of moral education must be based. However, it does more, it also suggests that the key to mature morality lies in the formation of socially desirable moral attitudes. Thus, although we now know that the principles of developmental psychology can be applied to this problem, they are inadequate alone. Such principles must be augmented by processes which lead to attitude formation. It will be seen below how both of these consequences can be built into a viable system of moral education.

BIBLIOGRAPHY

Barkley, K. L., 'Development of the Moral Judgement of College Students', in *Character and Personality*, No. 10, 1942.

Beller, B., 'Children's Attitudes Towards Honesty', *Journ. Soc. Psych.*, 1942.

Brennan, W. K., *The Relation of Social Adaptation, Emotional Adjustment and Moral Judgement to Intelligence in Primary School Children*, Unpub. M.Ed. Thesis, Manchester, 1961.

—: 'The Foundations for Modal Development', *Special Education*, Vol. LIV. No. 1. Spring, 1965.

Crane, A. R., 'The Development of Moral Values in Children', Pt. IV. 'Pre-Adolescent Gangs and the Moral Development of Children', *B.J.E.P.*, November, 1958, Vol. 28. Pt. III.

Durkheim, E., *Moral Education*, Free Press, New York, 1962.

Durkin, D., 'Children's Concepts of Justice—a Further Comparison with Piaget's Data', *Journ. Educ. Research*, 1959.

Goldman R., *Religious Thinking from Childhood to Adolescence*, Routledge and Kegan Paul, London, 1964.

Harding, D. W., *Social Psychology and Individual Values*, Hutchinson, London, 1953.

Havighurst, R. J., and Taba, H., *Adolescent Character and Personality*, John Wiley and Sons, Inc., New York, 1949.

Harrower, M. R., 'Social Status and Moral Development', *B.J.E.P.*, No. 4, 1934.

Hollingshead, A. B. *Elmtown's Youth*, John Wiley and Sons, New York, 1949.

Johnson, R. C., 'A Study of Children's Moral Judgements, *Child Development*, Vol. 33, No. 2, June, 1962.

Kerr, M., *The People of Ship Street*, Routledge and Kegan Paul, London, 1958.

Kohlberg, L., 'The Development of Children's Orientations Toward a Moral Order', *Vita Humana*, Vol. 6, Nos. 1-2, 1963.

Lerner, E., *Constraint Areas and Moral Judgement in Children*, Manasha, Wisconsin, Banta, 1937.

Loughran, R., 'A Pattern of Development in Moral Judgements Made by Adolescents Derived from Piaget's Schema of its Development in Childhood', *Educational Review*, February, 1967.

McKnight, R., *The Moral Sanctions of the Child*, Unpub. B.Ed. Thesis, Glasgow, 1950.

MacRae, D. Jr., *The Development of Moral Judgement in Children*, Unpub. Ph.D. Thesis, Harvard Univ., 1950.

—: 'A Test of Piaget's Theories of Moral Development', *Journal Abn. and Social Psychology*, 49, January, 1954.

Mays, J. B., *Growing Up in a City*, Liverpool University Press, 1956.

McPherson, D., *An Investigation into the System of Moral Instruction*, Unpub. B.Ed. Thesis, Glasgow, 1949.

Mead, G. H., *Mind, Self and Society*, University of Chicago Press, 1934.

Merrill, M. A., and Terman, L. M., *Measuring Intelligence*, Harrap, London, 1953; Houghton Mifflin, Boston, 1937.

Morris, J. F., *A Study of Value-Judgements in Adolescents*, Unpub. Ph.D. Thesis, London, 1955.

Newsom, J. and E., *Infant Care in an Urban Community*, Allen and Unwin, London, 1963.

Peck, R. F., and Havighurst, R. J., *The Psychology of Character Development*, John Wiley and Sons, New York, 1960.

Piaget, J., *The Moral Judgement of the Child*, Routledge and Kegan Paul, London, 1960; Free Press, New York.

Terman, L. M., and Merrill, M.A., *Measuring Intelligence*, Harrap, London, 1953; Houghton Mifflin, Boston, 1937.

Wechsler, D., *WISC Manual: Wechsler Intelligence Scale for Children*, The Psychological Corporation, New York, 1949.

Williams, N., Research Fellow in Psychology, Farmington Trust Research Unit into Moral Education, Oxford.

Sugarman, B., *Teenage Boys at School*, Unpub. Ph.D. Thesis, Princeton, 1965.

Swainson, B. M., *The Development of Moral Ideas in Children and Adolescents*, Unpub. D.Phil Thesis, Oxford, 1949.

Addendum

The original text of this book (particularly the present chapter) had to be considerably reduced. This may have produced a false impression here. The work of Dr. Kohlberg is more important than the necessarily brief reference suggests.

For those interested a list of his other publications to date is appended. It will be noted that he has yet to produce a major work. This may well be because the time-consuming task of scoring the material is still incomplete. In England this work is being done in a separate project by Douglas Graham of Durham University who has kindly corresponded with me on this subject.

The following are Lawrence Kohlberg's works:

The Development of Modes of Moral Thinking and Choice in the Years Ten to Sixteen, Unpub. Ph.D., Chicago, 1958. (Obtainable only as a positive microfilm copy, for five dollars.)

Moral Development and Identification in *Child Psychology*, ed. H. Stevenson, University of Chicago Press, 1963.

Development of Moral Character and Moral Ideology in *Review of Child Development Research*, Vol. 1., ed. M. and L. Hoffman, N. Y. Russell Sage Foundation, 1964.

Moral Education in the Schools; A Developmental View, The School Review, Vol. 74, University of Chicago Press, 1966.

The Development of Children's Orientations Toward a Moral Order: II Social Experiences, Social Conduct and the Development of Moral Thought, Vita Humana, Vol. IX, 1966.

Stage and Sequence: The Developmental Approach to Moralisation in *Moral Processes*, ed. M. Hoffman, Chicago Aldine Press, 1966.

(*Social Psychology*, R. Brown, Collier MacMillan 1965, reviews Kohlberg's experimental investigations in Chapter 8.)

CHAPTER 8

PSYCHO-SOCIAL DEVELOPMENT

The argument of this chapter can be presented simply. Without needing to become involved in depth psychology or psycho-analysis one can say that human behaviour is related to individual personality. Our conduct follows naturally from the kind of people that we are. If we are rational and altruistic then our conduct will mostly be rational and altruistic. If we are irrational and uncharitable persons then equally our conduct will reflect this. The motivation for our behaviour springs from our nature. This is why Peck and Havighurst, for example, speak of their work as a motivational theory of morality. They are therefore able to connect the stability of human personality with the consistency of human conduct by analysing some components of personality and relating these to the regularity of moral behaviour.

Introduction
The review of Havighurst and Taba, in Chapter Two, was over-simplified. The detailed structure of their methodology, the marked individual variations disclosed by their data, and the complex battery of tests used, make it difficult to generalize from these results.

It must immediately be admitted that at one stage they even appear to disclose evidence which points to specificity in moral behaviour. Rather in the manner of Hartshorne and May they conclude 'Moral beliefs are formed by accumulating reactions to immediate situations, not by a conscious formulation of a genera-lized code of conduct.'[1] At first sight this might deter an investi-gator from attempting to outline what Morris called 'The view that character development consists in the acquisition of a body of explicit principles to which conduct is consistently referred.'[2]

---

[1] R. J. Havighurst and H. Taba. *Adolescent Character and Personality*, p. 95.
[2] J. F. Morris, *A Study of Value Judgements in Adolescents*, p. 378.

But it should not do so. When studied with care it is clear that this conclusion refers more to the educational techniques employed in Illinois than to the children thus educated. The authors are simply showing that 'as the twig is bent so grows the tree', for they go on to say that the situational specificity, which they found in moral behaviour, 'reflects the fact that teaching of what is right and wrong is done with reference to isolated, concrete acts of behaviour' for 'relatively little effort is made to help young people generalize from these situations or to help them develop a coherent philosophy'.[1]

This observation is important for two reasons. Firstly it indicates that moral education should be conducted with due regard paid to a pattern of moral development. The moment a child is able to use formal operations, and so build up a 'coherent philosophy' teachers should accommodate their teaching to this maturational fact and pass from discussing specific moral situations to consider general moral principles.

Secondly it implies that the present postponement of moral maturity in our children may in fact be due to the teaching methods employed in schools rather than the maturational limits found in the children.

This has already been discovered in other areas of intellectual development. The operational level of thinking required for mathematics may be reached much earlier than the eleventh year of mental age. One can thus argue that evidence which at the moment points to the emergence of rational morality in the sixteenth year, is not so much a description of moral maturational levels as an indictment of the current form of moral education.

The most damaging criticism of such *laissez faire* moral teaching emerges as Havighurst and Taba conclude: 'The development of a personal and rational moral code, when it does take place, grows out of the accidents of personal make-up and patterns of adjustment. Under these circumstances maladjustment, rather than adjustment tends to be the stimulating force towards reflection, criticism and personal orientations.'[2]

It is the educational experiences of these children which produce this chaotic moral growth. Does this not then suggest that if

[1] R. J. Havighurst and H. Taba, *Adolescent Character and Personality,* p. 95.
[2] *Ibid.*

controlled and empirically confirmed techniques were employed in the sphere of moral education, one might find much younger children able to consider moral problems rationally? There is no evidence yet available to support this, and clearly some of the moral attitudes which ultimately produce moral behaviour may not be affected by this intellectual sophistication. But it has not yet been tried. That is the spur to endeavour. And one can only hope that the suggestions being made here will be of some help towards this end.

Personality Types

Havighurst and Taba found that their sixteen-year-old respondents were divided into two groups; those with high reputations and those with low reputations among adults and their peers. The former can be subdivided into self-directive persons, adaptive persons and submissive persons. The latter can be similarly classified as unadjusted and defiant persons. These must all now be studied since they provide an opportunity to marry this psycho-social analysis to the developmental scheme outlined above.

The Unadjusted Person: It will be argued later that children in this category seem to correspond, in their behaviour, to the earliest stage of moral development. It must however, be noted that this type of person is not yet a moral personality type. He may develop into a self-directive person, or a submissive person. Thus this level of development is really 'amoral'.

Havighurst and Taba described such a person very succinctly. He is 'discontented, insecure, frustrated. Usually he is having difficulties with his family. In school his work is not up to the level of his ability. However, he is not openly hostile to society or definitely maladjusted as is the defiant person. He is actively but as yet unsuccessfully seeking to establish a satisfactory relationship with his environment.'[1]

The Defiant Person: Again it looks as though it is possible to form some kind of link between this personality type and the behaviour of an 'amoral' person. Such a child has usually reached this stage as a result of persistent neglect, frustration and lack of social success. Therefore he is hostile to society and its institutions.

[1] *Ibid.* p. 165.

He is not, however, the moral rebel who refuses to conform in order to assist in the emergence of a higher code of conduct. He is truly anti-social in the sense that he is unable to co-operate with other people for any socially acceptable end. His lack of moral principles is apparent also in the consistently prudential form of his conduct. ('Prudential' is used loosely here, and refers to the fact that if he can see some gain for himself, even though temporary, he will lie, steal, cheat, defraud and violate every canon of morality.)

Jackson, in his study of the way in which social injustice breeds criminals, has described such a character in Manuel, the child of the Valparaiso slums. He too shows how often such amoral personality types can posses considerable personal charm. Havighurst and Taba describe this person. He is usually, 'openly hostile to society. He shows his hostility by doing poor school work, refusing to conform to social expectations and sometimes by attacks upon property which land him in jail. Because he has been neglected or mistreated by society he bears a never-ending grudge which prevents him from making any constructive adjustment to his age mates, to his family, to school or to a job.'[1]

The Submissive Person: Here one can find close affinities between personality type and moral control. This person has an attitude towards his environment which both Hoggart and Havighurst and Taba describe as 'passive acceptance'. He is lacking in self-confidence and tends to gain his desired sense of security by simple conformity to the standards imposed by stronger personalities. He feels more secure when following a leader than when initiating action himself. In situational conflicts he tends to withdraw.

On the whole, such people have a good reputation with authority figures who regard them highly because they conform to the required standards in a docile and uncritical manner. Such a person normally comes from a home dominated by authoritarian parents. He belongs to a social or ethnic group which lives by tradition. He associates with, and submits to, aggressive personalities. And he prospers in a school or class dominated by authoritarian teachers.

On the whole, such people tend to come from those social

[1] *Ibid.* p. 158.

classes which are traditionally expected to submit to authority. The one surprising element in such a person can be the display of a moral stubbornness when his conscience asserts itself. This, one would suppose, results from the inculcation of a strong sense of duty which perpetual submission to authority generates. This need not, however, be an anomaly. With such an undeveloped ego it is still possible that the super-ego should be both well-developed and severe.[1]

Clearly here is a person living by authority, and indeed Havighurst and Taba are quite explicit on that point. For them 'The submissive person is one who will not initiate action. He waits for others to take the lead. He never shows signs of overt aggression and rarely of covert aggression. He lives by authority.'[2]

The Adaptive Person: Here again the identification of this personality type with a form of moral control is readily made. This type of person seems to acquire a moral code simply by absorption from his social environment. Thus he acquires a value system without ever considering the nature of 'right' and 'wrong' or ever even being involved in moral conflict. Like submissive children, such people have high reputations since they are successful conformists and adjust easily and pleasantly to their peers.

Of this child Havighurst and Taba say 'The main characteristic of this personality type is the almost unconscious adoption of good patterns of conduct.'[3]

Such a person is usually highly intelligent (particularly if he belongs to the lower social strata of society) healthy, and energetic. He is an outgoing, friendly, almost totally aggressionless personality. For all these reasons he is absorbed easily into groups and assimilates group patterns of behaviour.

All this is interactive. Such a person more easily wins group approval and so tends to find it much easier to identify with the group. It is almost unnecessary to add that such children do not possess clearly defined moral codes.

The evidence suggests that they are most likely to be reared in an affectionate, permissive family, which provides security and love, and encourages social participation from an early age.

This is augmented by the fact that such a child has a fully developed ego. This enables him to have a view of both himself

[1] See pp. 211ff. below.   [2] *Ibid.* p. 146.   [3] *Ibid.* p. 143.

and society which produces ready response to social situations, particularly those which bring pleasure and success.

Through adolescence his ego tends to develop in the direction of group identification. The possession of a permissive conscience also helps. It enables him to act without self-recrimination and thus with self-assurance.

Havighurst and Taba sum all this up in terms which clearly point to the social controls of such a person: 'The Adaptive Person is sociable, friendly, vivacious and outgoing in manner. He has what is often called good "social intelligence". He fits readily into almost any social situation and seems to conform naturally to the expectations of the people with whom he is associated.'[1]

The Self-Directive Person: The profile of the self-directive personality type will show clearly that here one finds conduct directed by a personal moral control. These children have high reputations among adults and peers, not because they conform in any way but simply because they are known to be responsible and honest.

In essence this personality type is conscientious. His work is orderly. He persists to the end of a project and does what he sets out to do. He readily accepts leadership, even though he may not enjoy it, but does so from a sense of responsibility. He is not only self-critical but sets very high standards and then drives himself remorselessly to achieve them.

With such a strong will and personality he actually makes a good academic, compensating for any deficiency in intelligence by rigorous and persistent application. Moral problems perplex him for although he enjoys a high reputation he seems uncertain and critical about his own value-system. Yet he is self-sufficient and does not deliberately cultivate the friendship of others. He thus presents an ambivalent character. He appears to be poised and sophisticated because of his independence, and yet is afflicted by moods of self-doubt. All this is accompanied by a strongly developed conscience and an introspective tendency towards self-analysis.

This often leads to anxiety, but this anxiety is utilized in order to improve personal performance. Indeed it is achievement as a

[1] *Ibid.* p. 134.

personal feat that characterizes such a child. Thus the ego is developed still further and may lead to self-assertion and personal ambition.

The evidence suggests that personalities of this type have come from families where warm, loving acceptance was at a minimum. Probably the parents and related adults were themselves self-directive persons, or self-made men, and so achievement-based status is built into the psyche.

Such people usually succeed in life. Not only have they intelligence and an anxiety-directed drive, but they are equipped to face society. Crane makes an interesting point here. Discussing pre-adolescent gangs he points out that these organizations form a bridge between the kinship-based, ascribed status of the family and the achievement-status of society. Thus the self-directive person is orientated from early childhood towards the conditions of life in society at large.

On the whole such people seem to be produced by the child-rearing procedures of the higher social classes, who thus provide the nation with a supply of ambitious, responsible, conscientious individuals. Kipling describes them in his poem 'If'.

A Developmental Scheme Derived from Havighurst and Taba
The implicit relationship between personality types and moral controls is clear from the above survey. However, since Havighurst and Taba intended only to outline the personality types, it remains for this relationship between them and a scheme of moral development to be made quite explicit.

The defiant personality type can be located at the egocentric level of Piaget and the prudential amoral level of control suggested by Kennedy-Fraser. This is quite clear from the comments of Havighurst and Taba. For them: 'The Defiant Persons have rejected the generally approved moral beliefs and principles ... They are ruled by selfishness and aggressive impulses ... The Defiant Person has a very weak conscience and a poorly developed sense of self. This type of person lacks both inner and outer control over his impulses and thus is selfish, dishonest, disloyal and irresponsible.'[1]

In the submissive personality type one has a person directed by authoritarian controls. The conclusions of Havighurst and

[1] *Ibid.* pp. 183–4.

Taba leave one in no doubt on this point. 'Submissive Persons', they write, 'are worried not by the problem of whether or not they are living up to their own principles and whether or not those principles are the correct ones to follow, but by whether or not they are living up to the expectations of persons who are in authority over them.'[1]

This is evidence enough, but there is an even more impressive parallel here. McKnight spoke of both the prudential and authoritarian controls and argued that they: 'may be said to correspond with Piaget's first stage, the stage of moral realism'.[2]

Havighurst and Taba also make an implicit identification of this kind. For them the submissive person, as well as the defiant person, can be identified with this first stage since: 'For submissive persons the question is not "Is this really the right thing to do?" but rather, "Is this really the thing to do to keep me out of trouble?"'[3]

With the adaptive personality the relationship between moral control and self-concept is even clearer. Whereas the submissive person has a severe conscience and a weak sense of self, in the sense that they have a loose hold on reality and tend to retire from any attempt to impress people, the adaptive person has a permissive conscience and a well-developed sense of self. This leads naturally to a clear notion of how to establish and retain good social relations. There is, in addition, a desire to impress others and so succeed in all social relationships. Again the identification of this personality type with the social level of moral control is quite explicit. 'Adaptive Persons take on the beliefs and principles of their social environment readily without much question and without much inner commitment.'[4]

The final identification can be made with equal certainty. 'Self directive persons are reflective and critical concerning morality . . . they are characterized by self-doubt and turmoil over the moral choices they must make. They are engaged in the painful process of working out moral principles for themselves . . . They are worried by the problem of whether or not they are

[1] *Ibid.* p. 183.

[2] R. K. McKnight, *The Moral Sanctions of the Child,* p. 18.

[3] R. J. Havighurst and H. Taba, *Adolescent Character and Personality,* p. 183.

[4] *Ibid.*

living up to their own principles and whether or not those principles are the correct ones to follow.'[1]

These personality types form an ascending scale which reflects the different levels of moral control. Since this is related to individual ego-development one would expect the self-directive person, whose conduct is characterized by a personal level of moral control, to have a well developed sense of self. Indeed this is so, 'The self-directive person has a strong and severe conscience combined with a well developed sense of self. His sense of self consists of cold and objective understanding of the relations between himself and other people and of a drive for achievement and independence in those relationships.'[2]

Conclusion

It can be seen that Havighurst and Taba argue implicitly for a developmental scheme of moral development, but it may be objected that the above analysis has been little more than a manipulation of terminology. A further comment shows that this criticism can be met.

That this is a developmental scheme is clear from two chapters of this report. There it is argued that children should advance in their moral development. Now this does not mean that each personality type must become more morally adroit or ethically sophisticated. They must progress through the levels of moral development until they reach the personal or rational stage. This, it is presumed, will result from the influence of varying factors. Among these may be listed adult approval and disapproval; punishment and rewards; and verbal teaching. This use of different techniques has as its aim the accelerated progress of each child through the amoral and pre-moral stages to the moral stage. Thus they say: 'As boys and girls grow up we expect them to formulate an increasingly conscious and rational code of conduct.'[3]

When Havighurst and Taba conclude with their suggestions for moral education they further imply that it is the last stage in this sequential development which must be the goal for educational endeavour. They envisage the teacher's task as one in which he encourages the intellectualization of values and moral experiences. 'Thinking about moral experience leads to the

[1] *Ibid.*   [2] *Ibid.* pp. 183–4.
[3] *Ibid.* p. 81.

formation of moral principles. Applying moral principles intelligently to the various situations of modern life requires practice under guidance—guidance such as an educational institution is best fitted to give. The school has the greatest opportunity to supplement moral habits with moral thinking.'[1]

To support this developmental argument, one may turn to more evidence supplied by the work of the Committee on Human Development. Havighurst and Neugarton used data from Prairie City to make some comparisons with the development of Red Indian children. This showed moral growth continuing. Whereas the 1949 data indicated that the sixteen-year-old respondents in Prairie City, had yet to complete their moral development, the 1960 data of Peck and Havighurst revealed that many of them had done so. Thus it was concluded that the number of self-directive persons would grow still larger. In fact, they tabulated their expectation of a further development in moral responsibility[2] on this assumption.

If to this one now adds the evidence from Gesell that: 'It has taken sixteen years of development to bring it (i.e. the ethical sense) to its present level of functioning *and there are many potentials yet* to be realised,'[3] it is quite clear that moral development can take place within the framework of this psycho-social scheme.

Before concluding, an inconsistency must be explained. At one stage the authors say that over one-fifth of the young people studied were self-directive.[4] Yet earlier they had noted that very few reach that stage of moral thinking characterized by rationality and reflection.[5] This can only be resolved if one makes a legitimate assumption.

The authors were not concerned with outlining developmental stages. They may therefore have considered that both those whose morals sprang from rational considerations, and those who displayed personal ambitions, belonged to the self-directive category.

[1] *Ibid.* p. 194.   [2] *Ibid.* p. 314.

[3] A. Gesell, F. L. Ilg, and L. B. Ames, *Youth: the Years from Ten to Sixteen,* Hamish Hamilton, pp. 469–70.

[4] R. J. Havighurst and H. Taba, *Adolescent Character and Personality,* p. 121.

[5] *Ibid.* p. 94.

PECK AND HAVIGHURST

Introduction

The central thesis of this report can be stated simply. The motivational sources of moral behaviour may be discovered in the social and personal aims which belong to different character types. Thus the argument is a continuation of the motivational theory of morality first expressed by Havighurst and Taba.[1]

There are five character types. These are the amoral, expedient, conforming, irrational-conscientious and rational-altruistic, and are located at different stages of personal development. Their sequential nature is made clear from the comment, 'a set of five character types was defined, each conceived as the representative of a successive stage in the psycho-social development of the individual'.[2] In the interests of clarity this analysis too must begin by describing each of these character types.

The Amoral Person

His conduct results from gross egocentricity. Other people's feelings are not considered in a life of self-gratification. This kind of person could be called a psychopath in that no mental disorder accompanies his emotional and moral instability. He seeks the immediate gratification of impulses which emerge from an unstable system of values. This internally disorganized and impulse-ridden psyche often produces a hostility-guilt complex. This hostility can lead to delinquent or criminal acts but if the basic emotional attitudes attract others, he can be charming but irresponsible.

The personality pattern of those who become fixated at this stage is rather complex. It was found that the respondents living at this level have weak ego-strength. They cannot perceive the structure of social situations, or define their personal goals, or control their impulses. They are hostile in a non-specific way. This results in their rejection of any social restraints. They have weak superegos and so lack an 'integrated system of internalized moral principles'. They are impulsive and have no mechanism for restraining these impulses. As a result they suffer from punitive but inadequate guilt feelings and are as hostile to themselves as

[1] *Ibid.* pp. 92–5.

[2] R. H. Peck and R. J. Havighurst, *The Psychology of Character Development*, p. 3.

they are to society. In short they are disorganized, impulsive, anti-social and unhappy people. For this reason it is more accurate to describe them as amoral rather than immoral.

The Expedient Person

His conduct is still egocentric. He is self-centred in his perspective and refuses to consider the welfare of others. The difference however, lies here. Conduct may now *appear* to be moral, since his behaviour is the means towards self-gratification. But where undetected immorality or socially approved unethical conduct are equally effective in achieving his end, such a person will conduct himself in an immoral way. This indicates clearly that there are no internalized moral principles. Equally, there is a weak conscience and superego. The only internalized principle controlling such a person is the achievement of self-gratification. In this sense they are hedonists.

With such emphasis on self-gratification one would expect that a well developed ego would define this moral type. But this is not so. Here one finds little ego-strength, for self-centredness is no indication of a strong ego. In fact the reverse is true. When gratification is achieved without any understanding of its consequences, there is clearly no autonomous ego in control. Such people seem to seek immediate gratification by taking the easy way out and so fit easily into their social world. In this way they subscribe to authoritative sanctions. This produces not active morality, but merely the absence of immorality.

The suppression involved leads to personal unhappiness and since the pleasurable gratification, which they seek, depends on making real social contact, they are frustrated in their hedonism. 'They give up much of their spontaneity, yet get little in return. The self-defeating nature of insincere expedient, adaptation to society could scarcely be more demonstrated.'[1]

Before passing to the next category of motivational psychological traits, it is instructive to note the tremendous influence exerted by parents. This suggests that moral education is needed to offset some parental influence, so that society is not corrupted. In a blistering passage Peck and Havighurst say: 'The crux of the problem is this, each generation tends to perpetuate its strengths and weaknesses of character, largely unchanged. A

[1] *Ibid.* p. 93.

sizeable minority of adults are heavily amoral or expedient in character. They treat their children this way and their children strongly tend to turn out just like their parents. This fraction of the population provides our criminals, probably most of our psychotics, and a great many who are never institutionalized but who lead drifting, fear-ridden, or hate-ridden lives. From among this group come the actively evil members of society; the viciously hate-filled sadists, the conscienceless exploiters, the men and women whose terrible greed corrupts our law-guarding forces in community after community. Such people are sick, with crippled distorted perceptions of life. But they are also dangerous and must be firmly controlled lest they destroy the rest of us, or corrupt our morals into "getting ours, too", or turn us so revengefully against them that we descend to their level of immorality in fighting them.'[1]

Such people have become fixated at the moral stage of development characteristic of early childhood. Perhaps it is our tolerance of this in the very young, which makes us less sensitive to it in the otherwise mature. And it needs a novelist with the imagination of John Wain to remind us of the nightmare quality of life natural to a five year old.

The Conforming Person
His conduct is controlled by a single internalized principle. 'He wants to and does conform to all the rules of his group. He wants to do what others do, and his only anxiety is for possible disapproval.'[2]

Such conduct is characteristic of our society. Whyte ascribes it to our absorption in a paternalistic, industrial organization. Riesman sees it resulting from conformity to society as a result of 'other-direction' in behaviour. And Remmers found it characteristic of American teenagers. Such people were described by Heidegger as unauthentic men possessing only *Dasein*. The unauthentic man is the one who is afraid to face the reality of his nature and his existence. Of him, Richardson writes a most pertinent paragraph, which includes the following sentence, 'He hides himself in the crowd, thinks what everyone else thinks, admires what everyone else admires, not daring to be himself.'[3]

[1] *Ibid.* p. 97. [2] *Ibid.* p. 6.
[3] A. Richardson, *Religion in Contemporary Debate*, p. 82.

The importance of understanding this level of moral development is made clear by Peck and Havighurst who indicate that
most people become fixated at this stage of development. 'The
unthinking conformer, who often does not want to think for himself, probably makes up the largest single group of Americans and
perhaps of humanity everywhere.'[1]

Such people display moral stability. But this is produced more
by superego dictates than the reasoning power of a developed
ego. This stability then results from conformity to the conventions
of their society. Their behaviour is influenced by what they believe others expect of them, for they have unquestionably incorporated into their own value system the requirements of
society. Society in turn views them as 'good children' since they
are invariably submissive and conformist.

Thus their behaviour is 'other-directed'. It is conformity to
the rules, and not personal gratification, which marks this moral
agent.

If a strong superego acts as a rudimentary conscience, then
they are guided by a conscience. This makes them uncomfort-
able when they break the rules. For them right conduct is that
which conforms to the regulations laid down by society. Whether
this harms or helps others, appears to be no concern of theirs.
The rules must be obeyed regardless of whether others are hurt in
the process.

Having such strong superegos also means that they are unable
to control the harsh punitive effect of their consciences. Such
people are therefore usually depressed and unhappy. With superegos mostly made up of moral prohibitions incorporated into
their value system, they live under the perpetual strain of self-
denigration. 'Weak ego direction and willing conformity to outer
pressures thus produce adequate morality in their behaviour, reinforced by irrationally held internal moral principles which
have been taken over without much question from the people who
run their world.'[2]

The Irrational-Conscientious Person

He is only really distinguished from the above by a difference of
degree. Both are characterized by weak ego and strong superego

---

[1] R. H. Peck and R. J. Havighurst, *The Psychology of Character*, p. 196.
[2] *Ibid.* p. 95.

development; but an irrational-conscientious person is distinguished from a conforming person by the fact that he has an even more powerfully developed superego. Thus he can rarely violate the moral conventions incorporated in the process of his own superego development.

The conforming and irrational-conscientious levels of conduct are both characteristic of the same stage of moral development; usually of later childhood. This marks the transition from heteronomy to autonomy since the criterion of moral conduct is now not conformity to the group code but conformity to internalized standards of right and wrong.

Having insufficient ego strength to query the requirements of this blind, powerful conscience, graphically called 'the heir of the parental superegos',[1] they live by faithfully following these internalized rules without ever bringing rational considerations to bear on the problems facing them. Though this automatic behaviour appears to emanate from morally responsible people, they act with no consideration for the welfare of others. Such personalities are easily recognized in the community. People fixated at this stage of development become pillars of the community. They possess little human warmth and so are respected but not liked. Their literal-mindedness and rigidity make them extremely difficult to live with, particularly since the process of reciprocity leads them to demand equally unbending and cold behaviour from their companions. Indeed he always wants *his* conscience to be *your* guide! 'More than any other consideration, they are ruled by the dictates of their conscience, which consists of a firm well-integrated body of moral rules.'[2]

In one sense they display all the symptoms of a compulsive personality structure. The motivation of their morality is a compulsive desire to follow the rules which they have uncritically internalized. Apart from this they are psychologically normal. Their source of pleasure seems to be the cold satisfaction of living an impeccable life. Fixated at this stage of moral development they lead lives which are unattractive to their friends, and envied by none. Since it is a form of autonomy, limited only by the demands of the superego, it can lead to the highest stage of all. Then coldness is replaced by altruism and irrationality by rational discourse.

[1] *Ibid.* p. 8.　　　　　　　　　　　　　　　　[2] *Ibid.* p. 95.

The Rational-Altruistic Person

His is the highest level of moral behaviour, 'on one thing the research staff and adolescents were in unanimous agreement. Both gave highest rank to those of rational-altruistic character. They were accorded the highest moral reputation.'[1] Thus the empirical data confirmed the original hypothesis which was that 'The rational-altruistic type describes the highest level of moral maturity.'[2]

His conduct is altruistic because he considers the welfare of others involved in his action. It is rational because each new action and its effects are assessed realistically. The operational quality of this moral conduct is clear. 'He observes situations accurately, sees implications beyond the immediate and can experiment mentally to decide upon the most moral course of action. He recognizes objectively what other people want and how they feel. He is able to feel as they do or know how he would feel in their position without losing perspective by completely identifying with them.'[3]

The altruistic element in this conduct is easily described. There is a genuine concern for the welfare of others and an ability to accept the need to sacrifice oneself. This is not done from neurotic personal motives, but simply in order to help others. His pleasure at seeing others live full and happy lives prompts the conduct which is directed towards fulfilling their needs. Thus social co-operation, a sense of responsibility and respect for all human beings characterizes his conduct. Moral principles guide it but they are applied situationally with due regard to the effect on others, i.e. by Piaget's equity.

Thus one essential element in the motivation of this conduct is an altruistic impulse. During the research it was found that those children who belonged to this group could not enjoy themselves at the expense of others. Even when acting on impulse, they anticipated the effect that their behaviour would have on their fellows. They were equally unhappy at the prospect of harming others. All this marks the strong autonomous, adaptable ego which is invariably accompanied by a feeling of high regard for people.

This integration of personality leaves them free to use almost all their emotional energy. Inevitably they direct this towards

[1] *Ibid.* p. 183.   [2] *Ibid.* p. 8.   [3] *Ibid.*

socially constructive, moral actions. They cannot do otherwise, since this is their psycho-social nature. 'They can scarcely help continuing to develop in wisdom, consideration, and knowledge of self and others, for it is in their very make-up to look life in the face, know it and live by principles that bring the greatest good to themselves and to those they love.'[1]

The rational element in this behaviour is less easily described. Clearly one has to define the criteria which determines what is rational in order to avoid the danger of confusing it with rationalization. Peck and Havighurst recognize this: 'Most of us indulge in rationalization to some degree to justify our actions. In the moral sphere this is an attempt to avoid guilt or blame by calling an immoral act something else that we can "justify" on other grounds. It is none the less a misrepresentation of moral responsibility. Rationalizing is not a realistic way of facing and accepting responsibility.'[2] But they nowhere lay down the criteria of rationality in moral behaviour.

The Criteria of Mature Morality
A swift perusal firstly of their character types and then their research findings, however, discloses material that could be moulded to form such criteria. It is said that behaviour of this kind comes from 'a stable set of moral principles',[3] which are used to judge and assess actions so that there is an objective assessment of the given act. Again it is said that mental experimentation, of the kind which Piaget calls operational and reversible, precedes the action in order to determine the most moral course of action. Furthermore, this conduct is situational, since it does not follow from the rigid application of immutable regulations.

As a result the actions of others are also judged situationally so that an action is assessed in itself. There is no generalized overall approval or disapproval either of a person or his conduct. When this is applied to the moral agent himself it means that there is no irrational guilt or anxiety. If he makes a mistake he feels guilty about that alone, and then takes steps to rectify it. Hence although this conduct springs from a coherent system of firm, internalized, integrated moral principles, these principles are themselves subjected to frequent critical inquiry and examination

[1] *Ibid.* p. 97.   [2] *Ibid.* p. 17.   [3] *Ibid.* p. 127.

to see whether they in fact work in practice. Such a rational-altruistic person is clearly what Heidegger called 'an authentic man', whom Richardson has described as the man 'who therefore has the possibility of freedom to speak his own words and live his own life'.[1]

Such people possess three moral skills. There is firstly the central skill, which characterizes the altruistic element in this morality. This is the ability to know 'what other people want and how they feel'.[2] Secondly, the competence to make situational judgments which pay attention to what Reeves has called 'hard' facts. Of this she says, 'we need to encounter the hard resistant quality of things and persons'.[3] Thirdly, the ability to examine moral principles and either augment or modify them.

From this one may conclude that Peck and Havighurst imply the existence of such moral criteria. The only point which needs to be emphasized here is that these criteria are clearly a mingling of the rational and the altruistic elements in human personality. They can now be listed simply:

(1) The ability to attend to other people's feelings.
(2) The ability to attend to the 'hard' facts of a situation, e.g. the consequences of any moral action.
(3) The ability to accept or reject and augment or modify moral principles.

These three criteria are also listed by Loukes as basic moral imperatives. He argues that mature morality involves one in:

(1) Acting in a way which treats people as ends and never means.
(2) Acting with due regard to the expected consequences.
(3) Acting upon principles which would enable the act to be universalized.[4]

Further, these three criteria coincide exactly with those suggested by Wilson. He argues that morality involves one in a

[1] A. Richardson, *Religion in Contemporary Debate*, p. 82.
[2] R. H. Peck and R. J. Havighurst, *The Psychology of Character Development*, p. 8.
[3] M. Reeves, 'Moral Education in Early Maturity', in *Moral Education in a Changing Society*, ed. W. R. Niblett, Faber, London, 1963.
[4] H. Loukes, *New Ground in Christian Education*, pp. 107–8.

rational consideration of other people's interests which must then be reviewed in the light of one's own. Thus he suggests that the criteria of mature morality (he prefers to call it rational morality) are:

(1) Attention to one's own and other people's feelings.
(2) Attention to empirical facts of a 'hard' kind, e.g. consesequences.
(3) The ability to formulate and modify rules or moral principles.

As one would expect from a modern philosopher, Wilson also adds a fourth criterion namely, the ability to use language logically and clearly.

This emphasis on rationality in moral thinking is also apparent in the report of Peck and Havighurst. 'In positive terms', they write, 'the development of reasoned self-control, in order to ensure other people's well being, is one of the hall marks of the ethical person.'[1]

Clearly the ideal mature moral agent would be one who always did that which his reason assured him was morally desirable. But everyone experiences moments of irrational desire. These unreasonable impulses then characterize our behaviour on those occasions. Thus this picture of an altruistic and rational level of moral behaviour represents an ideal towards which we may hope to move.

Before continuing with the developmental analysis of this material it should be noted that these critieria fit snugly into the view that mature morality can be understood in terms of basic moral attitudes. The first criterion, which refers to genuine concern for people, clearly reveals an altruistic attitude. The second, which affirms that one should always consider the consequences of a moral action, is the conduct which would be expected from a morally responsible person. The third criterion deals with the rational appraisal of moral regulations and principles. And finally since moral maturity cannot be displayed where coercion is a factor, such a moral agent must be

[1] R. H. Peck and R. J. Havighurst, *The Psychology of Character Development*, p. 17.

autonomous. Thus once again we are left with the same list of attitudes to mark the morally mature, viz:

(1) Altruism.
(2) Rationality.
(3) Responsibility.
(4) Moral independence.

Durkheim, Piaget and Peck and Havighurst each place different emphasis on these attitudes. Durkheim emphasized responsibility.[1] Piaget stressed autonomy. For Peck and Havighurst rationality and altruism are the essential attributes of moral maturity. But obviously they are all necessary. Thus it must be finally emphasized that in a morally mature personality one would expect to find all these moral attitudes in a developed form.

The Developmental Scheme

It now only remains to show that these different character types can be located in a sequential scheme of moral development. This is a motivational theory of morality and must therefore be conflated with the pattern of moral controls listed in Chapter 5.

The amoral type is clearly both egocentric and prudential in his moral conduct. 'He considers himself to be the centre of the universe and sees other people or objects as means to direct self-gratification. He may form temporary alliances with people, but will abandon them the minute he sees a richer source of gratification.'[2]

The expedient type of child displays an authoritarian moral control. He is still egocentric but his prudence is replaced by a respect for authority. 'He adapts his behaviour sufficiently to (adult) standards to increase the possibility of gaining satisfaction for himself.'[3]

The conforming type of person is most often seen in a stable folk society. He learns by habit rather than insight and is motivated by group conformity since it is this conduct which a folk society most rewards. 'This kind of person has one general internalized principle; to do what others do, and what they say one

---

[1] As did Swainson. cf. p. 56 above.
[2] *Ibid.* p. 5. cf. also pp. 35–6, 43–5.
[3] *Ibid.* pp. 112. cf. p. 6.

should do. He wants to and does conform to all the rules of his group. He wants to do what others do.'[1] Clearly he lives at the moral level of social control.

The irrational-conscientious type of child is on the brink of mature morality. He has internalized a system of moral values. But this introjection resulted in moral demands which are not amenable to reason. He lives by 'conformity to a code he has internalized and believes in. The irrational component is visible in the individual's customary rigidity in applying a preconceived principle'.[2] In this rigid system there is no room for altruism. The application of a moral principle is far more important than consideration for people. Finally, the rational, altruistic person stands at the apex of moral development.[3]

A Two-factor Analysis

At this point in the argument there is an important observation to make. Hitherto this book has attempted to avoid psycho-analytical terminology. Psychologist readers will have realized this already. In a book designed for the non-specialist student and teacher it was thought advisable to avoid technical jargon, but a brief incursion into this realm must now be made.

Readers of Peck and Havighurst will know that they are Freudian in their orientation. This fact can now be used to gain a clearer understanding of their motivational theory of morality.

For them the amoral person has a weak ego and a weak super-ego. The expedient person has a weak ego but a 'significant amount of super-ego control'. The conforming character has a weak ego with a 'weak to moderate super-ego'. The irrational-conscientious personality has moderate ego-strength but is 'utterly guided by super-ego directives'. Finally only the rational-altruistic type has both a strong ego and a strong super-ego; indeed they say 'It scarcely seems accurate to describe them as having a separate compartmentalized super-ego.'[4]

Now with two co-ordinates representing ego strength and

---

[1] *Ibid.* p. 6. Note particularly the comment 'I do what everybody else does, so I guess they probably think the same thing of me'. *Ibid.* p. 60.

[2] *Ibid.* p. 7. *cf.* also pp. 95–6.

[3] *Ibid.* pp. 66f. *cf.* also pp. 162–3.

[4] R. F. Peck and R. J. Havighurst, *The Psychology of Character Development*, pp. 89–97.

super-ego strength one may make a two-factor analysis with a four cell lattice and distribute the different personality types among them. (See Fig. 2.) In addition to thus distributing the personality types among the cells of this lattice this model serves to emphasize another important point. Each child remains located within his own lattice cell. That is, his basic personality pattern is stable. If he begins as an expedient child or a conforming child the probability is that he will remain as such during the period of his normal development.[1]

FIG. 2.

A TWO-FACTOR ANALYSIS OF MORAL DEVELOPMENT
(BASED ON PECK & HAVIGHURST)

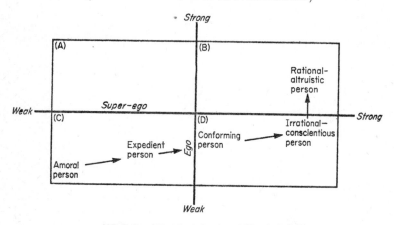

N.B. Peck and Havighurst found no child to fit Cell (A).

Of course there are difficulties with this lattice model for all moral studies abound with them. The first is that not all the cells are occupied. The second that the measurement of ego and super-ego strength involves one in a mechanical model of psychic functioning.

The first difficulty is immediately apparent if one glances at the diagram of this two factor analysis. The strong ego/weak super-ego cell is empty. This is simply because Peck and Havighurst found no candidates to fill it. Presumably some could be found to

---

[1] This notion of a development *within* the psycho-social types advances on the earlier view that development was *through* the different types. See pp. 199ff. above.

qualify as candidates. Recidivists spring naturally to mind. Here a strong ego acts with no moral restraint and so can become habitually criminal in a legal society such as ours. But there is also a further problem here. This is a Freudian model and the weak ego/strong super ego cell *should* be empty. It isn't of course since the Conforming and Irrational-conscientious person is located here. One would have expected an inadequate ego to imply the formation of an inadequate super-ego since the super-ego is formed, in analytic terms, by introjection, and so leave this cell unoccupied. Not all analysts would agree on this problem. The least then that one can say is that this is a paradoxical situation.[1]

The second difficulty is more easily resolved. Although techniques measuring ego strength and super-ego strength may be suspect this is not an impossible task. Peck and Havighurst are careful to record the techniques used in their research and claim that ego and super-ego strength can in fact be measured by tested methods employed by trained research workers. And powerful support is now given to this by Cattell. His factorial analyis of ego and super-ego strength in terms of source traits shows that objective measurement is possible. He claims that his source trait 'C', i.e. ego strength, and his source trait 'G', i.e. super-ego strength can both be accurately measured by questionnaires.[2]

Conclusion

Before concluding this scheme of psycho-social development three important points must be emphasized. Firstly, no individual represents a pure moral type yet he can be accurately classified as such. Secondly, there is a consistency in moral conduct despite the fact that the moral agent is maturing. Thirdly, this psycho-social developmental scheme does not imply that moral development is inevitable.

Each point can be presented briefly. All the Peck and Havighurst respondents were seen to act from a mixture of motives and reveal some confusion of character type. 'None the less when the

[1] I am indebted to Norman Williams the Research Fellow in Psychology at the Farmington Trust Research Unit at Oxford for discussing these points with me; and continuing this with a protracted correspondence from which I have drawn freely.

[2] R. B. Cattell. *The Scientific Analysis of Personality*, pp. 62–102.

dominant type of each individual's profile was used to classify him at the appropriate point on the ascending scale of maturity of character, it turned out that the subjects who fell in each type group showed some highly significant psychological features in common, and equally important differences from the subjects of the types above and below them on the scale.'[1]

Secondly, although each child passes through a series of different stages, each of which is characterized by the conduct expected of different moral types, yet he nevertheless displays a consistent personality pattern while doing so.[2] 'Studying these children from ten to seventeen with reported data going back into their early years in most cases, revealed a characteristic personality and character pattern which was largely laid down by age ten and changed little thereafter. Earlier data tended to fall in the same line in each case wherever it could be obtained. Briefly this suggests that the child of each character type starts very early to develop along that type path, and that growth simply makes him more and more that kind of person.'[3] Thus we may conclude that, 'A basic qualitative difference exists between the psychological maturation pattern of children who are becoming rationally altruistic in their character patterns and those who remain fixated in more primitive patterns.'[4]

The third point is adequately dealt with in the following chapter since it is integral to the arguments used there. For the moment one must be content simply to affirm that those who have made a study of child morality agree that there appears to be a decline of moral standards in early pubescence. (*See* p. 233ff.)

The educational implications of this material are enormous. It can however, all be reduced to a single question, 'How may we help children to become altruistic in their relationships and rational in their approach to moral problems?' At first sight it looks as if we can do little. It all seems to depend upon the individual's personality and thus involves the educator in techniques which facilitate changes in the child's character. *Indeed this is the situation.* Character change is inevitably involved in a scientifically constructed course of moral education. Both this and the companion volume[5] point clearly in the direction that

---

[1] *Ibid.* p. 166.   [2] *Ibid.* pp. 17–18.   [3] *Ibid.* p. 157.   [4] *Ibid.* pp. 172–3.
[5] *Moral Education: a Sociological Study of the Influences of Home and School.* A. W. Kay. A forthcoming volume.

we must go. When we arrive the educational terrain may as yet be unmapped, but it is some consolation to know that we are moving in the right direction.

BIBLIOGRAPHY

Cattell, R. B., *The Scientific Analysis of Behaviour*, Pelican Original, London, 1965.

Crane, A. R., 'Pre-Adolescent Gangs and the Moral Development of Children '*B.J.E.P.*, November, 1958.

Durkeim, E., *Moral Education*, Free Press, New York, 1960.

Gesell, A., *et. al.*, *Youth: The Years from Ten to Sixteen*, Hamish Hamilton, London, 1956; Harper & Row, New York, 1956.

Hartshorne, H., and May, M. A., *Studies in the Nature of Character*, Three volumes, The Macmillan Company, New York, 1928–30.

Havighurst, R. J., and Taba, H., *Adolescent Character and Personality*, John Wiley, New York, 1949.

Havighurst, R. J., and Neugarten, B. L., *American Indian and White Children*, University of Chicago Press, 1955.

Heidegger, M., *Sein und Zeit*, Neomarius Verlag, Tübingen, 1953.

Hoggart, R., *The Uses of Literacy*, Penguin, London, 1957; Oxford University Press, New York, 1957.

Jackson, C., *Manuel*, Jonathan Cape, London, 1965; Alfred A. Knopf, New York, 1964.

Kennedy-Frazer, D., *The Psychology of Education*, Methuen, London, 1944.

Loukes, H., *New Ground in Christian Education*, S.C.M. Press, London, 1965.

McKnight, R. K., *The Moral Sanctions of the Child*, Unpub. B.Ed. Thesis, Glasgow, 1950.

Morris, J. F., *A Study of Value-Judgements in Adolescents*, Unpub. Ph.D. Thesis, London, 1955.

Peck, R. H., and Havighurst, R. J., *The Psychology of Character Development*, John Wiley, New York, 1960.

Remmers, H. H., and Radler, D. H., *The American Teenager*, Bobbs-Merrill, Indianapolis, 1957.

Richardson, A., *Religion in Contemporary Debate*, S.C.M. Press, 1966; Westminster Press, Philadelphia, 1966.

Riesman, D., *The Lonely Crowd*, Penguin, London, 1961; Yale University Press, New Haven, 1950.

Wain, J., 'Master Richard', in *Nuncle and Other Stories*, Macmillan, London, 1960.

Whyte, W. H., *The Organisation Man*, Jonathan Cape, London, 1957; Simon & Schuster, New York, 1956.

Wilson, J., *Logic and Sexual Morality*, Penguin, London, 1965.

Wilson, J., *et. al.*, *Introduction to Moral Education*, A Pelican Original, London, 1968.

CHAPTER 9

THE ATTITUDINAL MODEL OF MORALITY

INTRODUCTION

This book has been specifically concerned to present evidence which can clarify our understanding of moral development in children. It was seen that just as intellectual development may be broken down into subordinate factors, in this case, the development of specific concepts and intellectual skills, so moral growth can be reduced to the four component elements dealt with above. Therefore, to understand moral development one must know firstly, something about the quality of behaviour natural to each stage; secondly, the characteristic sanctions which operate at each level; thirdly, the nature of the moral judgment exercised as children grow; and lastly, the personality or psycho-social maturity of the children concerned. These must be brought together before a comprehensive picture of moral development can be drawn. (See Fig. 3.)

This of course is only in the context of psychological considerations. It will be seen in the next volume[1] that a further complicating factor is the influence of home and school with familial and subcultural variations producing more modifications in the morality of each individual child.

At least one thing can now be said with certainty. None of the writers reviewed above were actually dealing with moral development. They simply selected one psychological element or dimension of moral growth and dealt with that to the exclusion of the others. Moral development as such must include all of these elements and further be concerned with the total development of each child. This will necessarily take the researcher into the areas of sociology, social psychology and philosophy; the last since in such a complex cross-discipline study the concepts used must be clarified to eliminate unnecessary confusion.

This is a very helpful conclusion to reach for it suggests that the many varied contexts within which discussions on morality

[1] *Moral Education: a Sociological Study of the Influence of Home and School.* A. W. Kay. A forthcoming volume.

FIG. 3.

A COMPREHENSIVE PLAN OF MORAL DEVELOPMENT

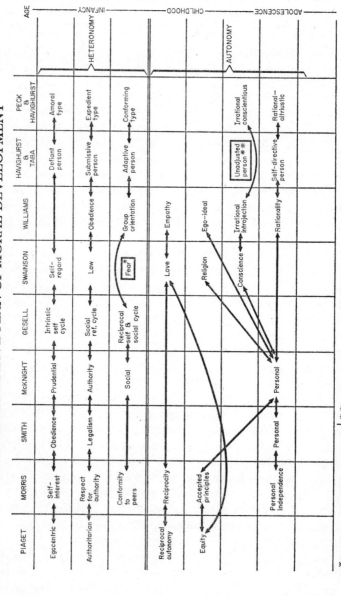

*Fear is a portmanteau sanction | **An unadjusted person may develop into one of the 4 personality types.
see p. 115 | see p. 193

take place, can now be unified within this multi-dimensional system. To realize that such discussions must necessarily be approached in this way enables one to see that each discipline makes a complementary contribution to our understanding. And when further it is realized that each of these can also be reduced to its component elements, a plan of the whole area emerges.

Such an analysis is extremely valuable for it shows that both lay and technical discussions which refer to many apparently unrelated aspects of this subject are actually taking place within the boundaries of this one, complex, yet clearly defined area. This must surely be welcome if for no other reason than that it will enable discussions to continue. Whereas they now inevitably founder upon apparently irreconcilable and mutually exclusive ideas, this dialectic view suggests that a synthesis will emerge. Thus the discussions between Christians and Humanists, psychologists and sociologists, philosophers and laymen can be continued in the knowledge that each has something of value to contribute to the whole. Even where the clash of opinion seems to be sharpest it can be seen now that this is a confrontation of many dimensions within the one study and not a conflict between the true and the false.

<h2 style="text-align:center">THE 'MODEL' AS AN AID TO UNDERSTANDING</h2>

Here then is the psychological aspect of this multi-dimensional picture of moral development. The evidence was presented above in a thematic form which lays bare its component parts. But how must one consider the whole? It is clear that this unity is moral development itself. But what is its nature? Is it like intellectual growth or physical growth? What analogy will best enable us to understand it?

Here it is necessary to digress very briefly, for one of the most fruitful contributions of modern philosophy to educational thought, is that of the 'model'. Ramsey deals with this subject simply and clearly. He believes that once we have discovered the appropriate 'model' we are better able both to understand and communicate the essence of the subject being studied or discussed.

Verbal models have had a central place in human thought for centuries. By using allegories Plato made his meaning more clear;

by using metaphors Jesus did the same. This device was used in Chapter 1 above where the models of a tomb and a frog were amongst those used to clarify our understanding of human development.

There are also non-verbal models which fall generally into two classes; the picture model and the disclosure model. Children make many of the first type in schools. In order better to understand the nature of the terrain of this country three dimensional relief models are made of the British Isles. These show what the real thing looks like yet offer a view seen only by astronauts. In this way they help children to understand the geography of the British Isles more clearly. The second type of model is also used in school since it is valuable in scientific studies. In order to help pupils to understand the structure of the solar system, for example, a teacher might whirl a sphere about his head on the end of a length of string. Here one has not so much a picture as an insight into the structure of that which is being studied. These models only throw *some* light on *some* aspects of the object of study. To confuse the models with the reality diminishes their value. They are aids to clearer comprehension which must be discarded as soon as this understanding is reached.

Now the reality here is moral development. What model can help us best in our attempt to understand it? Or rather, since models can be complementary to each other, 'What models, can help us best to understand it?' This question becomes more intelligible if the possible alternatives are listed.

POSSIBLE MODELS FOR MORAL DEVELOPMENT

There are at least six models from which to choose. Firstly, the model of intellectual growth. This enables us to understand moral development as a sequential process similar in form to the pattern of ever increasing conceptual understanding. This model is the one most used by educators for reasons which will be made clearer below. Secondly, there is the attitudinal model in which moral growth is deemed to be a process of developing moral attitudes. It will be argued below that this is equally satisfactory as a model not only because it aids the student in his attempt to understand all the characteristics of morality, but also because this model enables one to bring together the findings of the psychology and the sociology of moral development. Furthermore, it lays the foundations upon which a viable, practical system of moral education can be built.

The remaining four models are all valuable but have deficiencies not found in the first two. It merely remains therefore to list them briefly. There is, thirdly, the evolutionary model described in Chapters 3 and 4 where moral development can be understood in terms of different moralities so suited to a particular stage of development that they each displace the morality which preceded them. Fourthly, there is the ethical model described in Chapter 5 which focuses attention on a series of emerging sanctions. The fifth model is essentially sociological for it presents one with a pattern of cumulative development in which the emerging morality co-exists with, but finally predominates over its predecessor. The subdued element then persists like an underprivileged minority group barely tolerated in a alien community. Finally, there is the psychological model described in Chapter 8 which explains moral conduct in terms of a sequence of maturing forms of psycho-social development. Each of these has some quality to commend it, but attention is inevitably directed more closely to the first two models described above.

THE MODEL OF INTELLECTUAL DEVELOPMENT

It is not difficult to see why the intellectual model so readily commends itself. Piaget's theory of intellectual development is probably the most well-known amongst educators in this country and it seems to be tailor-made for the task. This is not merely because Piaget produced theories about both moral and intellectual development. The two schemes are themselves so similar that it is very easy to consider them both in terms of the same model. Furthermore, when one remembers that many consider mature morality to be essentially rational, the development of morality would seem to coincide with the development of rational thought.

In order to understand this argument more clearly it is necessary to know something of the detailed features of Piaget's developmental theory. This is inordinately complex. Fortunately for the busy student the late Nathan Isaacs wrote an introduction to Piaget's work. It is not generally known that Nathan was the husband of the late Susan Isaacs. We thus have one of the most brilliant interpreters of Piaget's theories married to one of the most implacably hostile opponents of his views. However, apart from some misleading statements, which the compression of complex work cannot avoid, this book stands as a monument to the unbiased objectivity of Nathan Isaac's treatment of Piaget's work.

For those who then wish to read Piaget himself the best book is probably *Logic and Psychology*. This is not only a presentation of the mature thought of Piaget but constituting, as it does, the material of some university lectures it is marked by an unexpected clarity and succinctness. If one then desires to read further in this subject, the whole range of Piaget's publications constitute an intellectual Eden in which the innocent educator can stroll for years.

In this analysis of intellectual development there appear to be three clearly defined and separate stages. There is firstly the pre-operational stage, secondly the stage of concrete operations and finally the stage of formal operations, with each successive stage depending upon its predecessor.

In the first stage an egocentric child thinks unsystematically, using intuition and transductive[1] processes in which a verbal or visual similarity is deemed to form a logical relationship, when in fact no such relationship exists. Operations can only emerge when this egocentricity is left behind. Since such a child does not then see everything exclusively from his own point of view and can therefore isolate himself from the external world he can do in his head what he before would only have done in reality. Thus by transferring the scene of his activity from the external world to his own mind he is free to go backwards and forwards over processes or arguments or ideas. This is why operations are reversible. But at this second stage he still cannot think in conceptual terms. He can only understand time in terms of specific periods of waiting or activity, so he speaks of *playtime, hometime* and *lunchtime*. He understands space only in terms of the relationship between tangible points; and number only in terms of specific objects. However, there comes a moment when he can dispense with these concrete representations of the ideas and consider the concepts themselves. He can then talk sensibly about abstractions like *time* and *space* and *number*. Thus he is able to understand the principles of history, geography and mathematics.

[1] See p. 227 below.

This, of course, is an extremely simplified version of a complex theory and since our purpose here is to see how easily one may understand moral development in terms of this model only the relevant features need to be discussed. For this purpose reference must be made to the critical periods which separate these three stages. The first usually occurs early in the junior school and the second early in the secondary school, though it is now recognized that there are wide individual differences to be accounted for.

There are two experiments which reveal vividly and dramatically how a child sheds his egocentricity and is prepared to think operationally in a way which allows him to reverse the constituent elements of a particular mental process. Both are extremely simple and any attempt to try them with young children can produce illuminating results.

Firstly, all one needs to do, as Piaget did, is to place some children before a *papiermâché* three dimensional landscape. Position a small figure of a child somewhere in it and ask, 'What can that little boy see? Egocentric children will not fail to describe not what the model of the boy would see but what *they* actually see. If one does this with the same child during a critical transition period the sudden change to describing what the model *itself* would see is unbelievably revealing. Suddenly they can put themselves in the position of that other 'child'.

Piaget's second experiment is equally simple. If one takes say six wooden beads and paints four of them white any child can now be asked 'are there more white beads or wooden beads?' (the point being of course that they are all wooden beads but that some of them have been submitted to a process which conceals this). Young children will say that there are more white beads. But again if one perseveres with the same child during this critical phase suddenly he will answer, 'There're all wooden and only some are white.' He has simply reversed the painting process in his mind; a process which reveals that the white beads are still wooden. In this way he reaches a logical answer.

These two features mark the transition from the egocentric stage to the stage of reversible concrete operations. This in turn can be seen clearly in transition to the final stage. Here ideas in themselves can be comprehended without making recourse to tangible and concrete manifestations of them. Again two simple experiments can indicate when this change takes place.

If one reads a nonsense sentence to a child in this critical stage he begins by concentrating on the concrete data and slowly passes to a review of the logic involved. If the sentence used is 'I am very glad I do not like onions, for if I liked them I would always be eating them and I hate eating unpleasant things',[1] at the level of concrete operations a child will discuss the verbal data and say 'Onions aren't unpleasant', or 'You should eat onions'. At the higher level of formal operations however he would ignore this and strike to the heart of the logic involved. Then he would argue about the logical contradiction between 'If I liked them' and 'onions are unpleasant'. That is, he passes from considering the tangible literary manifestations of an idea to considering the idea itself.

The second test is equally simple. Children love collecting and classifying things, as any boy's pocket or girl's handbag will testify. Piaget deals at great length with the different systems of classification used by children since they give reliable clues to the mental processes involved.[2] Supposing, for example, that a child is presented with a collection of two dimensional shapes. He could classify them first into two groups; those that are round and those that are not. As his mind works on the problem he may then classify the same shapes into two different groups; those that are triangular and those that are not. So far all is well. He is handling material presented to him in concrete form. Now ask him to classify mankind. He may begin by speaking of the British (who inevitably surround him in the classroom) and those who are not British. Children who still think in concrete terms cannot go beyond this. But if this is done during the critical transition stage it will suddenly occur to the child that he can do more than classify mankind in terms of the British and the non-British. He can speak of the French and those who are not French; of the Germans and those who are not German, of the Chinese and the non-Chinese. In fact the whole world is now open to him and he can classify in those terms which are not presented to him in a concrete form, for there are no French, Germans or Chinese in the class with him. He has simply passed from the stage where he understands the concept of race in purely concrete terms, to that

[1] J. Piaget, *Logic and Psychology*, p. 18.
[2] J. Piaget and B. Inhelder, *The Early Growth of Logic in the Child: Classification and Seriation*.

stage where he can use the concept without needing a concrete example of it before him. This operation is called 'vicariance'.[1]

The pattern is now clear. Ignoring the first stage of early infancy and the last stage of mature adult thought, there are these three stages. The first is marked by egocentricity and is left behind as reversible and reciprocal thought emerges. The second stage is then marked by an inability to comprehend abstract ideas. At the third stage ideas and abstract principles can be comprehended clearly.

This model appears to be entirely suitable to illuminate our understanding or moral development. In the first stage children's morality is essentially egocentric. They are selfish in their prudence and cannot comprehend that others have equal rights with them. At the second stage they can begin to think morally, even though this morality is in a very concrete form. Piaget shows this clearly. He records that children at this stage believed that a boy who accidentally broke fifteen cups was more guilty than a boy who broke only one even though he did it while stealing some jam from the larder.[2] They think that the greater the physical damage the more guilty a child must be, despite the intentions involved. Many other researchers have also found that this stage is marked by a slowly emerging recognition that abstract motives are important.

In addition this stage is marked by reciprocal thought. This is the moral corollary of reversibility. In effect each child says, 'I've worked it out this way, now I shall go back over the data and work it out from *his* point of view'.

Finally, mature moral thought transcends a concern for specific laws and grapples with abstract moral principles. Hitherto concepts of right and wrong, and justice and equity were understood purely in terms of their tangible effects. Now they are understood conceptually and rarely need concrete illustrations to indicate their nature. Many people can of course remain fixated at an earlier level and will never reach this stage of morality: but this does not affect the argument.

By the use of this model one's understanding of moral development can obviously be increased. It is also extraordinarily attractive as a model since it both confirms and supports what parents

1 J. Piaget, *Logic and Psychology*, p. 31.
2 J. Piaget, *The Moral Judgement of the Child*, p. 118.

and teachers may know of intellectual development; and the familiar is always far more acceptable to us.

In addition there is a further reinforcement for this conclusion. Recent studies in the growth of religious understanding have unreservedly supported and confirmed that the intellectual model is valuable in attempting to understand religious development. This is important because there appears to be a close relationship between religious and moral concepts. The evidence for this comes from both America and Great Britain.

Harms discovered three simple stages of development. These correspond roughly to the chronology of Piaget's scheme. He found that in the first stage, thinking was egocentric, unsystematic and credulous. Such children viewed religious stories from their own limited vantage point and thought of God as a giant in a fairy-tale world. At the second stage religion was almost entirely concrete in form. God was a localized tangible figure; and the relative reality of any religious idea was judged solely on the basis of possible historical confirmation. Finally at the third stage religion became personal and spiritualized. God was viewed here as a spiritual power and not a physical force. The religious realities were then accepted as intangible and non-material. Consequently concepts such as faith and hope were increasingly understood. This is seemingly an almost exact transposition of Piaget's findings into the area of religious thought.

Now a far more sophisticated confirmation has emerged from the work of Goldman. The title of his book *Religious Thinking from Childhood to Adolescence*, may be an entirely unselfconscious literal echo of Piaget's *The Growth of Logical Thinking from Childhood to Adolescence*, but the contents certainly provide massive evidence to support the Piagetian scheme of development, possibly, it may be argued, because he studies religious *thought*, not religious *behaviour*. All this evidence is distilled into a short chapter.[1] Here Goldman shows precisely why he concluded that there were specific stages in the development of religious thought. He too proposes to argue that there are three clearly defined levels of such thinking and a cursory reading shows that these correspond exactly to Piaget's scheme. (That he also indicated the existence of two intermediate stages between

[1] R. Goldman 'Operational Thinking About Religious Stories', in *Religious Thinking from Childhood to Adolescence*, pp. 51ff.

these is irrelevant here.) He calls these three the stages of intuitive religious thinking, concrete religious thinking and abstract religious thinking.

Considering just one item of evidence it can be shown that the intuitive stage contains thought that is egocentric, and transductive. When asked for example why Moses thought the ground was holy when he stood before the Burning Bush one child showed undiluted egocentricity by arguing that it was 'Because there was grass on it'. Presumably that child's experience of parks led him to conclude that since grass should not be walked on and holy ground could not be walked on, it was holy because it had grass on it. Another showed clear transductive thinking by suggesting that it was holy in order to induce Moses to take off his shoes; the purpose of this being to ensure that God and Moses would be friends. 'God wanted a friend and because God had his shoes off, they'd be friends.' This is subtle but clearly still primitive transduction. God does not wear shoes. Thus just as two young girls can secure and cement their friendship by wearing identical clothes, so God and Moses would be linked by this transductive relationship.

The stage of concrete religious thinking is delineated equally clearly from evidence provided by the children. For example when asked why that ground was holy, children at this stage argue that it was 'Because the holy would go down through God's feet into the ground and make it holy.' Here 'holiness' is understood not in terms of a spiritual quality but a physical substance.[1] This is clearly the stage of concrete operational thinking.

The level of abstract religious thinking produced responses of an entirely different kind. When explaining why Moses thought that the ground was holy, such children respond conceptually. They say for example, 'God is holy and the world is sinful.'

At first the adult reader is not aware of the tremendous step that such a child has taken. He does not realize it because he is now at home in his own thought-world. But such a child for the first time discusses the problem with no reference to the tangible bush and historical character or a specific time on a particular day. He discusses it only with reference to the abstract principles of holiness and sin. He has no need at all to refer either to the concrete

[1] This must not be confused with *mana* which is 'altogether distinct from physical power', see Codrington, quoted by Spinks, p. 37.

data of the narrative or to couch his conclusions in concrete form. He has reached the stage when he can dispense with them and can mentally manipulate abstract principles and propositions. This is equally clear from other responses provided by children at this stage of development. Some comments are profound, others merely ingenious, but they all illustrate the point. These children think in formal operations. 'Everywhere is holy where people believe and worship God', said one. 'The presence of God would hallow it like a magnetic field. The magnetic field is everywhere but the pole is in one spot. God is concentrated there', argued another, clearly grappling with the inconsistency between claiming holiness for one particular area of ground when the holy God was deemed to be omnipresent. Indeed one boy moulded this problem into his answer, 'Can God have a greater degree of presence? I'm not sure. Wasn't it supposed to be the Lord's mountain? Wasn't it a volcano and what they couldn't understand they called holy, something dangerous to be left alone.'[1]

INADEQUACIES OF THE 'INTELLECTUAL MODEL'

It may be argued that such support as Harms and Goldman provide is entirely predictable. Religious thought is nothing more than ordinary thought exercised on religious ideas. It may grapple with the ideas in a more meaningful way and at a more profound depth, but it is still the normal intellectual apparatus of children which is exercised in this way. This is undoubtedly true, yet as such it only serves to sharpen the argument at this point. Since this is true of religious thought presumably it is also true of moral thought. Therefore, one tends naturally to use the model of intellectual growth to understand moral thinking. But one must question whether this is true of moral conduct any more than Goldman's scheme is true of religious behaviour. It may be true of moral *thinking*. This is nothing more than normal intellectual powers exercised on moral problems. But is it true of moral *behaviour*?

In moral education one is also concerned with conduct; probably more concerned with conduct than with ethical thought. It is one thing to know the good. It is another to do it! And in

[1] Goldman, *op. cit.* p. 60.

morality the latter is supremely important. Is the model of intellectual growth adequate then to explain moral *behaviour*?

It has been argued that this could be so. Reciprocity in moral behaviour is only made possible by reversible, operational thinking. And the ability to act upon moral principles is only possible at the level of formal conceptual thought. There is also the fact that moral sanctions show a sequential development (See Chapter 5 above), which suggests the scheme normally associated with intellectual growth. Here it can be seen that the sanction slowly becomes active as egocentricity diminishes. It then emerges in tangible form firstly as prescriptions from authority, then as pressure from society, until it is finally integrated into the internal mental system of the moral agent.

This may be so and such a simple Freudian model of introjection can illuminate this area of inquiry. Yet the value of this consideration lies elsewhere. In directing attention to moral sanctions the way is opened to develop the present argument and consider whether the attitudinal model is helpful. This arises from the fact that sanctions act as motives and under certain circumstances motives are indistinguishable from attitudes.

This rather bald assertion will be examined more carefully later.[1] For the moment it may be accepted that such a relationship between moral sanctions and moral attitudes exists. This is clear even when the technical meaning of attitude is not known. For an authoritarian sanction to be effective one must have a positive attitude to that particular authority.

But clearly the intellectual model is inadequate when attention is turned from ethical discourse to moral conduct itself. And it is precisely at the point where the developmental model becomes inadequate that the 'attitude' model becomes appropriate. Thus one is justified in pursuing this search to discover whether morality can be understood more clearly when it is also viewed in terms of moral attitudes.

In this quest there is a danger to be avoided. In any new subject where the stage of clarification attracts most attention the temptation to erect complex all-embracing hypotheses is extremely seductive. Thus the important question at this stage must be 'Is the model of sequential intellectual development ade-

[1] Forthcoming companion volume, *Moral Education: the Influence of Home and School.* A. W. Kay.

quate?' Only if it isn't is one justified in seeking to augment it. At this stage simplicity is essential because a crucial educational decision must be made. The intellectual model may be extremely helpful but it must be admitted that it cannot adequately explain many of the accepted features of morality. It cannot do this because it is primarily related to intellectual processes whereas morality is primarily displayed in conduct. Recent work in social psychology[1] has shown that a study of behaviour is most helped by a consideration of the attitudes which produce it. The developmental model must therefore be augmented by viewing moral development in terms of attitudes.

What then are these features of morality which the intellectual model cannot explain but which the attitudinal model does? The two most obvious can be discussed briefly and then discarded for more important and less ambiguous considerations. Firstly, unlike intelligence, morality appears to be more independent of genetic factors. There is as yet no moral quotient in the sense that there is an intelligence quotient. The recently discovered connection between chromosome abnormalities and conduct only links genetic factors with socially aberrant conduct. It does not establish that morality depends upon inherited characteristics. However, there is sufficient uncertainty concerning the environmental influences on intelligence and the genetic influence on morality, to warrant leaving this consideration aside. The nature-nurture controversy referred to in Chapter 1 above indictated the balanced form of the evidence available, and to continue would merely add further weight to each side of the argument. One may, for example, add force to the contention that heredity is a factor in morality by referring to the evidence in Chapter 9. There it was shown that psycho-social personality patterns determine the nature of an individual's conduct and it could be argued with some force that in general moral traits and the personality profile are a markedly inherited feature of each person. There is the further more common-sense fact that some people find it easier to be good. They have inherited a personality which enables them to be altruistic and responsible far more easily than others. Christian pastoral psychology has made this distinction clear. Newman, for example, speaks of 'the once-born and the twice-born': of the former he says 'Of human sin they know

[1] e.g. Krech, Crutchfield and Ballachey, *The Individual and Society.*

perhaps little in their own hearts and not very much in the world; and human suffering melts them to tenderness.'[1] William James makes much of this distinction. 'Some persons are born with an inner constitution which is harmonious and well-balanced from the outset. Their impulses are consistent with one another, their will follows without trouble the guidance of their intellect and their lives are little haunted by regrets. Others are oppositely constituted.'[2] Yet on the other hand Mead showed clearly, as indeed have many other anthropologists, that society is a dominant determinant in morality. The moral man amongst her Arapesh Indians was the social outcaste amongst the Mundugumor, and vice versa.

The second consideration is related to this. Morality seems to have a non-cognitive element. Even when rational discourse provides a logically coherent solution to a moral dilemma men may still think that action other than that dictated by reason is called for. They will say, 'That is true but in this instance I *feel* that it is the wrong decision.' Presumably this is connected with the fact that while rationality only influences our thinking, altruism affects our behaviour. Further to this, responsibility creates categorical imperatives. When one knows the right thing to do, this knowledge is invariably associated with a belief that one should act upon it. Thus the moral use of the terms 'right' and 'wrong' is not identical with their logical use. Logic does not exhaust the content of morality for it is conative as well as cognitive. So here again the intellectual model is inadequate to explain our moral conduct.

Now interesting and even weighty though these considerations may be, empirical evidence has shown three *far more important* features of moral development which disclose the inadequacy of the intellectual model.

The first finding goes back to the work of Hartshorne and May. They discovered that morality was specific to each situation. Without being aware of any inconsistency in his conduct an individual displays different degrees of moral maturity in different situations. In one he will act like an egocentric child; in another as a mature adult; in yet a third like an irresponsible and

---

[1] F. W. Newman *The Soul: its Sorrows and its Aspirations*, 1852. Quoted by William James *The Varieties of Religious Experience*, Longmans, London, 1923, p. 80.   [2] James, *op. cit.* p. 168.

authoritarian schoolboy. But no attention is drawn to this because it is an expected and unmarked characteristic of morality. Otherwise morally upright and honest men may steal office stationery or elude paying bus fares. As an experiment the writer once asked a group of highly indignant students, who were all proclaiming their honesty, to indicate if they had no book on their shelves which did not belong to another person to whom it should have been returned long ago. As one would expect no student raised his hand.

Social class factors enter here of course, and will thus be dealt with in the forthcoming companion volume to this work. For the moment, however, one may point to the illuminating stories told by Kerr. She records that the working-class inhabitants of Liverpool were scrupulously honest in their dealings with each other, yet limited honest behaviour to these situations. On one occasion some boys who had made money by breaking into gas meters admitted the crime but proclaimed their alleged honesty with this revealing reservation, 'We never stole from our own block.'[1]

The intellectual model may *appear* to account for such discrepancies if one uses the Piagetian scheme of development. Reference has already been made to the work of Beard who showed that a child may be normal in his understanding of number, advanced in his concept of time and retarded in his appreciation of space. Thus intellectual specificity is possible. This is supported by Piaget's view that during the stage of concrete operations the notion of conservation (i.e. that an object remains quantitatively identical although its configuration is changed) is applied to mass, weight, and then volume in that order. Thus while grappling with the idea that the weight of an object remains identical even though its shape is changed, a child will already have reached the stage of knowing that mass is unaffected by this process yet not able to see that volume is also unaffected. Given a piece of clay he will argue that its mass remains constant, its volume is changed and its weight may or may not be changed when it is kneaded into another shape.

The deficiency of this parallel lies here. It deals with the conceptual elements of intellectual growth, not intellectual growth itself. The closest parallel would be with the elements of moral growth not moral growth itself. But since it will be argued that

[1] M. Kerr, *The People of Ship Street*, pp. 118–19.

the elements of morality are best understood as attitudes, this line of attack emerges as a claim that the attitudinal model is necessarily the one to employ!

It must be admitted that many can claim with some justice that an individual whose intelligence does not vary very much from situation to situation can be intellectually successful in one and not in another. Yet this is not strictly parallel either. Intelligence tests do indicate a relatively stable level of intelligence which can be measured under differing circumstances and shown to be reasonably consistent. That is, it is not specific to a *situation*, but is specific to a *person*. Tests of moral development however, show that circumstances affect the level of morality displayed. The same child will constantly display a different level of morality in each. In this case the morality is specific to the *situation* and not the child. Here then is the first inadequacy of the intellectual model. It cannot take account of this undisputed feature of morality.

The second characteristic of this kind is an inexplicable moral decline. The developmental model not only emphasizes the genetic nature of evolving maturity, it implies also that this growth is inevitable. Yet this has been found not to be true of moral development. At the onset of puberty there is a stage where morality declines. The evidence of this and its implications for our understanding of the emerging 'youth-culture' will be discussed in the companion volume. For the moment it is sufficient simply to state that many researchers have confirmed this phenomenon.

Macaulay and Watkins concluded from their studies that eleven to thirteen years is the period during which children are most amoral. Hartshorne and May found little improvement in behaviour from ten to fifteen years. Beller discovered from a study of attitudes towards honesty that not only was there no development during the twelfth and fifteenth years, but there was in fact a deterioration in this respect. Swainson found that the greatest degree of maladjustment (i.e. the enjoyment of wrong-doing) appeared at thirteen or fourteen years and observed, 'The moral ideas of the period of puberty are characterized to a greater extent than any other stage by a negative attitude.'[1] Morris also

[1] B. M. Swainson, *The Development of Moral Ideas in Children and Adolescents,* p. 92.

concluded that this period of early adolescence was characterized by a decline in value judgments. He attributed this to the psychological and physiological changes of adolescence, particularly the uncertainty concerning relations with those in authority. Perhaps the most educationally important observation was that this occurred because younger adolescents were not allowed to exercise sufficient responsibility. However, his evidence was clear. The school had a system of allocating 'black stars' for misconduct. In one term, chosen at random, it was found that the third and fourth forms had a much higher proportion of these than any other.

It is thus not without significance that the setting for most literary accounts of schoolboy anti-authoritarian conduct is the fourth form. Greyfriars and St Dominic's are classic cases of this. Finally, Edwards concluded that the moral attitudes of his boys deteriorated during their attendance at a secondary modern school.

The empirical evidence thus suggests that there is a period of moral decline, or at least a period of arrested moral growth in early adolescence, but it must be made perfectly clear that the evidence can be interpreted in another way. These moral agents are school-children. They belong to an essentially authoritarian, heteronomous organization. In view of this it is equally true to argue that the development of moral autonomy in this context will *inevitably appear to be* a decline in morality.

This seems to be a much more satisfactory explanation than that of Webb. He concluded that children acted as they did to preserve some sanity. In his sociological survey of a secondary school he argued: 'It is therefore not too much of an exaggeration to say that sanity is only possible by being, when not working, irrepressible, spontaneous and rule-breaking.'[1]

It is thus no surprise to the educational psychologist to see such banner headlines in the national press as, 'Age of Highest Criminality Now Only Fourteen'.[2] It clearly surprises the general public, otherwise tough-minded realists like journalists would have used a different headline. Perhaps it even surprises school-teachers, who seem destined to spend staff meetings discussing the vagaries and peccadilloes of the second, third and

---

[1] J. Webb, 'The Sociology of a School', p. 267.
[2] *Guardian Journal,* June 9, 1967.

fourth form boys, and then in passing on to a selection of prefects express astonishment that young Jones or Smith has come on so well in the fifth and sixth forms. It is the universal acceptance of such conduct amongst boys in early adolescence which tends to make us take this for granted, but it is this second feature of morality which cannot be explained in terms of intellectual growth.

The third characteristic of morality which cannot be explained in terms of the intellectual model of development is difficult to describe although readily recognizable in practical conduct. As children develop they accumulate different 'moralities'. This was seen clearly in the above review of moral development. In a discussion of morality it must be recognized that there are a whole series of qualitatively different 'moralities' which operate with the same person at different times. As he grows the number of 'moralities' accessible to him for behavioural expression, increases. Psychologically this is rather important, for it suggests that when a person moves from a higher morality to a lower, one does not have to speak of regression, and so make reference either to the reversion of the libido or to some psychological fixation. One has merely to accept that in this instance the moral agent has used an accessible 'morality'. It may be true to say that this is appropriate to an earlier level of development, but it does not require the hypothesis of regression to explain this particular conduct. This seems to result from the simple fact that as one grows morally, there is no irreparable jettisoning of earlier 'moralities'. These survive and co-exist with the new.

Now this is not true of intellectual development. Under stress one may regress to primitive modes of thinking: the most commonly observed being the egocentricity which emerges when an argument is going badly. At such moments cornered academics can be recognized in flight from rational thought into egocentric thinking by their reiterated claim, 'I'm afraid I can't see it that way.'

Just as the pre-operational boy in Piaget's experiment cannot see the view from the vantage point of the figure placed in the landscape, so they cannot see the argument from their opponent's point of view. But this invariably happens only under stress and is quickly recognized for the reversion or displacement activity that it truly is. Yet in our behaviour we move from morality to morality in a state of calm and detached normality. We do not expect a teenager suddenly to revert to a pre-operational stage of thinking when confronted with a particularly tricky piece of calculation. Having once reached the level at which he understands that permanence and conservation are essential qualities of matter he cannot revert to the stage of thinking that by pouring water into a flat dish or a tall cylinder he thereby diminishes or increases the quantity of fluid.

Yet in moral conduct this is not so. A teenager can appear to be consistent and reasonable even though throughout the course of a single day his moral actions may be variously governed by prudence, authoritarianism, or personal principles. This is simply because while in intellectual development the characteristics of the earlier stages of thought are inevitably replaced by the later, in morality the earlier 'moralities' survive. They seem to have an enduring quality which makes it impossible to completely eliminate them. Again the intellectual model cannot account for this fact or throw any light upon it.

THE VALUE OF AN 'ATTITUDINAL MODEL'

The advantage of thinking of moral development in terms of moral attitudes can soon be made clear. It is at exactly those points where the 'intellectual model' is inadequate that the 'attitudinal model' is of value. Those otherwise inexplicable features of moral evolution become explicable when the process is thought of in terms of attitudes. But to understand why this is so one must first know something of the technical meaning of the term 'attitude'.

This is an extraordinary tricky concept. For that reason many writers on this subject prefer to leave it undefined and trust that the general interpretation of the term will be sufficient to make their work intelligible. However, it is possible to find some writers who have grasped this nettle, all of whom are in agreement on the essential elements deemed to characterize an attitude.[1] From

[1] 'The word attitude can be defined as a mental and neural state of readiness organized through experiences, exerting a directive or dynamic influence upon the individual's responses to all objects and situations with which it related (Allport).

'Attitudes are enduring organizations of motivational, emotional, percep-

these definitions emerge a simple list of the characteristics of an attitude.

All agree that an attitude:

(1) Is learned and can thus be modified.
(2) Has conative as well as cognitive features.
(3) Is an enduring orientation of mind.
(4) Predisposes one to act in a particular way.
(5) Leads to overt action when related to a specific referent.
(6) Is invariably associated with a specific social object.

It can be seen immediately that these are the qualities which have been emphasized throughout this book, as belonging essentially to morality and moral development. In fact the discussion so far now appears to have been about attitudes, even though the term has not been used. But when these features of an attitude are placed beside the deficiencies of the 'intellectual model' the reason for insisting that moral growth can be understood in terms of moral attitudes, grows even stronger.

Take the case of moral specificity. From the time of Hartshorne and May it has been argued that morality is specific to the situation in which it is displayed. Intellectual activity is not but attitudinal conduct is. One undisputed feature of attitudes is that they are specific to situations. There is therefore, little doubt but that the specificity of morality springs from the fact that it consists of conduct precipitated by a predisposing attitude.

This does not only clarify an otherwise obscure feature of

tual and cognitive processes with respect to some aspect of the individual's world' (Krech and Crutchfield).

'Attitudes are more or less lasting and imply a characteristic and selective response to relevant objects' (Sherif and Sherif).

'Attitudes, whatever else they may be, imply characteristic modes of readiness in reacting to particular people or objects or classes of these' (Sherif).

'Attitudes are patterns of behaviour in response to particular people or objects or classes of these' (Argyle).

'The attitude is the state of readiness for motive arousal. It is the individual's susceptibility to stimulation' (Newcombe).

'An attitude is an enduring system of positive and negative evaluations, emotional feelings and pro and con tendencies with respect to a social object' (Krech, Crutchfield and Ballachey).

'An attitude is learned in relation to objects, persons and values' (Young).

'Attitudes are often related to feelings and emotions' (Young).

morality, it also enables the reader to view Hartshorne and May with greater sympathy. One point which has been overlooked in almost all the discussion, subsequent to the publication of their findings, is that their observations on the specificity of morality was included in a chapter called, 'Data on the specificness of conduct, attitudes and motivation.'[1] Over forty years ago they were clearly aware of the fact that morality was an amalgam of moral attitudes!

The second inexplicable feature of morality was displayed by the evidence which shows that morality was modified in early puberty. But this is precisely what one would expect if the study of this behaviour was deemed to be a study of moral attitudes. Attitudes are learned and can therefore be modified. It is this variability which makes them so valuable. Since they predispose us to act in relation to social referents they must be variable. If they were not, human beings would find life infinitely less exciting and rewarding. Our response to social stimuli must perpetually be modified. This is the essence of social learning. Instead of responding automatically with an identical response to a range of similar stimulae, our response is modified to identify the referent with greater precision and mould our reaction with greater sensitivity. It is this which characterizes the learning of human beings. They are creative in new situations and meet each challenge with a new variation of an old attitude.

These changes can be either congruent (i.e. a strengthening or weakening of the attitude in the same direction) or incongruent (i.e. a reversal of the attitude). Thus in the congruent change of a pupil's attitude to his teachers he will either like them less or more; whereas if the change is incongruent he will pass from liking them to hating them. In the latter case the teacher is still the referent but the pupils pass from a positive to a negative response when the attitude is granted behavioural expression.

It is thus clear that if one is in fact dealing with moral attitudes in early puberty this could account for the otherwise puzzling decline in moral standards. In this case the variable moral attitude has undergone an incongruent change. The factors which are effective in this attitude change cannot be discussed here, but one thing is certain. At the onset of puberty the moral stress a

[1] H. Hartshorne and M. A. May, *Studies in the Nature of Character*, Volume I, *Studies in Deceit*, pp. 211ff.

child experiences in an authoritarian institution is sufficient to induce this change.

It will be argued in the companion volume to this work that one can clearly see an incongruent change in authoritarian attitudes and a congruent change in personal attitudes at this stage. Such a child thus moves from subscribing to authoritarian morality to the point where personal morality struggles to emerge.

However, the point is clear. This second puzzling feature of moral growth is perfectly explicable when understood in terms of attitudes. And to this one may add, for example, the evidence of Edwards. His view that morality declined in early puberty was the result of his research into moral attitudes. He nowhere defines the term, but this is perfectly clear from the title of his thesis: *A Study of Certain Moral Attitudes among boys in a Secondary Modern School.*

The third characteristic of morality is equally well explained when understood in terms of attitudes. This puzzling feature, whereby earlier and more primitive forms of morality survive into maturity, is precisely what one would expect if this behaviour was precipitated by moral attitudes. In addition to their variability attitudes have the quality of enduring psychological systems. As Allen says so succinctly, 'They are built to last'.[1]

One of their most obvious features is durability. Naturally this is inevitable if social life is to proceed. Our relationships with others are very largely dependent upon what we know of their attitudes. Thus we can predict how our colleagues will react to certain situations or ideas. In this way precautions can be taken to ease social intercourse and eliminate many otherwise inevitable interpersonal tensions. But the point is this. It is also the permanence of moralities which characterize them. Our understanding of this element in moral development can thus be increased by speaking of moral attitudes. This incidentally has an extremely important corollary for education, for if, as will be argued later, our task is the education of attitude, the durability of the moral attitudes created assures the educator that his work will not be entirely wasted.

[1] E. A. Allen, 'Attitudes of Children and Adolescents in School', p. 66.

AN ANALYSIS IN TERMS OF ATTITUDES

Both the developmental and the attitudinal models are therefore required if we are to understand moral development more clearly. But before concluding it is necessary to clarify still further.

If one speaks of moral development in terms of intellectual development the position is quite clear. Because there are different levels of development, conduct and thought appropriate to each stage can be clearly defined. How then is morality to be understood in terms of attitudes? The above arguments are convincing but they leave one with a hazy notion of morality. It is rather like saying that a house is made of bricks. It may be true, but this provides one with a very imperfect image of the building in question!

In its simplest form morality can now be considered as a series of stages in development, each level of which is characterized by a dominant attitude. At the level of authoritarian morality for example a positive attitude to authority figures dominates. Later, at the level of social morality a positive attitude to one's peer society dominates. Thus at every stage this complex of attitudes precipitates one which dominates and so induces conduct of a specific kind.

Of course this is an over simplification. A dominant religious attitude, for example, can be more clearly defined. As an attitude, it may be related to a whole series of referents. Thus one in whom the religious sanction is operating can have positive attitudes towards God, the Bible, a Church, a particular religious leader, or a religious code and each of these can dominate at different times. Equally, one in whom an authoritarian sanction operates will have positive attitudes to parents, teachers, policemen or any other authority figure in his social environment.

Yet in essence there appears to be a series of displacing attitudes. They rearrange themselves according to circumstances, but at any one moment a dominant attitude dictates the quality of conduct. Now these it will be observed can also be understood in terms of a developmental scheme. Thus for the moment morality, as understood under the model of attitudes, still fits neatly into the more readily recognized form of individual development. Yet these amoral, authoritarian, social and personal attitudes do not exhaust the content of morality. It would be extravagant to say that they are the least important, but they certainly must be subordinated to those moral attitudes which are of supreme importance. Now what are these further moral attitudes which are so supremely important?

If we briefly recall the evidence provided above to show the different dimensions of moral development, it will be remembered that there were certain features of moral maturity which emerged with startling clarity. The morally mature person must be rational; he must be altruistic; he must be responsible; and as the term autonomy implies he must be morally independent. Here one has four primary moral attitudes all of which in a fully developed form mark the morally mature. It may be argued by some that a rationally moral man is morally mature. But is he, if he is not altruistic? Again others may say that an altruistic, responsible man is morally mature. And again it must be asked, 'Is he, if he is not reasonable?' Indeed it is clear that moral maturity is not only indexed by rationality, altruism, responsibility and moral independence but consists of their co-existence in a developed form.

What picture now emerges of morality in terms of attitudes? Simply this; there appears to be a developmental series of displacing attitudes which mark the different levels of moral maturity. Co-existing with these are the four primary moral attitudes which slowly emerge as the moral agent matures. (See Fig. 4.)

His rationality and altruism etc. may have initially to operate within the limits of earlier moralities and his moral independence be circumscribed by them. Yet these slowly emerge and finally mark the morally mature.

Peck and Havighurst it will be remembered found that those adolescents who finally reached the highest level of rational/altruism in morality had displayed these attitudes in their childhood. Even in the pre-teen years, they had shown a tendency to respond to people with love and to moral problems with reason.

Thus co-existing with the displacing series of moral attitudes one finds an emerging complex of attitudes which slowly mature into genuine morality. This is interesting because in the maturing of these primary attitudes one has a clear illustration of the kind of development described by Isaacs and Fleming. It is a constant growth characterized by increasing complexity and understand-

FIG. 4.

MORAL DEVELOPMENT IN TERMS OF ATTITUDES

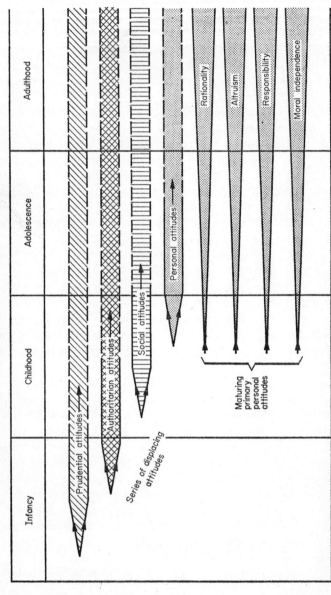

N.B. 1. These are generic terms referring to groups of attitudes, not specific attitudes.
2. The direction and duration of the broken lines as well as the relationship between the displacing series of attitudes is subject to individual personal variations.
3. For a clear analysis of personal attitudes see Evans *Attitudes and Interests in Education.*

ing with no critical phase to distinguish qualitatively different levels of growth. There will undoubtedly be critical moments. Rationality cannot but be affected by those crises in intellectual development outlined above. Moral independence cannot help being influenced by the pubescent tendency to become independent of authority. Altruism is certainly affected, as Swainson has shown, by the idealism of adolescence. Yet the growth of these primary attitudes is not inevitable, nor staggered into phases, nor entirely controlled by genetic factors, for even rationality in morals does not depend upon the level of intellectual development but is rather the ability to submit moral problems to the requirements of reason.

These primary attitudes will be more adequately defined in the companion volume. For the moment it should be sufficient to say that altruism is essentially that attitude which reveals a concern for people rather than things[1] and places the needs of others equal with one's own. Rationality is the willingness to discuss reasonably the moral requirements imposed on man. Responsibility is at least the willingness to accept culpability for one's own actions. And moral independence marks the degree to which one is willing either to depend upon another for moral support or to reach moral decisions alone.

CONCLUSION

That these two models both throw light on the nature of moral development, there is now no doubt. But what practical value have they? How can this help the parent and educator concerned with his responsibility to help children attain moral maturity?

Apart from the obvious value found in an academic clarification there are two advantages. Firstly the developmental model enables us to see more clearly that while each child needs help to reach the highest level of morality, the most effective help is that which is appropriate to his level of development. In this sense there appears to be a 'readiness for morality' which corresponds to 'readiness for reading' or 'readiness for writing'. In such instances parents and teachers will know that while the imposition

[1] The story of the small boy on a bus eating a toffee-apple illustrates this perfectly. His mother said 'Mind that lady's head with your toffee-apple; you might get hairs on it.'

of authority cannot lead to the highest morality, there is yet a stage where by his natural need for authority the moral growth of the child can be advanced by authoritarian means. Equally a social sanction alone cannot lead to mature morality, yet at the stage where he is impressed by it, teachers and parents may use it to facilitate his growth, in precisely the same way that materials are used in the primary school. They are aids to growth with which the grown child will ultimately dispense. This developmental model is thus invaluable is assessing whether teaching material is appropriate to a particular stage or not. In this way much unsuitable material at present being proposed through published and unpublished syllabuses on moral education can be eliminated before it has time to jeopardize the moral development of the children in our schools.

The attitudinal model is valuable in a rather different way. The developmental model makes it clear how far along the road to moral maturity each child has gone, but the attitudinal model shows which techniques may best help him to make further progress along it. If morality is to be understood in terms of attitudes, then moral education must be pursued by the education of attitude. The inculcation and strengthening of desirable moral attitudes will thus be the primary concern of the teachers involved in this work.

If it is objected that such a process is far too radical, that to be of any value this must involve the child in some fundamental personality changes, one can only reply that this is so. It is radical. Teachers must be left to decide whether the degree of change advocated is excessive or adequate. But one thing is clear from the preceding chapter above. In moral development one can trace a series of emerging stages in psycho-social maturity. This implies that moral education must be concerned with helping children to pass through these different stages of immature psycho-social growth. Indeed it may be argued that our function as teachers is the creation of fully formed human beings. And since when they first come under our care children are far from this ideal state, our teaching task necessarily involves us in the responsible job of moulding the personalities of these children. We do this incidentally at the moment, in all our work. No intellectual, physical, emotional, spiritual or aesthetic advance can be made without the personality of that child being changed.

Why then should this not be done consciously, using the techniques which are most adequate for this work? In this way we shall be more confident of helping children to become autonomous, responsible, rational and altruistic human beings.

BIBLIOGRAPHY

Allen, E. A., 'Attitudes of Children and Adolescents in School', *Educational Research*, Vol. 3, No. 1, 1960.

Allport, G. W., 'Attitudes', in *Handbook of Social Psychology* (ed.) C. Murchison, Clark University Press, 1935.

Argyle, M., *The Scientific Study of Social Behaviour*, Methuen, London, 1959.

Beard, R. M., *In Investigation of Concept Formation among Infant School Children*, Unpub. Ph.D., Thesis, London, 1957.

Beller, B., 'Children's Attitudes Towards Honesty', *J. Soc. Psych*, 1949.

Codrington, R. H., *The Melanesians: Studies in their Anthropology and Folklore*, Oxford University Press, London, 1891.

Edwards, J. B., *A Study of Certain Moral Attitudes among Boys in a Secondary Modern School*, Unpub. M.A. Thesis, Birmingham, 1959.

Evans, K. M., *Attitudes and Interests in Education*, Routledge and Kegan Paul, London, 1965.

Fleming, C. M., *Adolescence: Its Social Psychology*, Routledge and Kegan Paul, London, 1955.

—: *Teaching: a Psychological Analysis*, Methuen, London, 1959.

Goldman, R., *Religious Thinking from Childhood to Adolescence*, Routledge and Kegan Paul, London, 1964.

Harms, E., 'The Development of Religious Experience in Children', *Am. Journ. Soc.*, Vol. 50, No. 2.

Hartshorne, H., and May, M. A., *Studies in the Nature of Character*, Three volumes, Macmillan, New York, 1928–30.

Isaacs, N., *The Growth of Understanding in the Young Child*, Ward Lock, London, 1964.

Isaacs, S., *Intellectual Growth in Young Children*, Routledge and Kegan Paul, London, 1930; Schocken Books, New York, 1966.

Kerr, M., *The People of Ship Street*, Routledge and Kegan Paul, London, 1958.

Krech, D., and Crutchfield, R. S., *Theory and Problems of Social Psychology'*, McGraw-Hill, New York, 1948.

Krech, D., Crutchfield, R. S., and Ballachey, E. L., *The Individual and Society*, McGraw-Hill, New York, 1962.

Macaulay, E., and Watkins, S. H., 'An Investigation into the Development of the moral Conceptions of Children', Parts 1 and 2, *The Forum of Education*, IV.

Mead, M., *Sex and Temperament in Three Primitive Societies*, Routledge and Kegan Paul, London, 1935.

Morris, J. F., *A Study of Value Judgements in Adolescents*, Unpub. Ph.D. Thesis, London, 1955.

Newcomb, T. M., *Social Psychology*, Tavistock Publications Ltd., London, 1959; Holt, Rinehart & Winston, New York, 1965.

Newman, F. W., *The Soul: its Sorrows and its Aspirations*, London, 1852.

Piaget, J., *The Moral Judgement of the Child*, Routledge and Kegan Paul, London, 1932; Free Press, New York.

—: *Logic and Psychology*, Manchester University Press, 1953.

Piaget, J., and Inhelder, B., *The Early Growth of Logic in the Child: Classification and Seriation*, Routledge and Kegan Paul, London, 1964.

Ramsey, I. T., *Models and Mystery*, Oxford University Press, 1964.

Sherif, M., 'Group Influences upon the Formation of Norms and Attitudes', in *Readings in Social Psychology*, Maccoby, Newcomb and Hartley, Methuen, London, 1958.

Sherif, M. and C. W., *An Outline of Social Psychology*, Harper and Row, New York, 1956.

Spinks, G. S., *Psychology and Religion*, Methuen, London, 1963; Beacon Press, Boston, 1965.

Swainson, B. M., *The Development of Moral Ideas in Children and Adolescents*, Unpub. D.Phil. Thesis, Oxford, 1949.

Webb, B., 'The Sociology of a School', *B.J.S.*, September, 1962.

Young, K., *Handbook of Social Psychology*, Routledge and Kegan Paul, London, 1957; Appleton-Century-Crofts, New York.

CHAPTER 10

MORAL EDUCATION

INTRODUCTION

In concluding a book on moral development, it would be all too easy to raise controversial, ideological issues. To do this, even inadvertently, would be a mistake. As far as possible those who are working in this area must make educational and not ideological principles the criteria of all that they say and do. Only in this way will the question 'Can we reasonably hope to agree as moral educationists even though we differ in religion and philosophy?'[1] be answered affirmatively.

There are probably two propositions with which most teachers would agree. Firstly, that the moral education of children comes high in the list of educational priorities. As Taylor has said, 'Studies in the role of the teacher suggest that most teachers place first in importance moral training with instruction in subjects a close second.'[2] And secondly, that moral education may be conducted as an integral element of almost every school lesson.

Relevant to this second point is the classification of educational goals by the Association of College and University Examiners. They see two distinct types of educational objective. In their first handbook they speak of the cognitive domain. This refers to intellectual aims and involves the teacher in a consideration of the purely academic element in his work. Here one would place the data, principles and theories inherent in a particular subject. In the second handbook they refer to the affective domain, and Bloom reminds readers that the cognitive element does not exhaust the content of a particular subject. There is in addition the affective element which refers to values, beliefs, and attitudes. From this it would appear that with competent teaching the acquisition of values and beliefs is an inevitable process in every school lesson.

Roe goes even further. She believes that values and facts can become confused in the educational process. 'There is a subtle

---

[1] Elvin, H. L., *Education and Contemporary Society*, p. 197.
[2] P. H. Taylor, *Purpose and Structure in the Curriculum*, p. 166.

something about the way in which the three "R's" are taught which implies an intellectual morality of absolute rightness to the way words are spelled, for example, or the way grammar is constructed, or to the statement that two and two make four. Teaching those subjects in terms of "right" and "wrong" answers carries a strong moral connotation of considerable significance.[1] The moral influence, it seems, need not be limited to the affective element in teaching. It can also be inextricably involved in the cognitive content. But this only serves to underline the fact that *most* teachers in *most* subjects are necessarily involved in moral education.[2]

It is when one goes beyond these propositions that controversies emerge. Some would argue that adequate moral education results from the above pervasive influence. Others would say that it should become a separately time-tabled element in the school curriculum. Amongst those who subscribe to this latter view there would be further divisions of opinion. This clash is sharpest between those who think that it should be linked with religious education and those who consider that it would be harmful to do so. Of this conflict Cox has written. 'The popular view, endorsed by many teachers of religion, is that morality follows from beliefs on the argument, "I believe this, therefore, I should behave in this way", and on the conviction that religious belief can give the motivation and strength of character to put moral decision into practice. But there is a growing and responsible minority who maintain that an adequate morality can be found which can be justified on grounds other than religious ones, and that in the present state of religious confusion an education in morals that is tied to religious instruction is not the surest method of making an ethical society. Whatever the truth of this, the fact remains that most developed religions include a code of conduct and that a genuine religious education ought to have an effect, right or wrong, on the moral decisions of those who receive it.'[3]

[1] Anne Roe, *Personal Problems in Science*, p. 134.

[2] Such a statement may evoke dissent but many readers would surely agree if the case were put less pointedly. Taylor claims that 'Learning, as psychologists have made us aware, brings about a change in behaviour' (*op. cit.* p. 160). If this is so it is difficult to see how a practising teacher can avoid being involved in moral education.

[3] E. Cox, *Sixth Form Religion*, p. 148.

The present work is not intended to lead to similar controversy. It is merely hoped that the psychological evidence provided here will help those teachers who believe that specific moral education can be conducted in our schools. For such teachers the present psychological survey will have pointed to two subjects for discussion. Firstly, the fact that a developmental model of morality leads naturally to a consideration of the notion of 'readiness for morality'. And secondly, that the analysis of morality in terms of attitudes indicates the educational techniques which will be most effective for this work.

READINESS FOR MORALITY

There are certain tasks which are appropriate to particular stages of human development. Just as one would not ask a two-year-old child to shave his father with a cut-throat razor, or ask an octogenarian to refix a television aerial on the roof, so one would not ask a child to attempt tasks beyond his intellectual ability. We readily accept this without question in physical and intellectual matters. To make this mistake in the area of morality can have equally disastrous results.

In education this idea of 'readiness' is now an established axiom. There are stages when children are ready to learn. To anticipate this or attempt to defer it does untold harm. Thus we teachers are now talking more confidently of 'readiness for learning'. We say that a particular stage of development is one in which we can recognize a readiness for reading, or writing or numerical calculation. Cox, elsewhere, has suggested that this is also true of religious development. Basing his comments on Goldman's work he says, 'One of the most fruitful concepts in recent educational thought has been that of "readiness" . . . and . . . it is now being recognized that the idea of readiness can be applied to religious education.'[1]

This book has attempted to argue that one should now also be able to speak of 'readiness for morality'. In moral growth, just as in physical maturation or intellectual development, there are clearly defined stages, and each has tasks not only appropriate to it, but also essential for subsequent development. It is this which makes teaching such exacting but rewarding work. Once he

[1] E. Cox, *Changing Aims in Religious Education,* pp. 83–4.

realizes that children can only learn what they are ready to learn, the teacher finds three tasks before him.

Firstly, since the arrival of any stage of 'readiness' depends upon previous experience, he must see that children are given every opportunity to be involved in preparatory experiences. They must be prepared for understanding weight by weighing as many things as possible; for understanding number by counting as many objects as possible; for understanding time by measuring its duration and calculating relationships within a time-sequence; and for understanding morality by being involved in moral situations.

Secondly, there must be no attempt to force this development. This may be done by a well-meaning parent or teacher, but the results can be disastrous. If Junior School children are compelled to handle ideas before the stage of 'readiness' is reached, their development is not only hindered, it is positively retarded. Wanting to please parents and teachers, children will develop a verbal facility in the subject. They will talk knowingly of intellectual, moral and religious themes. An articulate child may even impress his relatives to the point where they nod their heads and predict a bright future for the boy. But none realize that the mental conditions producing this verbal facility will actually hinder the child from understanding later what he *appears* to understand now. Many a parent and teacher has found to his surprise that children who appeared to display so much potential as juniors fail absymally as seniors. Like the gilt on the mythical apples, this verbal facility soon wears thin and then reveals the shrivelled fruit which it successfully prevented from being ripened by the sun. So children intellectually gilded too early will never have ripened minds.

Then thirdly, it is the teacher's privilege to feed in the ideas which the developing mind can assimilate and handle. Like any growing organism the mind must be given intellectual milk until it has matured; but then the pappy diet no longer serves. *Then* is the moment to provide the meat of knowledge. To withhold this is almost as harmful as to give it too early. Thus the wise teacher may see his pupils grow under his watchful care. Indeeed the term 'kindergarten' conveys just such an idea. A classroom is a garden of children and the green-fingered teacher who knows their needs at every crucial stage can watch them grow and blossom.

All this can be applied to moral development. Havighurst is probably the one educator to draw this most forcibly to our attention in recent years. He argues that all of us face 'development tasks'. These, he says, are tasks which appear at critical points in an individual's growth. Their successful achievement leads to happiness while failure leads to unhappiness; and this unhappiness is made more bitter because society disapproves, the individual is frustrated and the successful achievement of later tasks is placed in jeopardy. Thus as a 'development task' emerges it must be mastered. If it is not, the whole personality is harmed.

Speech is an example of a developmental task. There is a point where this must be mastered, if it is not then articulate normal speech becomes almost impossible to achieve.[1] Infancy is crammed with these tasks. We must meet and master the art of walking, talking, reading, reasoning and relating to others. Now it is this last task which is of importance here. We must learn to relate to others. If we cannot, we become social cripples who are as handicapped as a child that cannot walk.

In adolescence there is one supreme task. Success here too means happiness while failure leads to rejection and social despair. This supreme developmental task is the acquisition of a mature moral system to guide our conduct. Thus the whole of a child's school days are involved in meeting each of these socially orientated tasks in order that ultimately he may meet and master this developmental task which should crown his educational life. He then, and only then, becomes an autonomous, responsible, moral human being.

In this pilgrimage to moral maturity there are, as we have seen, two factors which can facilitate progress. These are already accepted as axiomatic in intellectual development. Work must be appropriate to the particular stage; and each stage must be catered for if development is to continue.

McKnight makes the first point very clear. In moral education we should accommodate the material of a syllabus, to the limitations imposed by the developmental pattern of morality.[2] It is as useless to speak of personal moral sanctions to a child whose

[1] Gesell's life history of Kamala the 'Wolf Girl' illustrates Havighurst's thesis. After crawling on all fours for years Kamala was never able to run like a human being. *Wolf Child and Human Child*, p. 68.

[2] *cf.* L. Kohlberg, *Moral Education in the Schools. See* p. 190 above.

development has only taken him up to the level of authoritarianism, as it is to talk about time and space to a child still firmly embedded in the stage of concrete-operational thinking. Both will learn the language if this is attempted; but both will thereby be hindered from maturing further.

It follows that these stages are essential to moral development. It may be that one cannot reach moral maturity without passing through a prudential, an authoritarian, a reciprocal, and a social stage. This is not just because each system of morality contains valuable elements for society (cf. Chapter 3 above) but because progress is hindered if each stage is not negotiated. These can, of course, be telescoped together, but perhaps may not be omitted.

A very good example of this process comes from the history of religious evolution. Vriezen and Pfeiffer have argued that the pre-logical stage of man's development was essential for the emergence of Christian theology. The ability of pre-logical men to hold mutually inconsistent concepts, led to the highest level of theological thought. It is this pre-logical facility in the race which has partly enabled modern Christians to accept that God is both immanent and transcendent: One and Three; and the Dying Life-giver. This, it is argued, does not account for the inconsistencies. It merely explains how the highest truth which contains them can be understood by modern logical men. So Pfeiffer concludes that the sacred writers 'accepted inconsistencies without hesitation and thus established a successful church',[1] while Vriezen much more colourfully argues that the acceptance of contradictions 'speaks the truth in the form of a divine dialectic'.[2]

It can also be argued that morals transcend reason. If this is so then moral development is analogous to theological evolution. The heteronomous, amoral stages enable pre-logical human beings finally to accept a logical yet loving morality. Logic and love have as much in common as One and Three, yet in the last analysis they are conflated for morality is only that conduct which springs from *compassionate reasoning*. And these two apparently mutually exclusive qualities can be held in this creative tension because like the race, each individual has passed through a series of preparatory stages which enabled him to reach moral maturity in his personal development.

[1] R. H. Pfeiffer, *Introduction to the Old Testament*, pp. 197ff.
[2] Th. C. Vriezen, *Old Testament Theology*, pp. 75ff.

There is another dimension of growth too which must not be forgotten, for increasing attention is being devoted to the developmental analysis of subject syllabuses. Here educators are trying to discover the sequence of subject-matter most able to facilitate a pupil's progress. These attempts vary in intensity. At one extreme teachers can be found doing this every day with their subject in the classroom. They begin with material which is both easy to understand and naturally interesting. They then pass to more complex material which demands conscious attention. At the other extreme one enters the field of programmed learning in which behavioural psychology has had a powerful influence. Perhaps Skinner is the most well-known exponent of this, who, in 1958 received a citation[1] because 'he has invented a series of teaching machines designed to facilitate instruction from kindergarten through college'.[2] This internal sequence of development is clearly *also* necessary in any syllabus of moral education, but unless it is constructed with regard to the moral development of children its effectiveness will be considerably diminished.

THE TECHNIQUES OF MORAL EDUCATION

Because moral development may be understood in terms of moral attitudes, those methods which are able to induce *attitude formation and change* appear to be the techniques which should be employed in a course of moral education. There is now sufficient empirical evidence from this field of research to justify one in arguing that such methods are now available. Unfortunately, most of this work has been done in America, and English educators are on the whole unacquainted with this revolutionary aspect of social psychology. The day has now passed when such an educational tool can be stigmatized as an 'admass' technique used by Vance Packard's 'Hidden Persuaders'. It is a powerful educational instrument being fashioned and refined more and more by social psychologists dedicated to this field of research.

This is an extraordinarily complex subject in which the empirical data[3] suggests that few confident affirmations can be made.

[1] Awarded by the American Psychological Association.
[2] *American Psychologist,* Vol. 13, No. 12, December 1958. p. 736.
[3] Mostly found in the *American Journal of Abnormal and Social Psychology.*

Cohen and Halloran have both provided comprehensive surveys of the subject and other reviews can be found elsewhere.[1] Each of these writers organizes his material in a different way but one such structure is of value since it affords an easy transition to the classroom teaching situation. Hovland, Janis and Kelley speak of the three elements to be considered in any attitude change. These they refer to as:

(1) The communicator—who says it.
(2) The communication—what is said.
(3) The audience—who hears it.

In the classroom these three elements would be clearly identified as the teacher, the lesson material and the pupils. A detailed analysis of these will be undertaken in the companion volume[2] where it will be shown that most of what is known about the techniques which can induce attitude formation and change may be conveniently divided into these three categories. In this way many of the methods now being used to manipulate the values and tastes of the general public, can be conveniently transposed to the school system. There, instead of being used to exploit the public, they will be employed to produce morally mature young men and women. Succinct records of the research relating to this can be found in the works to which reference has already been made.

Clearly such techniques as are provided by these not only *can*, but *must*, be employed in education. This is an area where we dare not be Luddite in our thinking. Every possible technological device and psychological insight must be used to make education a process which produces more mature, informed, moral citizens. We accept this principle in other areas of work. Language laboratories have overcome the initial resistance to them and are now established in every well-equipped school. Teaching machines are the next inevitable innovation. Without doubt there will be more, and the educational scene will indubitably be transformed within the lives of the next generation of school chil-

---

[1] In, for example, publications by Brown, Evans, Jahoda and Warren, Sargent, Krech, Crutchfield and Ballachey. (See the bibliography of this chapter for full details.)

[2] A. W. Kay, *Moral Education: a Sociological Study of the Influence of Home and School,* to be published by Allen and Unwin.

dren. We dare not allow ill-formed prejudice to deter us in our attempt to establish a system of more effective moral education.

While other areas of education now employ the most sophisticated means to achieve their aims, we must not continue with our imperfect techniques in moral education. Common sense alone demands that we should be reasonable in this. Everybody agrees that physical health is desirable, and that modern medical techniques should be employed to achieve this. Equally everybody agrees that moral health is not only desirable for the individual but essential for the well-being of the community. Yet even though this is so, many educators appear to prefer outmoded techniques to achieve this equally laudable end. We would not submit to medieval medical practices to achieve physical health. Why then should we argue that modern techniques should *not* be used to achieve moral health? Although referring to culture in general Bantock's words are relevant here. 'It is odd that we ignore the methods of those who have most touched the "masses" in our times—the advertisers, the political dictators and the purveyors of cheap art in its various forms. . . . We must seek the sources of their strength—which are effective; and we must seek to direct the powers they have unleashed into better channels. We may, of course, fail in our efforts, for what is needed is a refinement of feeling, not a mere exploitation.'[1]

Undoubtedly some voices will be raised in a conscientiously held conviction that this may lead to brainwashing techniques in the classroom. But this may be dismissed as a failure to understand the nature of the proposed techniques. The far more important objection, however, may be the suggestion that in this way moral education will become a concealed form of indoctrination. Now this is a serious charge which is bound to be made by responsible educators and must therefore be met on its own terms.

Is this proposed scheme for the education of moral attitudes really indoctrination? Two considerations suggest that it is impossible to agree that this is so. The first has been argued by Hare. The essence of indoctrination, he says, lies neither in the content nor in the method of any system. It lies simply in its aim. It is not *what* we teach nor *how* we teach it, which determines whether we are indoctrinating or not. It is the ultimate *aim* which matters.

[1] G. H. Bantock, *Education in an Industrial Society*, p. 106.

Thus, apparently innocuous subjects, like History, can be shown to be indoctrinatory if they have as an implicit aim the laudatory presentation of a particular race or era. Now since the *aim* of moral education is the creation of morally mature citizens who can resist the blandishments of heteronomous values it is extremely difficult to see how this process can be termed indoctrinatory.[1]

This leads naturally to the second consideration. It is a development of the first but puts the case more sharply. If opponents of the moral education proposed here will insist on calling it indoctrination, the question must be asked, 'How is the creation of rational, morally independent, altruistic and responsible people indoctrination?' If the creation of mature moral agents who are autonomous and responsible *can* be termed a process of *indoctrination*, then the word has lost its meaning. Like Humpty Dumpty such objectors are making the word mean what they want it to mean.

In the first instance such criticisms may be sincere, but once an appellation of this kind is attached to a system it is in danger of having not only to fight reasoned opposition but irrational prejudice. Thus in moral education such incipient opposition *must* be met before it does irreparable harm. Therefore, it must be emphasized again that moral education of the kind envisaged here is not in any way a concealed form of indoctrination. Its aim is the creation of rational, responsible, autonomous and altruistic citizens.

To this end must be bent every modern technique and psychological insight. It is unreasonable to suggest that those techniques which clinical tests have shown to be the most effective in attitude formation and change should be ignored in favour of the

---

[1] One could, of course, be more subtle than this. If misgivings do remain concerning the process of moral education envisaged here, it can be argued that such a course in moral education is intended to induce resistance to its own influence. It would then be shown that such a course is essential for those who are influenced by it, but unnecessary for those who are not. When a moral agent is able to resist further heteronomous impositions upon his morality he is the kind of person that these techniques are intended to produce. And equally, while he is unable to resist them he is the kind of person for whom the course is designed. In a sentence: while the techniques are effective they are needed; when they cease to have any effect they are redundant.

current uninformed but well-meaning efforts of teachers. Instead of the 'frank' discussions, heart to heart talks, the headmaster's assembly reprimands, the 'I know what's best for you lad' techniques, and the naïve assumption that factual information on appropriate topics assures moral growth, teachers must brace themselves to this task and acknowledge its paramount importance by honouring it with the most efficient techniques available. After all, the *aim* has not changed. The history of western education shows that educators, with varying degrees of success, have always attempted to morally educate their pupils. It is merely that the *means* are now to become more efficient. It is simply hoped that such techniques will help to introduce effective moral education on a large scale.[1] Perhaps it is the ultimate effect of this which some teachers may really fear. Autonomous adolescents within any democratized school system will make inordinate demands upon the moral and personal resources of teachers. And it may well be precisely in these areas that many of us feel inadequate and insecure.

BIBLIOGRAPHY

Association of College and University Examiners, *Taxonomy of Educational Objectives: the Classification of Educational Goals*, Handbook 1, *Cognitive Domain*; Handbook 2, *Affective Domain*, Longmans, London, 1965.

Bantock, G. H., *Education in an Industrial Society*, Faber and Faber, London, 1963.

Bloom, Benjamin S., Editor of above A.C.U.E., *op. cit.*

Brown, J. A. C., *Techniques of Persuasion*, Pelican Original, London, 1963.

Cohen, A. R., *Attitude Change and Social Influence*, Basic Books, New York, 1964.

Cox, E., *Changing Aims in Religious Education*, Routledge and Kegan Paul, London, 1966.

[1] Although Ramage rejects Sargent's thesis he still says 'Dr Sargent is pointing out in his own way a fact of which we have long been aware—*viz.* that there *are* methods of "evangelism" and ways of trying to bring about conversions that are not very different either in principle or in basic technique, from brain washing and indoctrination.' *Battle for the Free Mind*, p. 15. This telling sentence can only enhance the argument presented above.

—: *Sixth Form Religion*, S.C.M. Press, London, 1967.

Elvin, H. L., *Education and Contemporary Society*, C. A. Watts and Co., London, 1965.

Evans, K. M., *Attitudes and Interests in Education*, Routledge and Kegan Paul, London, 1965.

Gesell, A., *Wolf Child and Human Child*, Methuen, London, 1941.

Halloran, J. D., *Attitude Formation and Change*, Leicester University Press, 1967.

Hare, R. M., 'Adolescents into Adults', in *Aims in Education*, (ed.) T. H. B. Hollins, Manchester University Press, 1967.

Havighurst, R. J., *Human Development and Education*, Longmans, London, 1953; David McKay, New York, 1953.

Hovland, C. J., Janis, I. L., and Kelley, H. H., *Communication and Persuasion*, Yale University Press, 1953.

Jahoda, M., and Warren, N., *Attitudes*, Penguin, London, 1966.

Krech, D. Crutchfield, R. S. and Ballachey, E. L., *The Individual and Society*, McGraw-Hill, New York, 1962.

McKnight, R. K., *The Moral Sanctions of the Child*, Unpub. B.Ed., Thesis, Glasgow, 1950.

Packard, V., *The Hidden Persuaders*, Penguin, London, 1961; David McKay, New York, 1957.

Pfeiffer, R. H., *Introduction to the Old Testament*, A. and C. Black, London, 1953; Harper and Row, New York, 1948.

Ramage, I., *Battle for the Free Mind*, Allen and Unwin, London, 1967.

Roe, A., 'Personal Problems in Science', in *Scientific Creativity*, (ed.) C. W. Taylor, John Wiley, New York, 1963.

Sargent, W., *Battle for the Mind*, Pan Books, London, 1957.

Skinner, B. F., and Holland, J. G., *An Analysis of Behaviour*, McGraw-Hill, New York, 1961.

Taylor, P. H., 'Purpose and Structure in the Curriculum', *Educational Review*, June, 1967.

Vriezen, Th. C., *Old Testament Theology*, H. Veenman and Zonen Wageninen, Holland, 1958.

INDEX

(Please note that none of the titles and subject matter contained in the bibliographies are listed in this index).